THE
NATIONALITIES OF EUROPE

TO MY WIFE
NORA KERSHAW CHADWICK

THE
NATIONALITIES OF EUROPE
AND
THE GROWTH OF NATIONAL
IDEOLOGIES

By

H. MUNRO CHADWICK

Hon. Fellow of Clare College, and formerly Elrington &
Bosworth Professor of Anglo-Saxon in the
University of Cambridge

CAMBRIDGE

At the University Press

1945

REPRINTED

1966

PUBLISHED BY

THE SYNDICS OF THE CAMBRIDGE UNIVERSITY PRESS

Bentley House, 200 Euston Road, London, N.W.1
American Branch: 32 East 57th Street, New York, N. Y. 10022
West African Office: P.M.B. 5181, Ibadan, Nigeria

Publisher's Note

Cambridge University Press Library Editions are reissues of out-of-print standard works from the Cambridge catalogue. The texts are unrevised and, apart from minor corrections, reproduce the latest published edition.

First published 1945
Reprinted 1966

First printed in Great Britain at the University Press, Cambridge
Library of Congress Catalogue Card Number: 46-2962
Reprinted in the United States of America

CONTENTS

PREFACE

THE question with which this book is concerned attracted little attention in this country until recently. There has been a general tendency, however, to regard nationalism as a kind of political disease which affects foreign nations and certain parts of our own islands—a disease which is due largely to economic causes, and capable of being cured by an improvement in economic conditions.

The events of the last few years have perhaps tended to cast some doubt upon this explanation of national movements and the remedy for them, as stated in this crude form. But on the whole they have probably strengthened the idea that nationalism is a disease. Has it not been responsible for the most brutal regime of which we have any record?

Yet it may be contended that this is a one-sided view. Nationalism is no doubt a vivifying and inspiring force. It makes for national unity and—when it is genuine, and not merely a cloak for political ambitions—it acts as a curb upon the selfish instincts of individuals, and of classes and professions. Its ugly side appears only when it is associated with aggression against neighbouring states, or with the coercion of alien or dissentient elements at home. And such aggression and coercion may of course arise from causes independent of nationalism.

I am not concerned, however, either to defend nationalism or to condemn it. My purpose is to call attention to the need for more knowledge, not only of national movements—their characteristics and causes, and the ideologies associated with them—but also, and more especially, for more knowledge of the nationalities themselves. I believe that the mistakes made by British policy in the past have been due in the main to ignorance of foreign peoples, including the non-British peoples within the empire. This ignorance and the negligence which accompanies it are themselves due in part to the fact that before the days of air warfare we believed our country to be comparatively safe from foreign aggression, but still more to an antiquated and defective system of education.

In democratic times it is essential that a knowledge of foreign peoples, including those of the empire, should be widespread and intimate. A knowledge of the political and economic conditions of the present day is of great value for certain purposes. But if we are to understand the characteristics and feelings, the ideologies, of other peoples, we must pay attention also to their past history, both political and cultural, their institutions, and the conditions which gave rise to their special characteristics. It is for this purpose that I undertook the following brief survey of the peoples of Europe.

The survey has been limited to Europe, because I have not sufficient knowledge of other Continents. Similar movements, however, can be observed or traced in many parts of the world. Arab nationalism is now in process of taking shape before our eyes.

The reader may perhaps think that I have devoted too much space to the past, and especially to the far past. My reason for doing so is that the early history of Europe, apart from Greece and Rome, is little known in this country; its importance for the conditions and the ideologies of to-day has not been sufficiently recognized. An additional reason is that this side of the subject is more closely connected with the studies which have occupied my life.

It may also be observed that the 'present' conditions occasionally referred to, especially in Chapters I and IX, do not always correspond to the political situation which actually exists to-day. Since the book went to press, events have been moving very rapidly; and the difficulties which now attend publication give the author of a book of this kind little chance of keeping pace with them.

My thanks are due to the Syndics of the Cambridge University Press for undertaking the publication of the book, and to the staff for the care with which the work has been carried out. My friends Dr C. E. Wright and Mrs R. C. Wright have, as on previous occasions, most kindly read the proofs for me. For their generous help and kindly criticism I am very grateful. Above all, I am indebted to my wife, whose wide knowledge and willing help have constantly been at my disposal.

H. M. C.

CHAPTER I

NATIONALITY AND LANGUAGE

No question in our time has given rise to more unrest in the world than that of nationality. The question abounds in complications, which are often difficult to understand. Yet no question of any importance has had less attention paid to it in this country.

It must first be observed that the word 'nationality' is used in two different senses, which are sometimes mutually exclusive.

In legal and official language a person of British nationality is one who is a British subject by birth or naturalisation, whatever may be his origin or the language which he speaks.

But the word is more generally used in a different sense—a sense which has its affinities in the words 'nationalist' and 'nationalism'. We hear frequently of conflicts of nationality within the territories of a single state; and the persons who represent these different nationalities are all usually natives of the country. Such conflicts often lead to a demand for independence on the part of a section of the population. Or, again, a minority of the population of one country may claim the same nationality as the majority of the population of another country; and such conditions may lead to a demand for the redistribution of territories.

It is not very easy to define what is meant by 'nationality' in this latter sense. Something in the nature of a common origin is perhaps always implied. Sometimes the feeling for nationality is derived from the former existence of an independent state or group of states, which have come to be incorporated—whether by conquest or by some peaceful process—with another state. Such is the case with nationality in Wales and Scotland, as well as in Ireland, which has now again become independent.

But on the Continent, in certain districts where differences of nationality are felt most acutely, e.g. Bohemia and Transylvania, separate nationality is claimed by populations which have lived side by side and under the same government for many centuries—in some cases for a thousand years or more—and which cannot be said to preserve any real memory of times when they were unconnected politically. Here nationality is bound up with language: those who speak different languages claim different origins. And it may be observed that in Wales and Ireland also nationality and language coincided not so very long ago, though now a considerable pro-

portion of the Welsh people and the great majority of the Irish have
lost their native languages.

It is true that this explanation does not apply to Scotland. Gaelic,
as well as English, is still spoken in a considerable part of the country.
But English had been the dominant language for some five centuries
before the Union of the Scottish and English crowns, in 1603; and
it is not at all certain that Gaelic was the language of the majority
of the population at any time within the last two thousand years.
Indeed, many scholars believe it to have been introduced from
Ireland at no very remote date, though this again is very doubtful.
At all events the movement for Scottish nationality is not—like the
Irish movement—bound up with the movement for the preservation
of the Gaelic language.

No certain analogy to the Scottish national movement is to be
found in Europe, so far as I am aware. In Norway the movement
for the restoration of the native language may be compared with the
movement for the preservation of Gaelic, but not with the Scottish
nationality movement; it has no separatist aims. A somewhat better
parallel may perhaps be found in the Serbo-Croatian dispute.[1] Here
we have two neighbouring peoples, speaking the same language,
but never connected politically with one another before their union
in 1918. The political, ecclesiastical and cultural connections of the
one had always been with the south and east, those of the other with
the north and west. Such a union, desirable as it doubtless was,
could not attain perfection in a day; and the speed with which
political unification was effected led, not unnaturally, to opposition
from the junior partner—or, to speak more accurately, from the
chief of the junior partners—which brought about the weakening
of the whole kingdom in the face of external danger. If this opposition is to be ascribed to a feeling for nationality, we must distinguish between 'Croatian nationality' and 'Yugoslav nationality';
for it was the growth of the latter feeling—for more than a century
past—which led to the unification of the various Yugoslav peoples.
At all events Croatia differs from Scotland in the fact that, by its union
with a foreign nation (Hungary), it had lost its independence more
than eight hundred years before its union with the other Yugoslavs.

Apart from this rather doubtful case, all nationality movements
on the Continent seem to be connected with language. The detailed
evidence for this statement will be reviewed in the next chapter.

Sometimes, as we shall see, the feeling for nationality is hardly

[1] I am speaking of the conditions which prevailed before the German invasion
in 1941.

more than an antiquarian interest, limited to more or less intellectual elements in the population. In other cases, however, it has come to be the strongest force in the life of the nation. The attainment of such strength would seem to need the stimulus of a powerful antagonistic force, either within the same country or beyond, but not too far beyond, its borders. It is no doubt by the absence of any such stimulus in this country that we are to explain the non-existence of any feeling for English nationality. In Yugoslavia, on the other hand, the feeling for nationality is well developed; but the stimulus is due, not to differences between Serbs and Croats, but to antagonism with external and alien peoples. In Germany a similar stimulus has been provided by antagonism towards the French, and still more the Poles and Czechs; in Poland by antagonism to the Germans and the Russians. In all such cases a difference of language seems to be involved.

It is often difficult or impossible to distinguish the feeling for nationality from patriotism—especially in countries where all, or nearly all, the population is of one nationality or language. Thus in England patriotism takes the place of nationalism; and English people frequently find it difficult to understand the feeling for nationality shown by other peoples. In Switzerland, on the other hand, a man may be a good Swiss patriot, whether his language be French, German or Italian; but his feeling for nationality will probably be governed, at least to some extent, by his language. Similar conditions may be found in Belgium and in Wales, and also in certain parts of Scotland where a linguistic boundary exists, or has existed. But in the last case the feeling for nationality is quite independent of Scottish nationalism; the latter feeling may be cherished equally by persons whose language is Gaelic or English. It would seem, indeed, that Scottish nationalism has more affinity with patriotism than with a feeling for nationality, as understood on the Continent.

Although patriotism and nationalism tend to coalesce, they are apparently of different origins. Both doubtless are natural and primary feelings; but the former seems to spring from love of home and the desire to preserve and protect it, while the latter is inspired by opposition or aversion to persons and things which are strange or unintelligible. Such opposition is not necessarily strong; under favourable conditions it may dwindle into insignificance. But it is liable to be strengthened if the difference of language is accompanied by cultural differences and a difference in religion, and especially if elements of fear or distrust are present, or if a conflict of interests arises.

The conditions of the Middle Ages were in general not very favourable to the growth of nationalism, except where differences of religion were involved. And even in such cases the religious element was usually stronger than the national—indeed, Christian armies fighting against Mohammedans or heathen commonly included contingents from various nationalities. Moreover, the ruling classes often spoke a different language from the mass of the population, while the Church was an international institution and employed an international language.

There were of course 'national' wars in which the religious element was absent, or not very obvious. We may instance the struggle of the Welsh against the Normans in the eleventh and twelfth centuries and that of the Scots against Edward I. But these were wars of conquest, involving a large amount of dispossession and spoliation; and the principle which animated the defenders may fairly be regarded as patriotism rather than nationalism.

In the fifteenth and sixteenth centuries we hear of some movements which seem to have been of a more truly national character. We may refer to the struggles of the Czechs during the Hussite period, and possibly to the war of independence in the Netherlands. But in both these cases the religious stimulus was probably the dominant force. On the other hand, the Swedish war of independence in the fifteenth century seems to have been due in the first case to misgovernment and spoliation by the Danish viceroys; and the movement for separation began in the industrial districts, among mineowners and miners. Probably therefore this movement ought to be described as patriotic rather than national. The same is true of the contemporary but unsuccessful movements for separation in Norway; and perhaps the war of independence in the Netherlands should be regarded in the same light.

The reason why one cannot speak more positively is that in the times which we have just been reviewing, and indeed down to the eighteenth century, nationalism can seldom be clearly distinguished from patriotism. The separatist movements and wars of independence of which we hear were almost always due to oppression and spoliation or extortion, which was very frequently combined with religious persecution. Those who strove to liberate their countries from alien oppression must be described as patriots. But a 'national idea', as distinct from patriotism, is hardly to be distinguished, except as a reminiscence of loyalty to a native ruler or royal family in the past: for the kingdoms and peoples of the Continent—apart from the Netherlands—were still regarded as the property of their rulers. It is apparently not until the latter part of the eighteenth century that we find this feeling or tradition of loyalty transferred from the ruler to the people itself—a change presumably connected in some way with the currents of thought which led to the Revolution in France. From this time onwards we may note the appearance of a feeling for nationality which differs somewhat from patriotism, and which does not necessarily require any cruel alien oppression or religious persecution to stimulate its growth.

It was in Austria, the hereditary dominion of the Hapsburgs, that modern nationalism seems first to have shown itself. In the sixteenth, and especially the seventeenth, centuries the Hapsburgs were responsible for more religious persecution than any other Christian dynasty of which we have record. As a result of this the Reformed religion was almost entirely destroyed, except in Hungary, the greater part of which was then under Turkish rule. The rigour of the persecution was somewhat modified after 1705; but it continued until 1781. In this year the traditional policy of the dynasty was completely reversed by the Emperor Joseph II, who was a free-thinker and zealous for reform in all directions, though, like other monarchs of his time, he regarded himself as alone entitled to decide—by decree—what changes were desirable. He abolished serfdom and other forms of oppression, and reformed the administration; he greatly reduced the number of religious establishments, but founded many new schools. In general his reforms were widely appreciated everywhere; but in the non-German parts of his dominions—in Hungary most of all—he aroused a storm of opposition by trying to enforce the use of German universally as the official language and the language of education.

This then was the period and these the conditions which produced modern nationalism. There was no question of religious persecution or of oppression in general. Freedom prevailed to an extent unprecedented in Austrian history—intellectually as well as in other respects. To most of the various peoples included in the Austrian dominions the next few years brought the birth or the revival of their native literatures. But Joseph's policy of enforcing the use of the German language—which has made him a hero to German nationalists—largely vitiated the effect of the benefits which he had conferred upon his dominions in general.[1] More especially was this the case

---

[1] His policy, however, seems not to have been entirely consistent. Owing to the opposition which he encountered from the Magyars, he is said to have encouraged separatist movements in Hungary. In particular, he founded schools for the Serbians in that country.

in Hungary, which had now recovered from its prostration in the
Turkish period, but which he refused to recognise as a separate
kingdom. It is true that he realised his mistake before his death in
1790. The obnoxious decrees were revoked; and Hungarian was
established as the language of education, and Latin restored as the
official language. A few years later, however, a new period of re-
actionary government began; and most of Joseph's reforms were
abolished. For more than half a century the new nationalism had
to limit its activities more or less to literature.[1] But the movement
had struck roots in all parts of the Austrian empire; and when—
from 1848 onwards—opportunities occurred again, it led to political
developments everywhere.

The constitutional movement in Poland, followed by the unsuccessful resistance to the Prussian and Russian armies, was contemporary with the reforms of Joseph II. The constitution was
proclaimed in 1791. But this was primarily a patriotic, rather than
nationalistic, movement. It was designed to save the country from
further partitions similar to that of 1772, though in fact it pre-
cipitated these disasters. In later times, however, the patriotic
movement assumed a nationalistic character, especially in Austria
(Galicia), where the situation was complicated by the existence of
a Ruthenian minority.

In the Balkans also nationalism was originally an outgrowth from
patriotism, which was largely affected by the conflict between Islam
and Orthodox Christianity. The Serbian war of independence—
from 1804 onwards—was primarily a patriotic movement. Many
of the leaders, including Kara-Gjorgje himself, had assisted the
Austrians in their abortive invasion of the country in 1788; and now,
when they saw that no more help was to be obtained from that
quarter, they undertook the work of liberation by themselves. The
Greek war of independence, which began in 1821, was likewise due
to patriotic feeling. And in principle the same may be said of the
contemporary movements in Rumania, though here the conditions
were more complicated.

In the period of liberation nationalism, as distinct from patriotism,
was more prominent in literature than in actual politics, though
outside Greece resentment was felt at the ecclesiastical privileges
enjoyed by Greeks, and in Rumania at their appointment as

---

[1] Great encouragement was given to the national aspirations of the Croatians
and Slovenians in 1809, when their lands were annexed by Napoleon; for their
languages came to be used officially and in schools. These privileges were abolished
after Napoleon's fall; but they had an important influence upon subsequent
history.

governors and officials. But the feeling for nationality gradually acquired strength, and in the latter part of the century it had become the most potent political force in the whole peninsula. It was believed that the Turkish empire in Europe was about to collapse; and each of the new states cherished claims to the heritage, which were in some areas irreconcilable. Indeed, the national movement had in view the political union of all the territories occupied by each of the nationalities, whether they were independent or subject to Turkey, Austria, Hungary or Russia—an object which was in large measure realised by the Treaty of Versailles in 1919.

In Italy the national movement followed a course which was in general somewhat similar to what we have noticed in the Balkans. Down to last century the country was divided among a considerable number of independent states, the ruling families of which were mostly of French or Austrian origin; Lombardy and (after 1815) Venetia belonged to Austria. Napoleon's campaigns transformed the country for a time and—though they impoverished it—introduced new ideas. But after his fall the previous conditions were restored, and a period of reaction and despotic government set in. A patriotic movement soon arose, which aimed primarily at the expulsion of the Austrians; but before long this developed into a movement for national unification. At first a federation was thought of; and in 1847 forms of constitutional government were established in most of the states. But this was followed by a series of abortive revolutions; and eventually it was decided to attempt the unification of the whole country under the king of Sardinia, who ruled Piedmont, and whose family was the only dynasty of native Italian origin. In 1859, by means of an alliance with France, the Sardinians expelled the Austrians from Lombardy—though not until 1867 from Venetia—and the rulers of all the other states were dispossessed by revolution. The final step was the occupation of Rome in 1870.

The national movement, however, was not satisfied with the unification of the peninsula. It was continued primarily with the object of liberating the remaining districts in Austria in which Italian was spoken, i.e. the Trentino (in South Tyrol) and certain districts on the Adriatic coast. But in course of time the nationalists began to cherish more ambitious designs and to include in their programme of annexations any region which it might be desirable to possess for strategic reasons or as a field for colonisation, whether it contained any Italian population or not. The first annexations carried out within the Mediterranean area were those of Tripoli with Cyrenaica, and Rhodes and the neighbouring islands, which were seized from Turkey in 1911–12. In 1915, when Italy entered the war against Germany and Austria, maps were issued, showing claims to large tracts of Austrian territory, in which the population was wholly German or Slovenian or Serbo-Croatian; and a very large proportion of these territories was in fact acquired by Italy at the Treaty of Versailles.

It will be seen then that in the history of Italian nationalism three phases may be distinguished—which we may call the phases of liberation, of unification and of aggression. The two first have been observed also in the Balkans; but in Italy the sequence was more rapid, and they overlapped to a considerable extent. It may be noted that since the beginning of the third phase—which followed the others after some interval—Italy has always been the chief enemy of the Yugoslavs and Greeks. Necessarily so, for their own unification is an obstacle to Italian schemes of annexation.

The national movement in Germany seems to have originated about the same time as that in Italy and under similar conditions. The two movements indeed had much in common, and were probably not unconnected. But the German movement had a more complicated history; and consideration of it must be deferred until a later chapter. The chief dates, however, may be mentioned here. The rise of national feeling took place during the war of liberation, which ended in 1813–14 with the overthrow of Napoleon. The first step towards national unification was the establishment of the German Confederation (with its Diet at Frankfort) in 1815. The next generation saw the growth of the Customs Union; the North German Confederation was established in 1866–7, the German Empire in 1871. The movement towards national aggression seems to have shown itself first in the eighties, unless we apply this term to the annexations of Sleswick-Holstein (1866) and Alsace-Lorraine (1871).[1] The movement acquired considerable strength by the foundation of the Pan-German League in 1894.

The case of Alsace-Lorraine is peculiar; it seems to be the only instance in Europe of national feeling moving in opposition to language. The provinces had belonged to the Empire down to the

---

[1] In both cases the majority of the population were German. But the former desired separation from Denmark and incorporation in Germany, whereas the latter did not desire separation from France. In both annexations the guiding force was Bismarck's policy for the aggrandisement of Prussia. The northern duchies were annexed to Prussia against their wishes. The western provinces were not annexed to Prussia, but placed under the personal authority of the emperor, who was king of Prussia. The influence of the national movement, however, is no doubt to be traced later, when large numbers of settlers were introduced from beyond the Rhine.

seventeenth century, when they were conquered by the French, for the most part during the Thirty Years' War (before 1648); and the great majority of the population still speak German. But the feeling has for a long time been French. I am not clear to what extent the annexation was prompted by German national feeling; but it certainly gave rise to a great movement of French national—or rather patriotic—feeling, both in the provinces themselves and in the rest of France. The situation which resulted from it may be described as a festering sore in the body of Europe.

Elsewhere in France there are several minorities with distinct languages of their own. Most, if not all, of these have a national consciousness, which shows itself in literary and antiquarian interests; but there are no separatist tendencies. In this respect the Basque and Provençal districts in the south show a remarkable contrast with the adjacent districts in Spain, as we shall see in the next chapter. In Brittany the Germans attempted to start a separatist (Celtic) movement in 1940; but the attempt seems to have proved a complete failure.

In these islands the history of national movements has been rather complicated. The Scottish National movement arose out of the negotiations for the Act of Union in 1702–7. The Scottish Parliament approved of the Union in principle, but objected to the actual terms, which practically robbed the country of its independence. In general the object of the movement has been to get these terms revised.

In this case, as we have noted, no question of a difference of language is involved. But the presence of a disaffected (Gaelic) element in the Highlands was no doubt a source of weakness to the Scottish cause. On the other hand, this element itself was actuated by dynastic, rather than consciously national, feeling. After 1745, however, the conditions changed. A Gaelic movement began to develop; but it was of the academic type, and limited to educational, literary and antiquarian activities. It seems to have shown no separatist tendencies.

In Ireland the national movement was in its earlier stages more of a patriotic character—due to misgovernment—than national in the strict sense. It is true that there had always been more or less hostility between the Irish and the English. But from the time of the Reformation this had been centred in religion; for the great majority of the Irish remained Catholics, and as such were placed under various disabilities. In 1782 the Irish Parliament, which was Protestant, acquired independence and proceeded to remove these disabilities; but the Crown intervened. This brought about a rebellion in 1798, which was punished with inexcusable severity. The Act of Union (1800) and the land-laws introduced new troubles, though the Emancipation of Catholics was passed by the British Parliament in 1829. A futile attempt at rebellion in 1848 led to the formation of plans, chiefly among the Irish who had emigrated to America, for the complete independence of Ireland. This movement resulted in the foundation, about 1858, of the 'Fenian Brotherhood', which derived its name from a military organisation of ancient Ireland—an indication that the objective was not the reform of abuses, but the recognition of a separate nationality. The movement, however, did not meet with much success at this time; and for the next half-century the Irish party, though they adopted the term 'Nationalist' about 1880, continued to press by constitutional means for the repeal of the Union and the reform of the land-laws. Then, in 1905, the movement for complete independence was revived by a new party, the Sinn Fein (i.e. 'We ourselves'), which after a time deprived the old Parliamentary party of nearly all its supporters, and eventually obtained the practical independence of the country by treaty in 1921. It was only this last movement which included in its policy the restoration of the Gaelic language, and thus brought the Irish movement into line with the national movements on the Continent. On the other hand, there seems never to have been any attempt to combine with the Gaelic-speaking inhabitants of western Scotland.

The Irish national (Sinn Fein) movement has a special interest attached to it by the fact that the language with which it is bound up is now spoken only by a small minority of the people.[1] It is as the language of Ireland in the past that it forms the backbone of Irish nationality. In this respect it may be compared with Hebrew in relation to the Jews. But the analogy must not be pressed too far; for Gaelic is not the language of the sacred books, whereas Hebrew lost its local connections long ago.

In Wales the national movement has always been bound up with the language, which is much more widely spoken than Gaelic (in either Ireland or Scotland). Its activities have been chiefly literary and educational, and include a number of valuable works. Much has been done for music and poetry by the Eisteddfod, which was

---

[1] Hence there seems to be a tendency in official circles to stress the geographical unity of Ireland, rather than the language, as the basis of Irish nationality. This is an argument of doubtful value when applied to maritime regions. To north-eastern Ireland connections with Britain would appear to be more vital than those with Ireland as a whole.

founded, or rather refounded, in 1798. Political activities are rendered difficult by the fact that more than half the population belong to Glamorgan and Monmouthshire, where more attention is paid to industrial than to national questions; but the national movement is now gaining ground. Extremists, who desire separation, seem to be few in number; but there are many people who feel that Wales has not received the recognition politically to which it is beyond question entitled on historical grounds.

The most outstanding feature of British history during the last hundred years has been the great and constantly increasing number of persons of Gaelic and Welsh origin who have attained distinction in political, commercial and intellectual life. The milieu from which our leading men are drawn has changed. Economic and political changes have brought to the surface new elements—new even in Scotland—which have strengthened and enriched the life of our country. For the British world of today 'Anglo-Celtic' would be a truer term than 'Anglo-Saxon'. Perhaps the Acts of Union have contributed to this end. But it is as individuals that these elements have entered into British national life. With the nationalities our relations—the relations of the central government—have been less successful. With Ireland they have led to dismal failure.

Yet to a Power which is the centre of a cosmopolitan empire and has interests and responsibilities throughout the world the existence of different nationalities in the home lands might have been a source of strength instead of weakness. To this end, however, mutual knowledge and appreciation between the nationalities is essential. And unfortunately the attainment of such knowledge and appreciation has been prevented by an antiquated and narrow educational system,[1] which knows nothing of nationalities or their aspirations, whether within these islands or beyond. It will be seen in a later chapter how this defect has affected, and still affects, our relations with foreign nations, as well as with India and colonial peoples.

As regards the milieu in which national movements have taken place a few words may be said here, though they must be of a

---

[1] We speak of the 'British Government', the 'British Empire', etc.; but the history on which we are brought up is still that of England only. The average educated Englishman knows of perhaps two incidents in the history of Scotland—English, not Gaelic, Scotland—but of Welsh or Irish history he knows nothing at all, apart from their relations with England. These lands are rich in historical associations; but for him they have no more than Tahiti or Timbuctoo. And how many people in England are aware that the Welsh are the modern representatives of a nation which once ruled not only the greater part of Britain, but also across the Channel, from Lisbon to Ankara?

summary character. In some cases fuller information will be given in the next chapter.

The movements have seldom, if ever, been initiated by persons of high position—princes, noblemen, generals, or even wealthy merchants. Usually the originators seem to have been literary men or teachers, sometimes also priests. In their initial stages there was apparently little or no difference between those movements which developed political activities and those which remained more or less academic. The beginning of political activities can generally be traced to large towns, where considerable numbers of people, chiefly 'black-coated workers', had received their education from the teachers, or come under their influence. Sometimes this took place even in foreign lands, to which there had been an exodus owing to oppressive conditions in the home land.

When a national or patriotic movement has taken the form of an armed rising,[1] the leadership has commonly come into the hands of countrymen who have gained experience and fame in guerilla warfare or brigandage. But the way has commonly been prepared for them by an intellectual movement. For an example we may refer to the Serbian war of independence in 1804. Kara-Gjorgje was a countryman, who had been a soldier and an outlaw. But the preliminary work had been done in the previous twenty years by literary men and teachers in the Hungarian towns and Vienna, where great numbers of Serbians had settled, to escape from Turkish oppression. In Greece, somewhat later, and in Bulgaria, much later, the course of events was similar, though in the latter case the fighting was done by Russian armies. The history of the Irish revolution, in 1921, was not very different.

National movements in general may be regarded as essentially democratic in their milieu and objectives, at least in so far as they are connected with political activities. Those which have no such connections, but are purely intellectual in their interests, are at least in no way antidemocratic; they have done much for the preservation of oral literature and other records belonging to their peoples, and are usually accompanied by educational work which is of considerable value. It is only when nationalism becomes aggressive that it tends to adopt policies—especially that of terrorism—which are incompatible with the principles of true democracy. Both Nazism

---

[1] In general such risings are better described as 'patriotic' than as 'national', especially when, as in Serbia, they are sudden, and provoked by an outbreak of persecution. But they are commonly preceded and accompanied by 'national' movements among intellectual people, which give permanence to the revolution. In Ireland the national element was the dominant orce.

and Fascism have strong democratic associations; and both have as their object the promotion of the interests of the German or Italian peoples. But they also associated themselves from the beginning with elements—military and capitalistic—which were essentially anti-democratic, for the purpose of promoting thereby the interests of their own peoples by the spoliation of other peoples. These anti-democratic elements possessed great political influence and, even before the appearance of Nazism and Fascism, had long been seek-ing,[1] with very considerable success, to gain popular support—a fact which is apt to be forgotten in this country. The way had thus been prepared by the earlier movements, chiefly through educational channels,[2] so that Nazism soon succeeded in permeating the younger generation of the German people[3] with doctrines—autocracy, terrorism, violence—which are subversive of the principles of democracy. Extreme nationalism, like the extreme forms of other popular movements, is no doubt liable to outbreaks of terrorism and violence—we may refer, for example, to the Irish Republican Army —but nationalism in itself cannot fairly be held responsible for the organised horrors of the last few years. With the military element we shall have to deal in a later chapter.

[1] Through earlier organisations, such as the Pan-German League.

[2] To educational sources must be traced also the 'superiority complex' which has influenced German opinion so greatly during the last half century.

[3] It would seem that this took place only to a much slighter extent in Italy. But I do not know the facts well enough to speak with confidence.

CHAPTER II

THE LANGUAGES OF EUROPE

THERE are now between forty and fifty languages spoken in Europe
—not including the languages of the Caucasus. As to the exact
number opinions may differ. Sometimes the languages spoken in
two or more regions may differ from one another so little that they
may be regarded as merely dialects of one language. Again, it is
uncertain whether we should count a few languages which are dying
out. But in any, case the number of distinct languages in actual use
cannot be said to be less than forty.

Nearly all these languages have a more or less developed feeling
for nationality associated with them, though the feeling differs of
course in intensity and scope.

Most of the languages fall into well-marked groups, as shown in
the notes to the map. The languages included within each of these
groups show more or less resemblance to one another; and these
resemblances were formerly much stronger than they now are.
Fifteen centuries ago the differences within most of the groups were
very slight; and the languages must have been mutually intelligible,
if not virtually identical. Between some of the groups also—those
which belong to the Indo-European linguistic family—there are
certain resemblances which likewise were greater in the past than
now. But these latter relationships date from more remote times—
three or four thousand years ago, or perhaps even more.

We will now take in order the languages which belong to each of
the groups in the Indo-European family, and afterwards the languages and groups of languages which do not belong to that family.
The direction to be followed in the survey will be roughly from west
to east. The numbers in the following paragraphs refer to the map.

The Celtic languages fall into two main branches, which differ
greatly from one another.

1, 2. The resemblance between Irish and Scottish Gaelic is so
close that they might fairly be regarded as dialects of one language.
But there is little or no feeling of common nationality, since the two
countries have long been divided, first by political history and then
by religion. In both countries Gaelic is now spoken only by a small
minority of the population, chiefly in the western districts. But a
good deal has been done to revive it, especially in Ireland, where
the movement for its restoration has in recent times been linked with

the movement for national independence, and where it is now recognised as the first official language. On the other hand, the revival of Scottish Gaelic is due to a feeling of the patriotic anti- quarian type, which is usually coincident with loyalty to 'our country', i.e. primarily the kingdom of Scotland (as a whole). This is of course in contrast with Ireland where, before the declaration of independence, loyalty (loyalism) and patriotism were antagonistic principles. The conditions in Northern Ireland are of course more complex.

3. Manx differs but little from Irish, and perhaps even less from Scottish Gaelic. When written, however, it gives a rather different impression, owing to the fact that its orthography was reformed, largely under English influence, in the eighteenth century. It is said to be very little spoken now; but there are still people who are in- terested in its preservation from a patriotic antiquarian point of view.

4, 5, 6. The Welsh, Cornish and Breton languages differ very greatly from Gaelic. On the other hand, they have much in common with one another, though the resemblances are not nearly so close as those of the Gaelic languages.

Both Welsh and Breton are still widely spoken. The former is usually bound up with a feeling for (Welsh) nationality, which is strongly developed, but is seldom in conflict with loyalty to Britain as a whole. The Breton language seems to have made much less pro- gress in literary and educational activities than Welsh, though it has long been the subject of patriotic antiquarian interest. I do not know how far the feeling for nationality has led to political aspirations; but the proposals for the independence of the country put forward by the Germans in 1940 have apparently not met with much success.

Cornish is generally believed to have died out more than a century ago, though there are persons now living who claim to have known it from infancy. It is the subject of a good deal of patriotic anti- quarian interest; and recently it has been used occasionally in church services.

The Romance languages are descended from Latin, which in the time of the Roman empire was spread over the greater part of southern and western Europe, and displaced the native languages. The languages indicated by the figures in the map are: (1) Portu- guese, (2) Spanish, (3) Catalan, (4) Provençal, (5) French, (6) Italian, (7) some Sardinian dialects, (8) the Alpine dialects, (9) Rumanian.

It is not much more than two thousand years since Latin, the parent language, came to be spoken in any of the countries outside

Italy; and individually each of these languages may be said to have had a life of about fifteen hundred years. Now the differences between them are such that in general two neighbouring languages are mutually intelligible with more or less difficulty, while distant languages are as a rule not mutually intelligible.

2, 3, 4. The political and social connections of Catalonia down to the twelfth century were with the south of France. From the Christian Spanish kingdoms it was separated by a broad belt of Moorish territory. In 1135, soon after the collapse of Moorish power in the north, it became joined to the kingdom of Aragon; and from that time, for eight hundred years, it has belonged, first to that kingdom, and then, from 1469, to the unified kingdom of Spain. Yet it has retained its own language, the connections of which still lie with the south of France. Indeed, Catalan and Provençal are hardly more than dialectal variations of one language. In the Middle Ages this was the most cultivated language of poetry in Europe. But in Provence from the sixteenth century, if not earlier, it was displaced by French as the language of the higher classes and of education; and it has never regained its position, although a revival in poetry took place last century.

The feeling for nationality differs greatly in the different linguistic areas. In Portugal, Spain—apart from Catalonia and perhaps the Basque districts—and France it coincides with patriotism towards the country as a whole. This is true even of Provence, where the dominant feeling is for France, though there is often also a (subsidiary) patriotic antiquarian interest in the native language, and especially in its literature. But in Catalonia the feeling for nationality is strongly separatist. It is often, but not always, combined with schemes of political and economic reorganisation.

6, 7. Italy, the home-land of the Romance languages, possesses numerous dialects, the differences between which are considerable; in some cases they are as great, and would seem to be at least as ancient, as any of those which are to be found between one Romance language and another. The most extreme examples occur in Sardinia. I do not know how far the dialects are associated with any feeling of (local) patriotism. The feeling for Italian nationality—indeed we may say Italian patriotism—itself seems to be a comparatively modern growth; but in the course of last century it had an immense development, even after the unification of the country. It has no doubt been much exploited by politicians; but the fact that they found in it the most promising means of advancing their own interests shows how great a hold it had on popular sentiment.

8. In eastern Switzerland and the eastern Alps a number of Romance dialects have survived from Roman times in high mountain valleys which, owing to their remoteness, escaped occupation by the German invaders in the fifth and sixth centuries. Some of these dialects have now acquired a more or less standard and literary form. That of the Engadin is recognised as one of the official languages of Switzerland.

9. Rumanian and the dialects related thereto would seem to have had a similar history. Outside Rumania these dialects are found in mountainous districts in various parts of the Balkan Peninsula. The speakers are mostly nomad herdsmen, who commonly know one or more other languages—Serbian, Bulgarian or Greek—as well as their own. The Rumanian language itself was probably preserved at one time under somewhat similar conditions, though by a larger and perhaps more compact population, It seems to have owed its survival to the Carpathians, which must have served as a refuge to the inhabitants of the surrounding country from successive waves of invasion, until better conditions allowed them to return to their homes.

The feeling for nationality in Rumania is acute. Like Italy, it was divided until recently among various governments. Wallachia and Moldavia had retained some degree of autonomy throughout the Turkish period. But they were under separate rulers; they were not united until 1859. Transylvania had belonged to Hungary for many centuries; it shared the fate of Hungary under Turkish rule and, later, under Austria. Bukovina was annexed by Austria in 1777, and Bessarabia by Russia in 1812. In the eighteenth and nineteenth centuries the two autonomous principalities were frequently occupied by Russian armies.

The national movement for independence and unification began early in last century, and was accompanied by educational reform and considerable literary activity. The union of the two principalities was effected in 1859; and in 1878 complete independence was granted to the new state—which in 1881 became a kingdom. But the remaining provinces,[1] Transylvania, Bukovina and Bessarabia, were not acquired until 1918. Unfortunately, all these provinces contain more or less considerable alien minorities which are a constant source of danger. Thus Transylvania contains about 1,500,000 Hungarians, nearly all of whom live in the centre of the province, surrounded by Rumanians. Before 1920 their isolation was of no

[1] Dobrudža was annexed in 1913. Changes which have taken place since 1939 are not taken into account here.

consequence, since the whole province was under Hungarian rule. But then the position was reversed, and these Hungarians became subject to Rumanian rule. The acute feeling for nationality, which prevails in both nations, precludes the possibility of settling this question by common consent. In Rumania, too, the difficulty of all such questions has been intensified by the influence of nationalistic organisations, which are prepared to resort to violence.

The Teutonic languages fall into three main branches. The differences between these branches are at least as old as the differences between the various Romance languages, and on the whole distinctly greater. They are not so old, and perhaps not quite so great, as those between the two main branches of the Celtic languages. But in general they are quite sufficient to prevent any mutual intelligibility.

1. The English language, in both England and Scotland, has many dialects, which differ considerably, usually in proportion to their (geographical) distance from one another. Some of these dialects have a good deal of patriotic sentiment associated with them. This is true especially of the Scottish dialects collectively, and next perhaps of those of Yorkshire. But in England generally the feeling for nationality—we may say the feeling for (exclusively English) patriotism—is probably less developed than in any other country in Europe. Its place is taken by what used to be called 'loyalty to king and country', but may be defined more accurately as patriotism towards Britain (as a whole) and the empire. In Scotland of course the feeling is not quite the same; a good-sized niche in the shrine is usually reserved for Scotland itself. With Scottish nationalists Scotland would come before Britain, though probably very few would leave the latter out altogether.

2. The nearest affinities of English are to be found in the Frisian dialects. The Frisians have no standard language, but only a number of dialects, which find their way into print only to a limited extent. These dialects are West Frisian, which is spoken in the Dutch province of Friesland, East Frisian, spoken on one or two islands off the mouths of the Ems and the Weser,[1] and North Frisian, spoken on the west coast of the province of Sleswick, between Tondern and Husum, together with the adjacent islands of Sylt, Föhr, Amrum and Heligoland. In the last case there is said to be a good deal of difference between the dialect of the coast and that of the islands.

---

[1] The language called East Frisian which is now spoken in the Prussian district of Ost-Friesland, to the east of the mouth of the Ems, is a Low German dialect, which has displaced the native Frisian.

The Frisian language was once much more widespread. A thousand years ago the Frisians occupied the whole coast of the North Sea from Flushing to the mouth of the Weser, and even beyond. The North Frisians of the coast are believed to be settlers from this region; but the language of the islands, it is thought, may have survived from the time when the English came to Britain from the peninsula, in the fifth century.

I do not know whether an Englishman could understand any of the Frisian dialects, if he heard it spoken. But he certainly could not read it without special study. A Dutchman might perhaps be able to make something of West Frisian; for the two languages have always been neighbours, and have clearly influenced each other very greatly. Probably all Frisians now understand either Dutch or German, as well as their own language.

Many West Frisians take a patriotic interest in their language and nationality; and a certain amount of literature, consisting chiefly of poetry and stories, is published at Leeuwarden. I do not know whether the feeling for nationality has led to any political activities. In East Frisian a considerable amount of legal literature has been preserved from the Middle Ages; but this dialect seems now to be almost extinct. I have not seen any modern literature in either this or the northern dialects, except a few specimens which have been collected by philologists—chiefly translations of passages from the Gospels. The North Frisian communities are, I understand, quite small.

3, 4, 5. The Dutch and German languages form a second branch of the Teutonic group.

Dutch may be taken as including Flemish, the language of the northern half of Belgium, with which it is virtually identical. Beyond this its original affinities lay with German, rather than with Frisian; but in course of time the two languages have come to differ so much that it would be difficult for a Dutchman to understand a German, or vice versa, without special study. There are, however, dialects— Low German or Platt-Deutsch—in the north of Germany which are intermediate between the two, and sometimes approximate very closely to Dutch. It is said that the true line of division between German and Low German runs from west to east through the Ruhr district, to the south of Magdeburg, and through the neighbourhood of Berlin; but actually the use of the Low German dialects is now more or less restricted to a few districts, of which the largest and most important includes Holstein, with southern Sleswick, and Mecklenburg. This district produced some noteworthy poets last century. Another, somewhat similar, dialect is the 'East Frisian'—

to the east of the mouth of the Ems—which has displaced the native Frisian dialect and taken its name.

There has been much linguistic displacement. In early times Frisian, which was then the language of the greater part of the present kingdom of the Netherlands, was largely displaced by Dutch, which in that period may be regarded as a variety of Low German. In later times Low German itself has been largely displaced by German (i.e. High German), which is much further removed from Dutch. In the Middle Ages Low German had a considerable literature; but towards the end of that period it had begun to give way to the southern language, which was that of the imperial court and of nearly all the more important principalities. Its decline was hastened by the publication of Luther's Bible (1522–34), which soon came to be generally accepted as the standard language of schools. By this time, however, the Netherlands were already drifting away from the Empire; their literary and educational activities developed on lines of their own, influenced no doubt by the Dutch, not the German, Bible. The gradual displacement of Low German by High German served therefore only to cut them off more effectively from their eastern neighbours.

The growth of the feeling for nationality in Germany was due in the first place to the currents of thought connected with the French Revolution, and then, more especially, to the disturbance caused by the French wars of aggression under Napoleon, which followed. The country was divided among a large number of states, great and small, each under a hereditary or ecclesiastical ruler, who was virtually independent. It is true that these states had belonged for a thousand years to the Holy Roman Empire, which was essentially a German empire, though it included some other peoples. But the authority of the Empire had for long been hardly more than nominal. The national movement set itself to bring about political and economic unity. It succeeded in establishing, and then gradually enlarging, a Customs' Union; and eventually, in 1871, it led to the foundation of a new German Empire. To this subject we shall have to return in a later chapter.

The national movement has been essentially bound up with the German, i.e. High German, language. It does not preclude interest of academic or local patriotic type in the Low German language; but it would never have tolerated a serious claim to separate nationality based on a language which is nearer to Dutch than to its own. The general effect of the movement has been to hasten the extinction or decline of Low German. Hence it is no accident that the area in which this language is best preserved consists of three provinces of which two were attached to Denmark down to 1864, while the third was the last of all the German states to join the Customs' Union.

Among the Dutch a national movement took place four centuries ago; but it was at least as much religious as national. It ended in the severance of the southern from the northern half of the people. Both Belgium and the Netherlands had belonged to the Hapsburg family. At the time of the Reformation the Netherlands secured their independence and maintained the Protestant religion. But the Hapsburgs succeeded in retaining possession of Belgium—which is half Dutch, half French—and in enforcing its adherence to Catholicism. In 1815 the two countries were united under the Dutch crown; but this arrangement lasted only until 1831, when Belgium revolted, and was constituted an independent kingdom.

In the Netherlands, as in this country, patriotism takes the place of national feeling. And the same seems to be true of Belgium, though among the Flemish population there is a feeling for nationality strong enough to secure that their language shall have equal rights with French. It is true that a more ambitious movement, aiming at total separation, made its appearance during the war of 1914–18, and has doubtless been at work again in recent years. But this cannot be regarded as an outcome of genuine and spontaneous national feeling. It was not directed towards reunion with the Netherlands, nor towards any object for the benefit of either the Flemings or the Dutch people as a whole. It was organised wholly for the benefit of the German Reich. There is no reason for doubting that it was one of the numerous organisations started by German agents for the purpose of spreading disunion and weakening the authority of the government in lands which they wish to gain possession of, and that the leaders of the movement themselves were actuated by the hope of reward, pecuniary or political, from the German government.

I do not know whether there is any feeling for nationality among the Flemish population of French Flanders—in the neighbourhood of Dunkirk.

The Scandinavian languages—viz. (6) Danish, (7) Swedish, (8) Norwegian, and (9) Icelandic—form the third branch of the Teutonic group. They are not intelligible to English, Dutch or German speakers without special study.

Danish and Swedish are near enough to one another to be mutually intelligible without much difficulty. But I do not think that an Icelander would be able to understand either of them. The native

language of Norway was similar to that of Iceland—which was a
Norwegian colony. But this language (Landsmål) now survives only
in dialects. For during the period when Norway was united to
Denmark (1387–1814) Danish became the standard language, and
still remains so, though in a slightly modified form (Riksmål). There
is a movement, however, to restore the old native language.

Færoese should perhaps be regarded as another distinct language;
but it differs very little from Icelandic. In the other colonies the
Norse language died out long ago, except in Shetland, where it
survived until last century.

In Scandinavian lands, as in England and the Netherlands,
patriotism takes the place of nationalism. Some feeling for nationality, however, is reflected in the movement for restoring the old
language of Norway. There is also a rather widespread tendency
towards a feeling for nationality in a much wider sense, viz. as em-
bracing the Scandinavian peoples generally, or at least those of the
three kingdoms.

Apart from the three branches of the Teutonic languages discussed above, there was formerly an eastern or Gothic branch, which
in early times was very widely distributed. The last remains of it
survived in the Crimea down to the seventeenth century.

The Slavonic languages are: (1) Russian, (2) Bulgarian, (3) Yugoslav (Serbo-Croatian), (4) Slovenian, (5) Slovak, (6) Czech,
(7) Polish, (8) the Lusatian dialects. It may seem arbitrary to treat
Russian with all its dialects as one unit, and at the same time to
take Slovak and Czech as two separate units; but from a historical
point of view this is on the whole perhaps the most convenient
arrangement.

The Slavonic languages in general show a somewhat closer resemblance to one another than either the Romance or the Teutonic
languages. This is true especially of the eastern and southern languages (Nos. 1–4). A Serbian or Croatian can understand Slovenian
without great difficulty; and even Russian or Bulgarian would hardly
be hopelessly unintelligible to him. The western (north-western)
languages (Nos. 5–8), however, differ more both from these and also,
except in the case of Czech and Slovak, from one another.

1. The standard language of Russia is Great Russian, and belonged originally to the region round Moscow. The dialects of White
Russia and the Ukraine (Little Russia and the regions to the south
and west of it) differ considerably from Great Russian. They produced an abundant literature in the past, and are still written to

some extent. In a later chapter it will be pointed out that Little Russia was the original nucleus of Russia. This region is the scene of the heroic stories which relate to the earliest times, and which are still preserved in oral poetry in the north of Russia.

2. The Bulgarians were originally a Turkish (Turco-Tataric), not a Slavonic, people. But they began to acquire a Slavonic language probably from the time when they first settled in the present Bulgaria—c. 680—if not before, for they had been known as raiders in this region for nearly two centuries. In the course of the next two or three centuries they became entirely Slavonised; about 900, or a little earlier, they adopted the Slavonic liturgy of Cyril and Methodios. From now for a considerable time they were the leading Slavonic people in the Balkans, and were largely responsible for the ecclesiastical Slavonic literature, which was current among all the Orthodox Slavonic peoples. The Turkish conquest in 1393, however, made a complete break, not only in the political but also in the cultural and literary history of the Bulgarians. The Church came into the hands of the Greeks, and the Slavonic liturgy was suppressed.

The modern Bulgarian language has affinities with both Russian and Serbo-Croatian; but a much larger proportion of its inflections has been lost—at least in the standard language—than in either of these. In literature there seems to have been a blank period of between three and four centuries; apparently no modern Bulgarian book was published before the latter part of the eighteenth century. The first school was established in 1835; but this was soon followed by many others. Literary activity may be said to have begun about the middle of last century.

3. The Serbians and Croatians speak the same language, which we may call either Serbo-Croatian or Yugoslav (i.e. South Slavonic). But the Serbians, who are Orthodox, use the Cyrillic alphabet, like the Russians and the Bulgarians, whereas the Croatians, who are Catholics, use the Roman alphabet, like the rest of the Slavonic peoples. The Serbians were the leading people in the Balkans in the thirteenth and fourteenth centuries, and contributed much to ecclesiastical Slavonic literature. Their literary activities, however, were reduced to a low ebb after the Turkish conquest, in 1459; and from this time not much was produced until the eighteenth century. Since then there has been a great revival. On the other hand, the Catholic districts were in general less affected by the Turks; their political connections were rather with Hungary, Venice and Austria. Consequently literature in the Roman character has flourished

continuously, at least in the coast-lands, from the fifteenth century. The Mohammedan Yugoslavs in Bosnia also now generally use this alphabet.

All Yugoslavs have a common oral literature, especially heroic poetry, which reaches back to the fourteenth century, and has been of great importance in the intellectual life of the nation. Some of the themes are current also in the western part of Bulgaria.

4. The Slovenians occupy the northernmost part of Yugoslavia—Carniola and southern Carinthia—and the adjacent districts in Italy. Their language differs but little from Serbo-Croatian; but their historical connections in the past have been with Austria. Literary activity began with the Reformation, but began to increase greatly towards the end of the eighteenth century.

5, 6. The Slovaks and Czechs speak closely related languages; but they have had different histories. The Czech kingdoms of Bohemia and Moravia—the former of which can be traced back to *c.* 620—were included in the Empire from the time of Charlemagne, with one or two intervals. Before the Hungarian invasion (*c.* 895) the territories of the Czechs and Slovaks probably extended to the borders of the Slovenians. It was here that Slavonic Christianity and the ecclesiastical Slavonic literature had their origin through the mission of Cyril and Methodios in 863. But the work of the mission was brought to an end in 885 through the influence of Rome, and especially the German Catholic bishops. It could never be renewed, since a few years later this region was cut off from the Greek world by the invasion of the Hungarians, who conquered and occupied the plain of the Danube. The Slovaks remained in occupation of the hill country to the north; but they were conquered by the Hungarians, and continued to be subject to them until 1920. The Czechs, on the other hand, remained attached to the Empire.

Literary activity developed among the Czechs in the thirteenth century, and flourished especially between the fourteenth and the sixteenth. In 1310 the kingdom of Bohemia passed to the Luxemburg family, who from 1347 to 1437 held also the imperial throne. Later it came to be united with Hungary, and in 1526 both kingdoms passed into the possession of the Hapsburg family. The Czechs had adopted the Reformation; and consequently they lost all their rights in the Thirty Years' War (*c.* 1620). The country was ruined, and literature came virtually to an end. The revival began under Joseph II (1780–90). Slovak literature began about the same date, or not much later. In earlier times the Slovaks had written in Czech.

7. The Poles, who were converted in 967, had in the tenth and eleventh centuries a large and powerful kingdom, which extended to the west of the Oder and sometimes included Pomerania. In the twelfth century their power was weakened by partitions of territory among the princes; but it was consolidated again in the fourteenth. In 1386 the kingdom was more than doubled in extent by the marriage of the heiress Jadviga with Jogaila, the ruler of the Lithuanians, who then held White Russia and Little Russia. But the union remained personal until 1569, when Lithuania, with all its subject territories, was incorporated in Poland. Poland was now the largest kingdom in the eastern half of Europe. Its territories extended from the Baltic to the Black Sea. The Kiev district, and from thence to the Black Sea, was annexed by the Russians in 1667; but, with this exception, the Polish territories remained undiminished until the first partition by Russia, Austria and Prussia in 1772. Further partitions followed—between Russia and Prussia in 1792, and finally between all the three powers in 1795. In 1815, after the Napoleonic wars,[1] there was some redistribution, whereby the Russian share was substantially increased.

The Poland restored by the Treaty of Versailles was not quite so large as Poland proper—without Lithuania—before 1569, since it did not contain the district of Lwow. But in the following years (1920–1) the Poles annexed considerable parts of Little Russia, White Russia and Lithuania, though not nearly so much of these regions as had belonged to Poland before 1772.

The peasants of eastern Poland have continued to speak Russian dialects. But the upper classes speak Polish both here and, for the most part, in Lithuania. In the latter country they would seem to be natives who became Polonised after—or even before—the union of 1569. In the former there are probably both Lithuanian and Russian elements.

8. The Lusatian Wendish communities in the upper part of the basin of the Spree are remains of the Sorbi, a Slavonic people who once occupied the whole of the region between the middle Elbe and the middle Oder. Now they are said to be not more than 100,000 in number. Other Slavonic peoples once lived to the west of the Elbe, and in Bavaria, Holstein and Mecklenburg. To these we shall have to refer in the next chapter.

A feeling for nationality is to be found perhaps among all Slavonic peoples. But it varies a good deal in intensity; and it has had a

---

[1] Napoleon had reassembled the greater part of Poland as a 'Duchy of Warsaw', which he presented to the king of Saxony.

different history among the different peoples. In the past it was
generally connected with religion.

The Russians are the people among whom it has been least developed, at all events until very recently. In its place there was a
strong feeling of devotion to the Church and the Tsar, which had
been inherited from early times. For illustration we may refer to
such expressions as 'Holy Russia' and 'the Orthodox Tsar', which
abound in traditional oral poetry. The strength of the feeling was no
doubt intensified by the fact that the wars waged by the Russians,
down to the eighteenth century, were almost always against Moslem
or Catholic peoples. The religious element was no doubt largely
eliminated by Peter the Great and some of his successors; but it is
not clear that their feelings were shared by anyone except the
highest officials. The frequent wars which they undertook seem to
have been inspired more by commercial and strategic considerations
than by any hope of freeing Russian communities from alien domination. Even the annexations of eastern Poland in 1772–95 can hardly
be regarded as exceptions. It is true that much of the population of
this region was really Russian—Little Russian or Red Russian. Of
this population, however, a considerable proportion—in Galicia—
was taken over by Austria, while Russia annexed other districts,
which were purely Polish. On the other hand, a strong feeling for
Russian nationality grew up later in Galicia itself.

In Poland before the partitions the feeling for nationality seems
to have been even less developed than in Russia. From 1697 to 1763
the kings were foreigners. The (Catholic) Church and the great
nobles were the only forces in the country which counted. But this
was all changed after the first partition. Before accomplishing the
second and third partitions, the invaders had to encounter a movement—patriotic rather than nationalistic in the strict sense—which
was strong enough to produce considerable, though untrained and
ill-equipped, armies. Since that time the feeling has never abated.

Most of the other Slavonic peoples were for some centuries subject
to the Hapsburgs. Among all of these the feeling for nationality
seems to have found expression in the reign of Joseph II (1780–90),
who introduced religious toleration and in general abandoned the
policy of repression followed by his predecessors.

In the times when the Czechs retained the government of their
own country, whether under the Hapsburgs or other dynasties, they
had adopted the Reformed religion. Consequently their autonomy
perished with their religion in the Thirty Years' War; and it was not
until a more liberal policy was initiated by Joseph II that their

feeling for nationality was able to express itself. The tangible results achieved did not at the time amount to much; for Joseph himself was intent on a policy of Germanisation, and the reform policy was abandoned a few years after his death. Yet the time had proved sufficient for the resurrection of the national language, which soon displayed considerable literary activity, in both books and journals. After 1848 more progress was effected. In the latter part of last century the Czechs succeeded in obtaining recognition for their language in official use and in education; but they failed in their attempts to get their kingdom restored on the same footing as that of Hungary.

The Slovenians came under German rule at a much earlier date than the Czechs. From the ninth century their land was gradually divided into a number of provinces, which were governed, under the Empire, by hereditary German dukes, though in one case[1] a curious ceremony of installation, conducted in Slovenian, suggests that at one time it had been necessary for a new duke to be elected, or at least approved, by the inhabitants. Very little literature—almost wholly religious—has been preserved from the Middle Ages, though the earliest texts date probably from the ninth century. But in the sixteenth century the Reformation produced great literary activity, which affected also the neighbouring Croatians. As among the Czechs, Protestantism was stamped out in the following century; but literary activity did not entirely cease. In the revival which took place towards the end of the eighteenth century it was associated with national aspirations; and the movement was greatly stimulated in 1809, when a large part of Slovenia, together with portions of Croatia and Dalmatia, was annexed to Napoleon's empire. The Slovenian language was used officially and in schools. The realisation of the Slovenians' hopes was frustrated, it is true, a few years later, when these 'Illyrian Provinces' were recovered by the Hapsburgs; and the connections with Croatia and Dalmatia were broken. But Slovenian literature has continued to flourish down to the present day.

The Slovaks and the Croatians were subject to Hungary for many centuries, the former from c. 900, the latter from 1102. This kingdom, in the eighteenth century was recovering after the expulsion of the

[1] The dukes of Carinthia were installed, down to 1414, near Maria-Saal (about five miles north of Klagenfurt), apparently on the site of the ancient Virunum, later called Carantana. The ceremony was conducted by a peasant, who had to inquire after the character of the new duke and slap him in the face. The first recorded German duke seems to have been the emperor Arnulf (before 887). Not many years before this the Slovenians had rulers of their own.

Turks. But it had the incurable weakness that the Hungarians (Magyars) themselves, who were the dominant element, formed only a minority of the total population. The national aspirations of both the Slovaks and the Croatians were awakened by the struggle between Joseph II and the Hungarians, and were perhaps encouraged to some extent by the emperor. The Slovaks were also much influenced by the national movement among the Czechs, whose language differs very little from their own. Slovak now made its first appearance as a literary language, while Croatian literature gained a new lease of life.

The struggle between the Hungarians and the Austrian emperors, Joseph's successors, continued through the greater part of the nineteenth century. The Austrians were supported by the subject nationalities, especially the Croatians, who in 1848 went to war against the Hungarian government; and all this period was favourable to national aspirations, which were accompanied by considerable literary activity. But in 1867 the Hungarians succeeded in securing complete independence within the borders of their kingdom; and for the next half-century—until after 1918—all movements on behalf of the subject nationalities were suppressed. Croatia nominally had an autonomous government of its own; but this was constantly coerced by the Hungarian governor.

All the peoples of Yugoslavia, except the Slovenians, speak the same language; but their political history has been very different. Dalmatia, or at least the greater part of it, belonged originally to the kingdom of Croatia, with which it passed in course of time to Hungary. But from 998 onwards it was occupied for shorter or longer periods by the Venetians, who from the fifteenth century held it continuously. In the south the conditions were more complex; some districts had been attached to Serbia in medieval times, and the inhabitants are regarded as Serbians. Ragusa (Dubrovnik), however, was an independent republic, under Turkish suzerainty, from the fifteenth century. Italian was much spoken in the towns, including Dubrovnik, especially by the richer classes, though in modern times it has been limited practically to Zadar (Zara). But Yugoslav literature flourished greatly under the influence of the Italian Renaissance, especially at Dubrovnik; and the themes were drawn largely from Yugoslav life. Eventually the whole of Dalmatia, together with Dubrovnik, was seized by Napoleon, when he destroyed the republic of Venice. Then after short periods, first of Austrian, and then of French rule, it was formed into a new Austrian province at the settlement in 1814.

The Serbians had in the Middle Ages a powerful kingdom which extended both to the Adriatic and to the Aegean. After the Turkish conquest, in 1459—and apparently to some extent even earlier— there was a movement of population northwards into Hungarian territory. These Serbians themselves fell under Turkish rule when the greater part of Hungary was conquered, in 1526. But when the Austrians expelled the Turks from Hungary, in 1688, they played an important part in the campaign. In the following year the Austrians conquered a considerable part of the old Serbian kingdom; and this conquest was repeated in 1739, and again in 1756. But on all three occasions the Austrians gave up their conquests after a few years; and in each case their withdrawal was accompanied by a large exodus of Serbians who had fought for them. In the latter part of the eighteenth century therefore a considerable part of southern Hungary had come to be occupied by Serbians. They were disliked and oppressed by the Hungarians, chiefly because of their Orthodox religion; but they were protected to some extent by the Austrian rulers, especially Joseph II, who encouraged them materially in their educational efforts. These efforts led to a widespread literary renascence, in which the leading figure was Dositije Obratović, the first great Serbian author. The renascence was accompanied by a wave of national feeling, which soon affected the Serbians south of the Danube, and led to the wars of liberation—first under Kara-gjorgje in 1804, and finally under Miloš Obrenović in 1815. The literary renascence then spread to the old Serbian kingdom, as well as to the small theocratic state of Montenegro, which had achieved its liberation about a century before. The chief names in this re-nascence are perhaps those of Vuk Karadžić, the collector of the national oral poetry, and Bishop Peter II (Njegoš) of Montenegro.

No nation in Europe has encountered greater difficulties in attain-ing to its unification than that of the Yugoslavs. In the Middle Ages it was divided among a number of kingdoms, some native, some foreign. Later, as we have seen, different parts of it became subject to four different foreign governments, while one or two small districts still retained a certain degree of independence. It may be added that no attempt has been made here to give a complete ac-count of these divisions. Thus, nothing has been said of Bosnia, which was a separate kingdom in medieval times, while later it long ad-hered to Turkey, because most of the landowners had accepted Islam. Yet in spite of all these divisions a feeling for national unity can be traced back at least to the sixteenth century; since the close of the eighteenth it has made steady progress. One of the chief factors has been the common possession of a great body of oral heroic poetry, which circulated everywhere. Historians drew largely from these poems—we may instance especially Mavro Orbini of Dubrovnik (c. 1600). It may be added that in the eighteenth century we find Catholic authors citing or quoting from Cyrillic works, and Orthodox authors from works written in the Roman character. Vuk Karadžić is said to have been much indebted to the Slovenian author J. Kopitar. In the political struggles of last century the Serbians in Hungary usually supported the Croatians against the Hungarian government.

Political unification was not attained until after the last Great War, in 1918–19. A democratic constitution was then adopted, with a representative assembly drawn from all parts of Yugoslavia, including Slovenia. This was a bold experiment, in view of the very different historical experience of the various provinces, and endangered the prospects of a movement for the success of which time was required. What actually happened was that the representatives of certain provinces devoted themselves to the special interests of those provinces, oblivious of the fact that the country was surrounded by predatory neighbours whose object was to encourage dissensions in order to be able to despoil and dismember the new kingdom.

The Bulgarians, as we noted above, had in the ninth and tenth centuries a powerful kingdom, which extended from the Black Sea practically to the Aegean and the Adriatic, and also, down to c. 900, included the greater part of Rumania. This kingdom was destroyed by the Greeks in 1018; and the Bulgarians remained under Greek rule down to 1186, when they recovered their freedom. In the next thirty or forty years they succeeded in regaining almost the whole of their predecessors' dominions; but their power was short-lived. The kingdom survived until 1393; but after 1241 they were expelled by the Greeks from their western conquests, including Macedonia. During the last century of its existence their kingdom was inferior in power, and sometimes subject, to that of the Serbians. The Turkish conquest, which took place in 1393–8, was more complete than in any other country. Even the Church was denationalised, and handed over to the Greeks; and the Slavonic liturgy of St Cyril, which had been adopted five centuries before, was suppressed, together with all the literature written in this language.

Nothing more seems to have been written for about four centuries, in the course of which time the language had changed greatly. The first modern Bulgarian work was a history of the nation by Paysios, a monk of Athos, published in 1762. In Bulgaria itself no schools were founded until 1835; and not much was written before the middle of the century. When public opinion became articulate, its first effort was for the recovery of the Church—which was effected in 1870. Then began a revolutionary movement—not on a large scale—which in 1876 led to fearful massacres by the Turks. In 1877 the Russians invaded Bulgaria, and in the following year imposed upon the Turks the Treaty of San Stefano, which was to create a principality of Bulgaria extending to the Aegean and the border of Albania, and therefore not much smaller than the Bulgarian kingdom of the tenth century. Owing to the opposition of the other Powers this Treaty was annulled a few months later at the congress at Berlin. By the new treaty which now took its place the Bulgarian principality was limited to the area between the Danube and the Balkans, while to the south of this a new autonomous province (Eastern Rumelia) was created, under a Christian governor. In 1885 this latter province by a revolution attached itself to the principality; and since that time Bulgaria has consisted of these two united districts.

Although the Treaty of San Stefano never actually came into force, it had an immense influence in arousing a militant national feeling among the Bulgarians. The new Bulgaria, even as augmented by the addition of the southern province after the revolution of 1885, was not nearly as great as the Bulgaria proposed by the Treaty; it did not include Macedonia, nor did it approach the Aegean coast anywhere. Revolutionary committees were soon at work for the annexation of these districts; and before long a reign of terror was produced everywhere, especially in Macedonia. The komitadji soon came to regard the Serbian and, more especially, the Greek inhabitants, rather than the Turks, as their chief enemies. This state of irregular warfare continued down to the formation of the alliance between the four Christian Balkan kingdoms, which led to the first Balkan war in 1912. When the Turks had been deprived of the disputed territories, the Bulgarians demanded a share of the conquests which their allies regarded as excessive; and thus arose the second Balkan war, in 1913, in which Bulgaria was defeated. Since that time the Bulgarian nationalists have looked to the Germans for support in the realisation of their ambitions.

There can be little doubt that the Treaty of San Stefano is largely —I will not say wholly—responsible for the troubles from which the Balkans have suffered during the last half-century. Before 1878 occasional outbreaks against Turkish oppression had taken place; but the violent antagonisms between the various Christian nationalities were as yet unknown. The Treaty, by the extent of the territories which it awarded to the Bulgarians, brought into existence ambitions which were incompatible, and incapable of peaceful settlement. Macedonia had belonged to the Bulgarians in the ninth and tenth centuries, and again for some thirty years in the thirteenth century. After that it had been Serbian for the greater part of a century. Moreover, Prilep, in the centre of the country, had been the home of Marko Kraljević, the most famous of all Serbian heroes. It is true that the language is Bulgarian, rather than Serbian; but the bearing of the linguistic evidence is not quite clear, as we shall see in the next chapter. As for the Greeks, they had owned the country before either the Bulgarians or the Serbians, and still occupy most of the coastal districts.

These mutually exclusive claims and the endless troubles produced thereby might have been avoided, e.g. by the formation of something in the nature of a federal union of the southern Slavonic peoples, and by granting the coastal districts to their Greek inhabitants, on condition that they allowed access to certain ports to their Slavonic neighbours. The question why nothing of this kind was attempted brings us to the root of the difficulty: the troubles of the Balkan peoples were not primarily of their own making, but due to external pressure. The Russian government were aware, when the Treaty was made, that the Austrians were then preparing to occupy Bosnia, with a view to a future expansion to the Aegean. Austria had recently concluded a close alliance with Germany, which involved a new orientation of her foreign policy. If the Russians ever thought of a scheme for uniting all the southern Slavonic peoples, they must have realised that any such proposal would lead immediately to war with the central Powers. They seem, however, to have thought that the creation of a 'Great Bulgaria' would encounter less opposition, though it would have the same effect in preventing the Austro-German domination of the peninsula. In this, however, they were mistaken; this proposal itself involved war—for which they were not prepared. The settlement adopted in place of it, besides keeping open the way to the Aegean, was bound to produce dissensions between the various Balkan states—which would give the central Powers an opportunity of intervening whenever they wished.

The Albanian language has no ancient history; but there can be no doubt that it has been spoken in the Balkans from time immemorial. Indeed, Albania is the only region in the peninsula which has retained its native language against the encroachments of Greek and Latin in ancient times and of Slavonic in later ages—though the country itself was subject to Romans, Greeks, Bulgarians and Serbians in turn. After the death of Dušan, in 1356, there was a short period of independence—about sixty years—under the rule of a foreign family called Balša. Then came the Turkish conquest. But several of the coast towns belonged to Venice in the fifteenth and sixteenth centuries.

After a long struggle against the Turks in the fifteenth century most of the inhabitants accepted Islam. At present 71 per cent of the population are said to be Moslems, 19 per cent (chiefly in the south) Orthodox, and 10 per cent (in the north) Catholics. Many of the Moslems used to enter the Turkish service; and sometimes they attained the highest positions. Such was the case with Mohammed Ali Pasha, who in 1805 founded the reigning dynasty in Egypt. In former times many Albanians settled in Greece; but there the language has not maintained itself.

There is a flourishing oral literature, including abundance of narrative poetry. The earliest written Albanian dates from the fifteenth century; and the Bible is said to have been translated in the sixteenth. Apart from a few religious works, however, little or nothing seems to have been produced before last century. Even then the use of the native language in education (and in publications) within the country itself was prohibited by the Turkish government; but in Albanian colonies, especially in Greece and Italy, there was a fair amount of literary activity. No standard form of language or writing had obtained general recognition. The northern dialects were usually written in Roman characters, the southern in Greek. Since the establishment of Albanian independence, however, these difficulties have been gradually overcome. A uniform type of language is now everywhere taught in schools, which are already numerous. Before the Italian invasion literature and journalism had begun to expand; and further development may be expected when better conditions are restored.

The Albanians were later than the other peoples of the Balkans in showing any feeling for nationality. This was due doubtless to the religious divisions in the population, and especially to the fact that the Moslems were the most numerous and powerful element. A movement in this direction took place as far back as 1878; but no widespread support seems to have been gained until after 1900. Indeed, I think that even then few people in this country had any knowledge of such movements. An unsuccessful rising took place in 1910. But in 1912, during the first Balkan war, Essad Pasha, an

Albanian who commanded the Turkish forces at Scutari (Skadar), proclaimed himself king. The Powers then recognised Albanian independence; but in place of Essad, whom they would not accept, they appointed a German prince, Wilhelm of Wied. After trying for two years without success to establish his authority, he left the country on the outbreak of the first World War, in 1914. Then, after various vicissitudes, its independence was again recognised in 1919–20.

The Greeks have a much longer history than any other people in Europe. Apart from good oral traditions dating from earlier times, they have had written records from the eighth century B.C. At that time they occupied not only the old Greek lands, i.e. the peninsula from Thessaly southwards and the adjacent islands; they had expanded to the east coast of the Aegean, and were founding colonies, many of which became rich and populous, in Italy, Sicily and other parts of the Mediterranean. In course of time most of these colonies became Latinised. Here we are concerned only with those regions in Europe which have preserved a Greek population, speaking the Greek language, down to our own times.

The regions in question comprise the old Greek lands, together with Epeiros, Macedonia and Thrace. Some of the Greek cities on the north coast of the Aegean had been founded in very early times; but in general the Hellenising of these northern regions did not take place until the Macedonian or even, in some cases, the Roman period. When in 330 Byzantium, which had been founded a thousand years before, was made the capital of the Roman Empire by Constantine I, a new orientation was given to the Greek world; for it soon became the intellectual, as well as the political, centre of the empire, and remained so until the end.

While the Roman Empire retained its power the Greek language was spoken far and wide, in both Europe and Asia. Even where it was not generally spoken it was the language of culture; and inscriptions show that it was known to many people even in this country. But evil times began in the fifth and sixth centuries. Before 600 Thrace, Macedonia and the old Greek lands were overrun by Slavonic invaders, who even in the Peloponnesos maintained themselves in some districts for several centuries. These were followed in Thrace and Macedonia by the Bulgarians, who began a struggle with the Greek subjects of the empire, which lasted as long as the two peoples preserved their freedom, and has sprung up again in our own times. Then, in 1204, Constantinople (Byzantium) itself was captured and plundered by the Venetians, accompanied by a host of adventurers (the 'Fourth Crusade') from France and Italy, one of whom, Baldwin of Flanders, was made emperor. At the same time most of the empire was parcelled out among the invaders. The foreign dynasty did not last long. The capital was recaptured in 1261, Macedonia and part of Thrace even earlier—though they soon became subject to the Serbians. But the old Greek lands remained for the most part in the hands of the foreign adventurers, while the Venetians retained many of the islands. Then, in 1356, the Turks crossed the Dardanelles, and soon conquered the greater part of Thrace and Macedonia, though the capital itself held out until 1453. In the following century they gained possession of all the old Greek lands, except a few islands. The last to hold out were the Venetians, who succeeded in keeping Crete until 1669, and in 1685 even re-gained the Peloponnesos for a short time. But the Greek world as a whole had fallen under Turkish dominion before 1500.

The series of invasions and alien dominations noted above had of course a disastrous effect upon the Greek provinces, especially after 1204. But Constantinople itself was less affected, except during the half-century after this date. Since Roman times it had been the capital of European civilisation and intellectual culture. It had had its university many centuries before any city in the west. And it maintained a considerable amount of literary activity in the old classical language down to the end. But after 1500 there was no scope for intellectual life except in the Church, which under Turkish government succeeded not only in keeping its position to a certain extent, but also in extending its authority over the non-Greek provinces of the new empire. It is not difficult to understand how such authority, dependent as it was upon rulers of an alien religion, led to much abuse, and contributed to embitter relations between the Christian peoples.

The old classical language was in regular use for literature down to the late fifteenth century, though its form had been stereotyped about eighteen hundred years before. After 1500 literary work was at an end in the Greek world, except in connection with the Church. A revival, however, took place towards the end of the eighteenth century. But the new literature used the spoken language, which for several centuries at least had differed greatly from the classical language. The latter was now by no means widely understood; but the choice of the spoken language is said to have been due largely to the popularity of the current oral poetry, especially the poems which celebrated the heroic deeds of outlaws against the Turks. At the present time, however, the new literature, which has continued to flourish and expand, shows perhaps in its language more latitude than any other literature in Europe; for some authors adhere more or less closely to the spoken language, while others try to approximate as nearly as possible to the classical.

In the old Greek lands the feeling for nationality seems to have shown itself first towards the end of the eighteenth century. The immediate cause is doubtless to be found in the two unsuccessful risings in the Peloponnesos which were brought about by the empress Catherine II in 1769 and 1789, in the course of her long struggle with the Turks. Down to the eighteenth century the chief opponents of the Turks in this region—the Venetians and others—had been Latins (Catholics). From Greeks the Turks had had nothing to fear, except from local leaders whom the tyranny and oppression of their governors had forced into outlawry and brigandage. But now the Latins had disappeared from the scene. In place of them the Turks were faced for the first time with the hostility of a powerful Orthodox sovereign. She is said to have planned the restoration of the Greek empire, and to have tried to get Joseph II to support her in the project.

The Russian plans failed. But the national consciousness of the Greeks was now awakened, and found expression in the new literature, especially in poetry, which began to pass from the heroic to the patriotic phase. The course of events was much the same as in Serbia; and the earlier stages were contemporary. But the war of independence did not actually break out until 1821. At the peace concluded in 1829 the independence of the southern districts was recognised; and other districts and islands were added later, from time to time. It was not until after the Balkan wars, in 1913, that Epeiros, Macedonia and western Thrace acquired their freedom.

Only two languages of the 'Baltic' group now survive: (1) Latvian or Lettish, (2) Lithuanian. Their resemblance to one another is very close; but the peoples themselves have had a different history.

In medieval times there were other 'Baltic' peoples, with more or less closely related languages. The best known were the Prusai or Prussians, who inhabited East Prussia, and whose name has been taken over by the Germans who conquered the country. Their language survived nearly to the end of the seventeenth century; and some written remains of it have been preserved. It differed from Lettish and Lithuanian more than these do from one another.

All these peoples remained heathen down to the thirteenth century

or later. Latvia was invaded *c.* 1200–2 by a German crusading
Order, the 'Brothers of the Sword', who eventually succeeded in
conquering the country. Prussia (i.e. East Prussia) was invaded in
1230 by another German Order, the 'Teutonic Knights', which had
been established originally for a crusade in Palestine. This invasion
was of an especially ferocious character. It soon assumed the form of
a 'holy war', and, when the natives refused to be converted, it tended
to become a war of extermination. In 1237 the two Orders were
amalgamated. German merchants and other settlers were introduced, and several bishoprics were established. Before long both
countries, together with the intervening coastal territory and also
the south of Estonia, were divided between the Knights, the bishops
and the merchant cities. In course of time Prussia became wholly
Germanised; but Latvia and southern Estonia, which were now
Christian, were in 1561 annexed by Poland (properly Lithuania).
In 1629 Livonia, i.e. northern Latvia and southern Estonia, was
transferred to Sweden, while Courland, or southern Latvia, remained attached to Poland. Later, both Livonia and Courland were
annexed by Russia, the former, together with (northern) Estonia,
in 1721, the latter, with the rest of Poland, in 1795. The termination
of German rule in 1561 prevented Latvia from becoming Germanised,
as Prussia was. But German influence remained very strong,
especially in the towns, while in the country the native population
had been reduced to serfdom. Not long before the Polish annexation
(1561) the Reformation had been adopted by both the Germans,
including the Order, and the Latvians.

  The Lithuanians have had a different history. The German pene-
tration of Latvia was mainly by sea. And the same is probably true
of Prussia to some extent; for the Order had no territories west of the
Vistula before 1310. But in those times the Lithuanians were still a
good distance from the sea; and consequently they suffered comparatively little from aggression by the Order. They retained their
independence and their native (heathen) religion. But on the
other hand, they did not escape the great invasion of the Tatars
(or Mongols), who devastated the larger part of Russia, as well as
Hungary and other regions, in 1237–41. But in 1242 they gained a
great victory, which gave them possession of White Russia and other
regions in western Russia, which had been conquered by the Tatars
in the preceding years. In later wars, under their king Gediminas
(*d.* 1341), they overthrew the Tatars again on the Dnjepr, and annexed the region of Kiev. This king's grandson, Vytautas, carried
his conquests to the Black Sea, and also, in 1410, broke the power of

the Teutonic Knights. The Lithuanians in general seem to have been very tolerant rulers. Some of their princes were Catholics, some Orthodox; but the majority remained heathen. In the Russian provinces from which they had expelled the Tatars White Russian was kept as the official language.

In 1386 the Lithuanian and Polish crowns were united by the marriage of the Polish queen Jadviga with Jogaila, another grandson of Gediminas, who was converted to Catholicism at the same time and became king of Poland (as Vladislav I). The complete unification of the two kingdoms did not take place until 1569. In the meantime Lithuania had—soon after 1410—expanded westwards to the sea and (much later) annexed Courland and Livonia. After 1569 Lithuania shared the history of Poland. Although it had larger territories, it was the poorer country; and it had gradually come to be in a position of inferiority. The nobility were almost entirely Polonised, and adopted the Polish language. At the partitions of Poland Lithuania was included in the Russian share.

Both the Latvians and the Lithuanians have abundant stores of oral poetry. The latter seem to have once had a good many heroic or historical poems, reaching back to the thirteenth century. But those which survive now are not numerous; and some of them are known only from Polish translations, made about a century ago. Written literature in both languages began in the sixteenth century; but, apart from religious works, not much seems to have been produced—very little in Lettish—before the middle of last century. Since then there has been a steady increase in literary activity in Latvia, and the country has been well supplied with schools. The use of the Lithuanian language was prohibited in Russia from 1863 to 1904; but the literary output since then has been very considerable.

The feeling for nationality was in both countries late in finding expression. The Latvians had been serfs under foreign rulers and landlords for over six hundred years before their emancipation in 1818–19; and they had no educated class to give them any lead. The Lithuanians had the advantage of a distinguished history in the past, which had not been completely forgotten; but their nobility had been denationalised for centuries. Moreover, they became involved in the Polish risings of 1831 and 1863, which brought upon them harsh repressive measures from the Russian authorities. Indeed, after 1863 the government aimed at the complete Russification of the country. The national movement seems to have been due primarily to the bitterness caused by these measures. The campaign was carried on at first in contraband journals and by students' societies. It began apparently in 1875; and in 1905 it led to a national congress, at which autonomy was demanded. This, however, was not obtained until after the war, in 1918. In Latvia the movement seems to have been contemporary and, in part, similar. This also was due very largely to the government's policy of Russification.

The only remaining language of the Indo-European family in Europe is Ossetian—which is spoken in one of the valleys on the north side of the central Caucasus, together with an adjacent valley on the south side. This language belongs to the Aryan or Indo-Iranian group; its nearest affinities are with Persian and other Iranian languages. There seems to be no doubt that the Ossetians are descended from the Alani, who occupied the south Russian steppe in the fourth century. In a later chapter we shall have to refer again to them and other Iranian peoples in the same region. In more recent times they have not, so far as I know, played any important part in European history. Their district is now an Autonomous Area —from which it may probably be inferred that they have a developed feeling for nationality.

Apart from the various groups of Indo-European languages, which we have noticed above, most of the remaining languages of Europe belong to the Ugro-Finnic and the Altaic (or Turco-Tataric) families. These are all limited to the eastern half of Europe. We will take the Ugro-Finnic family first.

(1) Finnish and (2) Estonian are two of a closely related group of languages spoken to the north and south of the Gulf of Finland and in the Russian districts which lie immediately to the east. (3) The dialects of the Lapps who, though few in number, are widely distributed in the north of Norway, Sweden and Finland, and in the Kola peninsula, are also rather nearly related to this group. More distantly related are the languages of (4) the Čeremis and (5) the Mordvin, who inhabit the middle basin of the Volga—the former to the east, between Viatka and Ufa, the latter to the south-west, between Nižni Novgorod and Samara. Still more distant are the languages of (6) the Votjak, to the north-east of the Čeremis, and (7) the Zyrjän, who extend northwards from the Votjak to the Arctic Ocean. These last two peoples, whose languages are closely related to one another, are sometimes regarded as a 'Permian' group. They are usually identified with the ancient Bjarmar (Beormas), who are frequently mentioned in stories of the Viking Age, and who then extended westwards as far as the White Sea.

It will be seen that the Finnic peoples—apart from the Ugrians—are distributed over a large part of northern Russia, as well as Finland and Estonia. But their numbers are quite small. The Finns, with the Karelians, may number over 4,000,000, the Estonians less than a million and a half, the Čeremis about 400,000, the Mordvin over 1,000,000, the Votjak and Zyrjän together about 700,000. In addition to these there are some small communities, chiefly in southern Karelia and the province of Leningrad, with languages of their own.[1] But the total for these, together with Lappish, hardly comes to 100,000. There can be little doubt, however, that these communities, together with the larger peoples farther east, are merely remnants of what was once a great Finnic population, and that the whole of northern Russia, from Latvia to the southern end of the Urals, must at one time have been occupied by peoples speaking languages of this type. In Chapter IV (p. 83 f.) we shall have to notice briefly how and when the Russianising of the region took place.

The Lapps are of a different race from the rest of the Finnic peoples. It is generally thought therefore that they must originally have spoken a different language from that which they now have, and that their present language must have been acquired from their neighbours. On the other hand, the Finns are generally believed to have lived south of the Gulf of Finland down to the early centuries of our era, though perhaps it still requires to be proved that they were not in Finland also. Mention may also be made of the fact that down to the Viking Age northern Sweden was occupied by a people, apparently of Finnic stock, called Kvænir (Ang.-Sax. *Cwenas*), who have subsequently disappeared. It is quite possible that in earlier times peoples of this stock were much more widely distributed in Scandinavia.

None of the Finnic peoples were politically independent before the end of the first World War. Finland (*Suomi*) belonged to Sweden from the twelfth century (*c.* 1157) down to the eighteenth. The Russians annexed the Viborg district in 1721, and a good deal more of the country in 1743. In 1809 the whole country was ceded by Sweden to the Tsar, who became Grand Duke. It was allowed to keep its own constitution, with a Diet and army of its own. Viborg was reunited with the rest of the country. No steps towards Russification seem to have been taken until *c.* 1880; and they did not become very serious till almost the end of the century. Then the Tsar Nicholas II proceeded to incorporate Finland with the rest of the empire. The

[1] Another Finnic language, Livonian, is still spoken in one or two villages in the peninsula which forms the west side of the Gulf of Riga. Finnic place-names are said to extend somewhat farther south in the coastal districts.

Russian language and Russian officials were introduced, the Diet was suppressed, and the army incorporated with the imperial army: Great opposition was encountered; but the imperial government, after some hesitation in 1905–7, continued its policy—in a somewhat modified form—until its collapse in 1917. The Finns then declared their independence. But civil war followed; and German troops were introduced. The throne was offered to a German prince; but the German collapse in 1918 prevented this from taking effect. A republican constitution was adopted in 1919.

National feeling, of an academic kind, is traceable back to about 1820, i.e. soon after the cessation of Swedish rule. Before that the Swedes—who still number about 11 per cent of the population—seem to have monopolised the intellectual life of the country, especially in the towns. But from that time onwards a growing feeling of national consciousness showed itself in the study of the native and kindred languages and native oral poetry and folklore. Political nationalism, however, seems to have made little headway before c. 1880. But from the beginning of the present century the repressive measures taken by the Russian government roused an intensity of national and political feeling perhaps unsurpassed in Europe. The Russian revolution, in 1917, led to the emergence of two parties, the 'Red', or Communist, which looked for support to the new Russian regime, and the 'White', or Militarist, which leaned upon Germany. The struggle between them led to great excesses during the next two years. These two parties still exist. Probably neither of them commands anything like a majority of the population; but the latter, which is now in power, is a source of grave danger to the country, the end of which cannot yet be foreseen.

Finnish written literature began before 1550; a translation of the New Testament appeared in 1548. But for nearly three centuries after this time Swedish was the regular language of literature; the output in Finnish was very slight. The change took place about the middle of last century, after the publication of the Kalevala and other oral poetry; and before long there was very considerable literary activity, in both prose and poetry. For more than half a century now Finland has been well to the fore in all branches of learning. Education is universal.

Little seems to be known of Estonian history[1] before 1219, when

---

[1] The Estonians (*Eesti*) are said to have been a warlike people; and early Norse records occasionally refer to them as pirates. Why have they the same name (Norse *Eistr*) as the people of East Prussia (Latin *Aestii*, King Alfred's *Este*)? I have not seen any satisfactory explanation of this. The latter appear to be the (Baltic) Prusai (cf. p. 36 f.).

the northern part of the country was occupied by the Danes. The southern part had already been invaded by the German 'Brothers of the Sword', who in 1237 were amalgamated with the Teutonic Order (cf. p. 37). In 1346 they also purchased the northern part from the Danes. Under their rule the whole of the land came into the hands of German barons; the native population were reduced to serfdom. At the Reformation the barons offered their allegiance to Sweden. Eventually, in 1561, after some warfare between Poland, Sweden and Russia, the northern part was annexed by Sweden, while 'Livonia'—i.e. southern Estonia with northern Latvia—was ceded to Poland. In 1629 the whole of Livonia was conquered by the Swedish king Gustavus Adolphus; but in 1721 all the Swedish possessions in this region were annexed by the Tsar Peter the Great.

In 1817 the Tsar Alexander I abolished serfdom; but the measure seems to have had little practical effect. The condition of the peasants continued to be very bad, and frequent risings took place. In other respects the Russians interfered little with the internal affairs of the provinces before 1881. The Estonians were still divided between Estonia and Livonia; and German, the language of the barons and the cities, was still maintained as the official language in both provinces. But in 1881 the imperial government instituted a systematic Russification of the country, just as in Finland. The effect of this process was to alienate the dominant German landowners, and at the same time to give a political impetus to such slight feeling for nationality as already existed among the Estonians.

This feeling seems to have been of an academic character at first, and to have shown itself chiefly in the collecting of oral poetry. It was apparently not until towards the end of the century that it took a political form. After 1905, when more freedom was allowed to the subject nationalities, the national movement gained great strength. Its objects were to get the northern (Estonian) part of Livonia united with Estonia and to secure autonomy for the whole. After the Russian collapse, in 1917, the first object was gained; and the Diet declared its independence. But the new Russian government refused to grant independence; and hostilities resulted. Then the landowners, who desired not independence, but union with Germany, intervened and obtained the support of a German army. The Russians had to retire. But by this time the World War had come to an end; and the German army also was forced to withdraw. Estonian independence was recognised, and a democratic constitution was established. A large proportion of the German population left the country soon afterwards.

The beginnings of written literature date from early in the seventeenth century. Parts of the New Testament were translated in 1632. But the number of books—mostly religious—published in Estonian down to *c.* 1850 seems to have been quite small. The intellectual life of the country was German, and concentrated chiefly in the University of Dorpat (Tartu). About the middle of last century, however, native oral poetry began to be published; and not long afterwards literature of modern types, both prose and poetry, made its appearance. Since 1900 the output has greatly increased. After the establishment of independence education was made compulsory; and the University of Tartu, which had been Russian since 1895, was nationalised.

For the Finnic peoples within Russia itself information is not readily available at present. So far as I know, these peoples have never influenced the general history of Europe. The Karelians, however, now have an Autonomous Republic, while the Zyrjän and the Votjak have Autonomous Areas—from which it may be presumed that they already possess a definite consciousness of nationality. I do not know how far literary or intellectual activities have been developed. The Zyrjän had some written literature, of a religious character, as far back as the fourteenth century.

(8) The Hungarian (Magyar) language is now perhaps the only representative in Europe of the Ugrian group, which are rather distantly related to the Finnic languages. A few years ago a related language called Vogul was spoken in the Urals, east of Perm; but it was dying out. Another similar language called Ostiak is probably still spoken by a few thousand people slightly farther east, in the direction of Tobolsk.

The Hungarians or Magyars are first heard of in the ninth century, at which time they occupied the steppe north of the Black Sea, between the Dnjepr and the Volga. They had arrived in this region not long before, apparently from the north-east. Their earlier home was probably in the territory of what is now the Baškir Autonomous Republic, and not far from the region where Vogul used to be spoken.

The westward movement of the Magyars was one of a long series of movements along the steppe from the east, which will require discussion in the next two chapters. All the other movements of this series, since the fourth century, were carried out by nomads of Turco-Tataric stock. The language of the Magyars shows that they were of a different origin from the rest. But the nature of their movements and their method of warfare render it practically certain that they must have contained a large—and doubtless dominant—element of this stock, which gave the impetus to their movements.

In 895 the Magyars crossed the Carpathians and conquered the central basin of the Danube, which since then has borne their name (Hungary). They destroyed or absorbed the Slavonic and other peoples of the plain, and reduced the inhabitants of the surrounding hill country to subjection. For the next sixty years their raids did immense havoc in central and western Europe; but after their defeat by Otto I in 955 they settled down; and towards the end of the century they were converted to Christianity. To their subsequent history we shall have to return in Chapter IV.

It was among the Magyars apparently that nationalism of the modern type first showed itself—in 1780—and it is still at least as strong there as in any other country in Europe. In earlier times the feeling had been bound up with religion. A large proportion of the Magyars accepted the doctrines of the Reformation, whereas the Hapsburgs, under whose rule Hungary had passed in 1526, were the most uncompromising upholders of Catholicism. The greater part of the country had indeed been conquered by the Turks; but in the parts which remained free a state of constant tension with the Austrian rulers prevailed, at least down to the beginning of the eighteenth century. A gradual movement towards religious tolera-tion then began, and was completed under Joseph II. But this king introduced a new source of strife by his Germanising policy. He sought to incorporate Hungary in his Austrian dominions and to enforce the use of German everywhere, in both administration and education. His decree provoked a great outburst of national feeling. After some twenty years of fluctuating policy, the Austrian govern-ment again took up an attitude of repression; but in Hungary the national movement only grew stronger, and led first to the unsuccess-ful revolution of 1848, and then to the recovery of full national rights in 1867.

The struggle now entered upon a new phase. In Hungary itself the Magyars formed only a minority of the population. The de-pendent peoples—the Slovaks, Croatians, Serbians and Rumanians—had tended to support the Austrians, and had already well-de-veloped aspirations of their own. For the next half-century the tension between these peoples and the Magyars increased con-tinually, until the former attained complete independence at the end of the first World War. Then, in 1938–40, when the opportunity occurred, the Magyars lost no time in reoccupying the territories which they had had to give up. Indeed, it would seem from various reports that the Germans have had a good deal of difficulty in preventing outbreaks of hostilities among their own allies.

The beginnings of Hungarian literature date from the twelfth century. A good deal of poetry is preserved from the sixteenth century onwards. But very little Magyar prose was written before last century; for Latin was the official language, as well as the language of education, and was regularly used even in the Diet. Since the beginning of last century, however, there has been a flourishing Magyar literature in all the ordinary modern genres; and learning and the arts are well advanced. National feeling is often very much in evidence; and in works relating to the country, but intended for foreign readers, there is a widespread tendency to propaganda, which is sometimes misleading in relation to questions of nationality. It is to be regretted that even distinguished authors have not always been free from reproach in this respect.

It was formerly held that the Altaic or Turco-Tataric languages were connected, though distantly, with the Ugro-Finnic family; and the name 'Ural-Altaic' was invented—not very happily—as a comprehensive term for both families. But I understand that this connection is now doubted, and that the remote affinities of the Ugro-Finnic languages are commonly thought to have lain rather with the Indo-European family than with the Altaic. In any case it seems to be generally agreed that the Altaic languages belonged originally to central and eastern Asia, and that they did not penetrate into Europe until comparatively late times.

The Altaic peoples were nomadic shepherds, who spent their summers on the steppe. They invaded Europe from time to time, in a series of great movements which lasted from the fourth century to the thirteenth and profoundly influenced the course of European history. These movements took place by way of the steppe to the north of the Caspian Sea. But the invasion of the Ottoman Turks, in 1356, came from a different quarter—by way of the Dardanelles from Asia Minor. Their ancestors had made their way into south-western Asia through Iran, from the steppe east of the Caspian. All these movements will require notice in the next two chapters.

1. The Ottoman Turks, when they were at the height of their power in the sixteenth and seventeenth centuries, ruled over a large part of Europe, in addition to their possessions in Asia and Africa. They held all the Balkan peninsula, the greater part of Hungary and Rumania, and nearly all the coast-lands of the Black Sea and the Sea of Azov, including the Crimea; and their language was spoken

everywhere, though often not by any considerable proportion of the population. But now their territories are limited to eastern Thrace; and beyond this region the language is not spoken by any considerable population (in Europe), except in the Crimea and the Dobrudža.

National feeling in the modern sense is of recent growth. Even down to the close of last century patriotism was bound up with religion (Islam) and virtually limited to Moslems. Loyalty was owed to the Sultan as Caliph, or head of religion, rather than as Turkish sovereign. The misgovernment of Abdul Hamid II led to a revolution in 1908, when a constitutional government was established. But many nationalities were represented; for the empire was still very extensive, and its population heterogeneous. Power soon came into the hands of a military clique, of German sympathies, whose chief concern was the strengthening of the army. After the first World War the provinces with non-Turkish population acquired independence. In 1920–1 a second revolution took place under Mustafa Kemal. What was now left of the empire was almost entirely Turkish; and a National Council was formed, with strong national feeling. The authority of the Sultan-Caliph was repudiated, religion eliminated, and a secular republic established. The capital and centre of gravity were removed into Anatolia (Ankara); but Kemal's policy in so doing was to bring Anatolia into Europe, and to make the Turks Europeans. Then followed the reform of education, with the substitution of Roman for Arabic script, and the attempt to eliminate all Arabic elements from the language.

Intellectual life down to last century was wholly under Arabic and Persian influence. Arabic, as the language of religion, was at least as widely known as Latin has ever been in the west, while Persian held a position similar to that of French in England during the Middle Ages. Poetry has been much cultivated, at least since the fifteenth century, and especially in the highest circles. Many of the Sultans composed poems, either in Persian or in Turkish, after Persian models. Prose literature also has had a fairly long history. It was only in the last century that European influence, especially French, began to make itself felt. The national movement brought with it the desire to introduce native elements into literature; but in practice its chief effect perhaps has been to substitute European for Arabic and Persian influence.

The rest of the Altaic languages in Europe belong wholly, or almost wholly, to Russia.

2. Kazan Turkish is spoken by about 200,000 people in the Tatar

Autonomous Republic, chiefly to the east of the middle Volga. These people are no doubt the survivors of the Khanat of Kazan, which was conquered by the Russians under Ivan IV in 1552. The Khanat itself had arisen through a revolt or secession from the 'Golden Horde' about 1445. The seceders, under a branch of the royal family, had made their way up the Volga and established themselves at Kazan, in what was at that time the territory of the Bulgarians—that portion of the Bulgarians which had not moved westwards to the Danube (cf. p. 71 f.).

3. Baškir Turkish is spoken by nearly half a million people in the Baškir Autonomous Republic, east and south-east of the Tatar Republic, and extending to the Urals. The early history of the Baškir is obscure; we shall have to refer to it in Chapter IV. They seem to have occupied the region where they now live long before the coming of the Golden Horde, and to have been connected in some way with the Magyars, though the latter were not Turks.

4. Čuvaš is spoken by about half a million people in the Čuvaš Autonomous Area, west of the Tatar Republic, and mostly west of the middle Volga. This language is said to differ a good deal from all the other Turkish languages. The Čuvaš are commonly thought to be descended from the old Bulgarians[1]—the part of that people which was not destroyed or absorbed by the Tatars of Kazan. Čuvaš then was perhaps the first Turkish language to penetrate into Europe. Unlike the rest of the Turkish peoples in Europe, who are Moslems, the Čuvaš are (nominally) Orthodox Christians.

5. In the Crimea two different Turkish languages are spoken. In the south the language is Ottoman Turkish, introduced while the Crimea was under Ottoman suzerainty (1475–1774). But the northern language is that of the Crimean Tatars, formerly the subjects of the Khanat of the Crimea, which was conquered by the Russians under Catherine II in 1783. This Khanat had its origin c. 1430 in a secession from the Golden Horde—like the Khanat of Kazan.

Apart from the four languages noted above, there are a number of Turkish languages spoken by small communities[2] in various parts of southern Russia, but now in process of being engulfed in the rising tide of Russification. Some of these are no doubt relics of the Khanat of the Crimea, which was at one time conterminous with that of

---

[1] The ruins of Bulgar, the old Bulgarian capital, are still to be seen near the Volga, about fifty miles south of Kazan, and rather less from the border of the Čuvaš Area.

[2] The Azerbaidžan Turks are a much more numerous people. But I am omitting them with the rest of the peoples of the Caucasus. I have no information worth recording.

Kazan. Others, farther to the east, are remains of the Khanat of Astrachan—which likewise owed its origin (in 1466) to a secession from the Golden Horde, and which was conquered by the Russians in 1556. It is generally believed now, I think, that all these dialects in the south—excluding of course Ottoman Turkish—are derived from the language of the Golden Horde. This Horde consisted of the descendants of the host led into Europe by Batu Khan, grandson of Genghiz Khan, in 1237. Their capital was Sarai, about thirty miles east of Stalingrad, which, after the three secessions mentioned above, was eventually destroyed in 1502 by the Khan of the Crimea.

Batu Khan and his family were Mongols; but it is believed that only an insignificant fraction of his army came from his own people. The rest were drawn from the Tatar peoples who had submitted to his family. With them were incorporated later the remains of the Polovci, who held the steppe north of the Black Sea at the time of his arrival, and who were conquered by him. It is possible that some of the Turkish dialects now spoken in this region may have preserved characteristics derived from them, or from even earlier peoples; but I am not qualified to discuss the question.

In much later times—about 1632—a Mongolian people, the Kalmuks, came from central Asia, and occupied the lands north-west of the Caspian, which are now called the Kalmuk Autonomous Area. In 1771, owing to some disagreement with the Russian authorities, a large proportion of them returned to their former home; but many of them seem to have remained behind. They are Buddhists.

I have no information as to the extent to which the Turkish peoples in Russia are affected by (separate) national feeling or have written literatures of their own. It may, however, be presumed that at least the larger communities, which give their names to Autonomous Republics and Areas, have some developed sense of nationality; and the Soviet Government, unlike their predecessors, seem to have no desire to suppress these feelings. Their languages are used officially and in education.

There still remains the Basque language, which is spoken by perhaps nearly three-quarters of a million people in the extreme south-west of France and the adjacent districts in Spain. This language seems to be quite isolated; at least, so far as I am aware, no connection with any other known language has been satisfactorily established. Most probably it has been spoken from time immemorial in the region where it is now found; but it may once have had a wider distribution in Spain, and perhaps also in France. Presumably it represents the language, or one of the languages, of the ancient Iberians. But little evidence is available, except from place-names. Basque literary records do not go back beyond the sixteenth century; and not much seems to have been produced before last century. Now there is a fair amount of literary activity, which follows the ordinary European lines.

The Basques have played no part in European history—apart from what we know of the ancient Iberians. Since Roman times they have always been under foreign rulers. They possessed, however, a certain autonomy of their own, in France down to the Revolution, in Spain as late as 1876. In France their feeling for nationality seems to be limited to cultural and antiquarian interests; but in Spain it became a vigorous political movement, which made a heroic struggle for independence in the recent civil war.

CHAPTER III

THE FORMATION OF THE LINGUISTIC MAP
OF EUROPE. I

THE linguistic geography of Europe is a product of long ages. Some of the languages are of comparatively recent introduction; but others seem to have existed, perhaps in their present positions, from time immemorial.

The most striking feature of the linguistic map of modern Europe is the predominance of the three chief groups—the Romance, Teutonic and Slavonic languages. Between them these three groups occupy at least five-sixths of the whole area, while in population their predominance is still greater.

The expansion of these groups has taken place for the most part during the historical period, and many of the movements of population by which it was brought about can be traced with more or less precision.

It is for the Romance or Latin group that the best and most detailed information is available. The expansion of the Latin language was due to the growth of the Roman Empire. In the earliest times for which we have any reliable evidence the Latin language would seem to have been confined to a quite small district in the centre of Italy. By the third century (B.C.) it had spread, with the expansion of the Roman power, throughout the peninsula, though it had not yet succeeded in ousting the other languages, native and Greek, which were current there. Then, through their wars with the Carthaginians, the Romans acquired possession of, first the Mediterranean islands, Sicily and Sardinia, and, later, the east coast of Spain. In the next two centuries further conquests followed, in Europe as well as in Asia and Africa, so that by the death of Augustus, in A.D. 14, the empire extended to the Rhine and the Danube, and included the whole of Spain and Gaul. Still later came the conquest of this country (from A.D. 43) and of Rumania (c. 106).

Everywhere in Europe, except in the Greek-speaking lands of the Balkan peninsula, the Roman conquest led to the introduction of the Latin language—partly no doubt through the armies of occupation, and partly through the traders who followed them. The upper classes of the conquered populations were encouraged to adopt it, together with Roman education and Roman civilisation as a whole.

Before the end of Roman rule Latin seems to have displaced the native languages throughout most of Spain and Gaul, and also throughout the southern part of central Europe, with the northern part of the Balkan peninsula. This was the origin of the Spanish, Portuguese, Catalan, Provençal, French and Rumanian languages. They were originally dialects of Latin, which owed their differentiation to the fact that the regions in which they developed were separated from one another by physical obstacles, such as ranges of mountains, or by political boundaries of post-Roman times. In the eastern Alpine and Danubian regions Latin itself was displaced in later times by new movements from the north and east—though Latin dialects still survive in some isolated valleys, while in others the former existence of Latin-speaking communities is attested by place-names. But it was only in remote lands, like Britain, and in poor countries, like the Basque provinces and Albania, that Latin failed to secure a lasting foothold and the native languages were able to maintain their position.

Rome was a strictly national state in the early days of its expansion, when its territories were still small. But in course of time the state came in a sense to embrace all Italy, and then the provinces beyond Italy. Before A.D. 100 the soldiers of the regular army and the highest officials in the government—indeed, even emperors themselves—might be drawn from the outer provinces. By the third century the empire had become practically cosmopolitan; natives of all provinces were now Roman citizens. Some of the emperors both spoke and wrote Greek. A Syrian at South Shields put up to the memory of his British wife a monument with an inscription which is partly in Syriac. Yet political unity was almost always preserved. The government was still centred in Rome; and Latin remained the official language. The Britons apparently were proud to regard themselves as Roman citizens even for some time after Roman rule had finally disappeared from this country.

The expansion of the Teutonic peoples had begun before they came into contact with the Romans, i.e. before the earliest times for which we have contemporary records. It is clear from place-names that they had conquered nearly the whole of western and southern Germany from Celtic peoples. When the Romans began the conquest of Gaul, in 59 B.C., they had already reached the Rhine; and one army had recently established itself in territories to the west of that river. But the Roman conquest put a stop to expansion in that direction for several centuries.

A great predatory expedition to the south of Europe, that of the Cimbri and Teutones, had taken place half a century before this time. But the first permanent conquest from the Roman empire was that of Rumania (Dacia) in the third century. This was part of a great movement of expansion by the Goths, who inhabited Poland. In addition to Rumania, their conquests extended over the Ukraine and as far as the Crimea. In the west, however, the expansion of the Teutonic peoples can hardly be said to have begun before the fifth century. It is the fifth and sixth centuries which may be regarded as the great period of Teutonic expansion.

The Rhine frontier was first broken by the Vandals in 406, who, after spending some time in Gaul and Spain, passed over in 429 to North Africa, which they conquered and occupied. They were followed by the Visigoths, who, coming from the lower Danube, invaded Italy and captured Rome (in 410), but soon afterwards moved on to southern Gaul and Spain, which they conquered and occupied. Then came the Burgundians from the middle Rhine, who (c. 440–3) conquered and occupied eastern Gaul. The rest of that country was gradually conquered in the course of the fifth century —especially between 431 and 486—by the Franks, chiefly the Salic Franks, the ancestors of the modern Dutch. The regions south of the Danube were conquered, not much later, by the Alamanni, the Bavarians and the Rugi. The last-named, who had come from the coast of the Baltic, occupied what is now Lower Austria and the adjacent regions; but they were overthrown in 487 by an army from Italy. Two years later Italy itself was conquered by the Ostrogoths, from the lower Danube, with the survivors of the Rugi. The kingdom of the Ostrogoths was destroyed in 553; but within fifteen years of this event the north of Italy was conquered by the Langobardi, who had come from the lower Elbe and (c. 489) taken possession of the regions evacuated by the Rugi. Contemporaneous with these movements on the Continent was the conquest by the English of the eastern half of southern Britain.

When the Teutonic expansion was at its height (c. 500), practically all the western half of the Roman empire had come under Teutonic rule. But much of this expansion was transitory. The Vandals were destroyed in 534 and the Ostrogoths in 553 by Roman armies from Constantinople. In Italy, Spain and the greater part of Gaul—which had now become France—the Teutonic conquerors were absorbed and Romanised in the following centuries. South Russia and the region of the lower Danube had been evacuated by them, apart from the Crimea and one or two other pockets, when the Ostrogoths moved westwards. The permanent expansion therefore won by the Teutonic peoples in this period consisted of a belt of territory—varying from 50 to 150 miles in breadth—which had been conquered and occupied by the Franks, Alamanni and Bavarians, to the west of the Rhine and the south of the Danube. To this must be added the part of southern Britain which grew into England.

It will be seen from what has been said above that the Teutonic expansion differed greatly from the Roman. There was no 'Teutonic Empire', no political unity or central authority of any kind which was recognised by all the various peoples. As a rule each people was wholly independent. From time to time we hear of alliances, or rather hegemonies or suzerainties, which extended over very large areas. Such were the 'empires' of the Gothic king Eormenric (c. 370), the Hunnish king Attila (c. 450) and the Ostrogothic king Theodric (c. 500). But these empires were of short duration; usually they collapsed as soon as the kings who established them died. And they never included the whole of the Teutonic peoples. We never hear of these peoples acting as a single body, or with any central organisation, whether against the Romans or any other enemy.

During the period of expansion Teutonic society was of the unsettled, barbaric type which may best be described as 'heroic'. The dominant factor was the young prince who was out for adventure and 'glory', and who attracted numerous young followers by the hope of riches and plunder. There was little or no feeling for nationality. Princes of the same family were ready to fight against one another. Very frequently they took service under the Romans against their own countrymen. So also the armies which the Romans encountered were often by no means homogeneous. The Vandals, when they invaded Gaul in 406, were accompanied by a large force of Suebi, who established a kingdom of their own in the north-west of Spain, and also by Alani, who were Iranians but became merged in the Vandals. The Ostrogoths, in their invasion of Italy in 489, were accompanied by Rugi, while the Langobardi, when they carried out a similar invasion, in 567–8, employed a considerable force of Saxons, who subsequently returned to Germany. The English forces which conquered this country in the fifth century cannot have been supplied wholly from Angel itself; they must have included contingents from a wider area. Indeed, it is clear enough that wealthy and successful kings had little difficulty in gathering forces sufficient to enable them to conquer large tracts of country. Their primary object, however, usually was not the conquest of lands, but the acquisition of wealth (treasure) and prestige for themselves and of abundance of good food and drink for their followers.

The hosts which conquered the Roman provinces were doubtless drawn chiefly from the younger and more active elements in their nations; and when they settled down in conquered lands, they were like armies of occupation. It was due to this that the Vandals and Ostrogoths, after their defeats, melted away and vanished within a few months, while the Visigoths, the Langobardi and many of the Franks soon became denationalised. By the eighth century little was left of what had once been the eastern Teutonic peoples—the Vandals, Goths, Rugi, etc.—except a few remnants in the Crimea and perhaps in Transylvania or the Banat.

Warriors of this kind, when they had settled down in civilised lands, were not well adapted to carry on the administration of government. The kings therefore soon became dependent upon educated Romans, whom they attracted into their service. As these were usually ecclesiastics, the result was a great increase in the wealth and influence of the Church.

The process of expansion of which we have been speaking affected first those of the Teutonic peoples who were nearest to the frontiers. But these were at the same time pressed from behind by more distant peoples, who were impelled by the same process. Thus, while the more vigorous and warlike elements of the Franks were engaged in the conquest of Gaul, their less enterprising and more peaceful elements were themselves being conquered and absorbed by the Saxons, who came to occupy most of the old Frankish territories. The more eastern part of the Teutonic world, however, was subject also to external pressure. Thus the movements of the Visigoths and Ostrogoths seem to have been influenced—in different ways—by the invasion of the Huns, a Turkish people from the steppe, while the Langobardic invasion of Italy may have been due in part to the Avars, a similar people, who arrived later from the same region. Subsequently, all the eastern Teutonic peoples were under a more lasting pressure from a different source, of which we shall have to speak below.

We have been speaking of the Teutonic expansion which took place in the fifth and sixth centuries, and which was virtually at an end, except in Britain, by 570. But it is to be borne in mind that this expansion began in much earlier times, though it was checked by the Romans for over four centuries. The Romans themselves reached the Rhine in 58 B.C., and later effected a transitory conquest of a large area beyond it. In the first century of our era they were fairly well acquainted with the western Teutonic peoples; and their literary men, especially Tacitus, give us a good deal of information. Society was already of the heroic type, but in a much less advanced form than in later times. There was little wealth and, though predatory warfare was extremely popular, the warriors were for the most part poorly armed. Tacitus gives the impression, perhaps wrongly, that kingship was exceptional among the western peoples, though he recognises the existence of royal families;[1] and he says that even such kings as there were had only limited power. The 'states', i.e. independent peoples, were numerous in the west, and must have been quite small. Many of them were included in the territories which later (c. 400) belonged to the Franks and Alamanni, whose names first appear in the third century. It would seem then that the first four centuries must have seen a considerable growth in the size of the states—whether by conquest or otherwise—as well as in wealth, military equipment and the power of the rulers.

The Slavonic peoples are first mentioned—under the name Veneti or Venedi—in the first century of our era. Their home at this time would seem to have been in the central and lower part of the basin of the Dnjepr, and extended westwards, perhaps as far as the Dnjestr. It is not until the sixth century, however, that we hear much of them.

Even in the sixth century it is only for the lower Danube and the Balkans, where they were in direct contact with the Romans, that we have any precise information. From 527 onwards we hear of frequent raids in the Roman territories, as far as Thrace, Macedonia and Greece. Before the end of the century—in 582 and the following years—a large part of the peninsula seems to have been occupied by them, including even the southernmost district of the Peloponnesos. The invaders are regularly called Sclavenoi (Sclavinoi, Sclavi)— a name which is applied to them even before they crossed the

---

[1] E.g. *Ann.* xi, 16; *Hist.* iv, 13. The most probable, though not universally accepted, explanation of the word 'king' (Ang.-Sax. *cyning*, O. Germ. *cuning*, O. Norse *konungr*) is that originally it meant a member of the *cyn*, or (royal) family; and there is English and Norse evidence that the title 'king' was given to a royal prince, if he had any position of authority or even a comitatus (Ang.-Sax. *(ge)dryht*, O. Norse *drótt*), or body of armed followers. An older word for 'king' is Goth. *þiudans* (βασιλεύς), which is preserved also in Ang.-Sax. and O. Norse poetry (*þeoden*, *þjóðann*)—from *þiuda*, etc., 'people, nation'. A still older term is probably preserved in Goth. *reiks* (ἄρχων) and in derivatives elsewhere, such as Ang.-Sax. *rice*, 'kingdom'. This appears to be a loanword from Celtic *-rix*, 'king'. Yet another word for 'king'—*hendinos*—was used by the Burgundians, according to Ammianus Marcellinus, xxviii, 5, 14, unless this form is a scribal error for *theudinos*.

Danube—though occasionally we meet with a number of names which are obviously those of communities or constituent sections of the nation. But before the end of the seventh century the eastern half of the Balkans was conquered by the Bulgarians (cf. p. 23). These were a Turkish people; but before long—perhaps even before they crossed the Danube—they began to adopt the language of the Slavs who had become subject to them. The two peoples soon became fused; but the name by which they were known from henceforth was that of the conquerors, though the true Bulgarian language entirely disappeared within the next two or three centuries.

Farther to the north-west the Serbians and Croatians are said to have been allowed by the emperor Heraclios (610–41) to occupy the lands which they now inhabit, including Serbia, Bosnia, Dalmatia and Croatia. It is thought by some scholars that they had crossed the Danube somewhat before this time, and that the emperor's permission was no more than a recognition of conditions which already existed. This may be true. Hardly any information, however, is available; and the question is complicated by the rather uncertain relations of these peoples with the Avars—another Turkish people from the steppe—to which we shall have to refer later.

Still farther to the north-west, the Slovenians bear the same name as the people who invaded the Balkans in the sixth century. *Sclavenoi* (Σκλαβηνοί) is merely an earlier form of the old national name *Sloveni*, in Greek orthography. The Slovenians themselves[1] also are usually called *Sclaui* or *Sclauini* by our earliest authorities, which are Latin. Sometimes, however, we find the name Carantani, derived from a Roman city called Carantana (earlier Virunum), the site of which can be traced between Klagenfurt and St Veit. It was here that the curious installation ceremony of the dukes of Carinthia, referred to on p. 27, took place; and the name of the province itself seems to be derived from the same locality.

The date at which the Slovenians invaded the lands which they now occupy is never definitely stated, but can be determined within certain limits. Its previous owners had been the Langobardi, who descended into Italy, apparently with all their belongings, in 567. An even later *terminus a quo* may perhaps be inferred from the fact that an ecclesiastical council at Grado in 579 was attended by certain bishops from this region; for the Church was destroyed by the invaders. On the other hand, Paul the Deacon, iv, 7, states that in 595 the Bavarians carried out a great raid into the 'province of the Sclaui'—which suggests that they had been in possession of the

---

[1] The term in regular use now (in the narrower sense) is *Slovenci*.

country at least for some little time. Their arrival would therefore seem to coincide approximately with the invasion of the Balkans by the southern Sclaveni, in 582. It may be noted indeed that the Spanish abbot John of Biclar—a contemporary authority—records devastations of both Thrace and Illyricum in this year, and evidently connects the two movements. Illyricum at this time meant the provinces west of the middle Danube.

In the centuries which immediately followed their settlement in the Alps the territories possessed by the Slovenians were much larger than the area where the language is spoken now. It has practically disappeared from the northern half of their territories. In the west they extended to the source of the Drava, near Innichen in Tyrol. Northwards they included all Carinthia and Styria, and extended as far as the Salzach, the Enns and the Ybbs, in the provinces of Salzburg and Austria (both Upper and Lower). In Lower Austria, however, and in Hungary it is impossible to determine the boundaries between them and the Avars. The relations between the two peoples are also far from clear. At all events it is obvious that, when the Slovenians came from the east, they must have possessed, or at least traversed, a large part of Hungary.

The most northern Slavonic peoples were separated from the Slovenians by territories—in Lower Austria—which in the seventh and eighth centuries belonged to the Avars; but in 791–6 these lands were conquered by Charlemagne, and then soon became German-ised. For the northern Slavonic peoples very little information is available before this time. In early records, which are all of German origin, but written in Latin, they are usually called Winidi, which is the term used for the Slavonic peoples in general in all Teutonic languages. From the eighth century we begin to find Sclaui (later Slaui); but this is a learned form, transferred from the southern Slavs (Slovenians), and was never used either in German or by the northern Slavs themselves.

These northern peoples occupied territories which in the early centuries of our era had belonged to the eastern and central Teutonic peoples—as far as, and including, the basin of the Elbe and the upper part of that of the Main. Unfortunately, however, very little information is available for these regions before the ninth century; and consequently it is impossible to determine with precision when the westward movement or movements of the Slavonic peoples took place, or what was the time of their greatest expansion. But at the time when our information begins we know, chiefly from casual references in legal documents, that the boundary between Germans and Slavs ran along the course of the Saale—all modern Saxony was Slavonic—and that, farther north, it passed, from south to north, through the Harz Mountains and across the Elbe, a little to the south-east of Hamburg, and from thence on to the Danish frontier at the Eider, not far to the west of Kiel.

For the ninth and following centuries our information is supplemented by some short tracts on political or ethnical geography. The first (in Anglo-Saxon) is contained in King Alfred's translation of Orosius's 'History'. The king evidently recognised that the sketch of geography with which Orosius begins his work was inadequate and out-of-date; and he has supplemented it by an account, from some unknown source, of central and northern Europe, which seems to represent the geography of his own day (c. 890), shortly before the Hungarian invasion. He gives the names and indicates the positions of a number of the northern Slavonic peoples, as well as the Slovenians (*Carendre*) and the Bulgarians. A somewhat similar (Latin) list—of Slavonic peoples only—is preserved in an astronomical MS. from Regensburg, dating from the close of the eleventh century.[1] This list may perhaps have drawn from the same source as Alfred; but it is followed by more detailed lists, which are quite independent. A third list of Slavonic peoples (in Russian) is to be found in the introduction to the ancient Russian Chronicle, formerly attributed to Nestor, and believed to date from c. 1113, though it may contain somewhat earlier elements. The introduction gives a brief account of the distribution of Noah's descendants, which ends with a rather more detailed notice of the Slavonic peoples (*Slověne*), among the descendants of Japhet. It says that the Slověne originally lived 'beside the Danube, where now are the lands of the Hungarians and the Bulgarians', and traces their expansion from that region. Lastly, mention must be made of the (Greek) work 'On the Administration of the Empire', written c. 952 by the emperor Constantine VII (Porphyrogenitus), which refers to many Slavonic peoples beyond the borders of the empire.

The largest and most important peoples north of the Danube, in the west, were the Czechs and the Sorabi. The former are apparently not mentioned by their own name (Česi) before the Russian Chronicle (c. 1100). In early (western) records they usually bear the names of their two kingdoms, Bohemia and Moravia, which were sometimes united, sometimes separate. The former is derived from the earlier occupants of the land, the latter from the river

---

[1] A short list (of the northern peoples only), dating from about the same time, is given by Adam of Bremen, *Gesta Hammaburg. Eccl.* II, 18.

March. The date of the Slavonic conquest is not known; but it can hardly have been later than *c.* 600. In 623 the Bohemians[1] chose as their king a merchant named Samo, from Sens, in France. It would seem that in early times the Bohemian conquests extended well into Bavaria, since later we find Slavonic populations in the upper basin of the Main.

The Sorabi or Surbi occupied territories which were apparently not much smaller than those of the Czechs. They stretched from the Saale in the west probably to the Oder in the east, and thus included the whole of the modern kingdom of Saxony, together with much more to the west, east and north-east. There is no record of their invasion of this region. We hear of them first *c.* 630, when they were at war with the Franks in Thuringia and in alliance with Samo. To their downfall in the twelfth century we shall have to return later. Their language now survives only in the basin of the Spree (cf. p. 25).

North of the Sorabi the most important people were the Wilti, between the Elbe and the Oder. In the same region there were also a number of smaller peoples, among whom we may mention the Obotriti (called by Alfred *Afdrede*) in Mecklenburg. They were allied with Charlemagne in his wars with the Danes. Farthest north of all were the Wagri, in the district round Kiel and Lübeck. All these peoples disappeared in the course of the Middle Ages; but their languages in some parts long survived them. Even to the west of the Elbe, not far from Salzwedel, Slavonic was spoken until near the end of the eighteenth century.

For the date of the Slavonic conquests in the west as a whole some evidence is perhaps to be obtained from the story of a journey told by Procopios (*Gothic War*, ii, 15), who wrote about 550. The journey is said to be made on more than one occasion, and therefore probably follows a recognised route, from the Roman frontier on the Danube to 'Thule', i.e. Scandinavia. The travellers belong to the Eruloi, a Teutonic people, part of whom had entered the Roman service; and the date is apparently *c.* 512–20. The starting place is, at least on one occasion, Belgrade. The travellers are said to pass through 'all the peoples of the Sclavenoi in succession', and then to traverse an extensive waste country, after which they come to the Warnoi, a Teutonic people who occupied Mecklenburg before the Obotriti. From here the travellers made their way through the peoples of the Danes, and then arrived at the ocean and embarked for Thule. The

---

[1] He is called king of the Winidi; but his kingdom must have included Bohemia, though it may have extended farther west.

goal of the journeys was the land of the Gautoi, where some of their
royal family were settled.

Since the travellers pass through the 'peoples of the Danes' before
they come to the ocean, their route would seem to lie through Holstein and Jutland and not via Warnemünde. The 'ocean' then must
be the Cattegat, and the end of their journey is to be sought in
Västra Götland—perhaps at Göteborg, or in the neighbourhood.
The Warnoi may already have begun to move or expand westwards.
Their subsequent history presents some difficult problems; but it is
known that some of them settled within the dominions of the Franks,
against whom they revolted unsuccessfully in 595. At the time of the
journeys, however, they were in alliance with Theodric, king of the
Ostrogoths; and it is hardly necessary to suppose that they had
moved far, if at all, beyond their ancient borders. In any case it
would seem that the 'waste country', through which the travellers
passed before they came to them, must have lain between the Elbe
and the Oder. The first stages of the route would presumably lead
through the Hungarian plain, to the east of—and not very far from
—the Danube. After this the most natural course would be through
Slovakia, Moravia and either Silesia or Saxony. The first stages led
through 'all the peoples of the Sclavenoi in succession'; but unfortunately we do not know where these end and the waste land
begins. There is no reason for doubting that eastern Hungary was
at this time largely occupied by the Slovenians, or at least by
Slavonic peoples. But we have no information for the regions farther
north. The lands between the Elbe and the Oder had once been the
homes of powerful Teutonic peoples, the Semnones, the Burgundians
and (farther south) the Vandals. The fact that this region is now
called 'waste' would seem to point to devastation through widespread and long-continued raiding.

In 561, or a little later, Thuringia, which then apparently extended to the Elbe and had recently been conquered by the Franks
and Saxons, was invaded by the Avars, a people from the steppe,
who down to this time are known only to the north and east of the
Black Sea. In one battle, which took place on the Elbe, Sigiberht,
king of the Franks, was defeated and captured by the Avars. Peace
was then made; and the Avars, together with a Saxon army, moved
south to join the Langobardi in an attack upon the Gepidae, a
Teutonic people, who then occupied the Banat and northern Serbia.
After this war, and probably through some agreement connected
with it, the Langobardi moved into Italy, and the whole of the
plain of the Danube, from Austria to the Rumanian frontier, came

into the possession of the Avars—who soon became a serious danger to Constantinople. But they did not desist from their operations in the north. About 596 we hear of them invading Thuringia again, though they were bought off by the Franks—who in the meantime (apparently *c.* 567) had settled their frontier in the basin of the Saale with forces drawn from various Teutonic peoples from the northern coasts.[1] Among these were almost certainly the Warni, whose revolt in 595, referred to above, may have been connected in some way with the Avar invasion. The activities of the Avars themselves in the north were brought to an end by Samo, in whose territories, presumably Bohemia, they had been accustomed to make their winter quarters. In the basin of the Danube, however, they maintained their power until near the end of the eighth century, when they were overthrown by Charlemagne.

From *c.* 600 Slavonic armies are frequently mentioned as serving under the Avars. Perhaps the earliest instances occur in 601–3, when we hear of Slavonic—or rather Slovenian—forces sent by the king of the Avars to support the Langobardic king Agilulf in his wars in Italy. There can be no doubt that about this time the Avars had a widespread suzerainty over Slavonic populations. Indeed, one writer,[2] late in the seventh century, states that all the Sclavinioi were subject to the ruler of the Avars, though this may be an overstatement, especially if he means the Slavonic peoples in general, and not merely the Slovenians. No cases seem to be recorded from the sixth century. Yet it is difficult to see how the Slovenians can have reached the eastern Alps without authority from the Avars, who possessed western Hungary from 567 onwards. So also, farther north, we find the Avars invading Thuringia about 561 and again about 596, while about thirty years after the latter date we find the Sorabi invading the same country from the same quarter. Moreover, the Sorabi at this time were apparently under the suzerainty of Samo, who had just expelled the Avars from Bohemia.

On the other hand, there is no ground for supposing that the Sclavenoi who were raiding in the Balkans in 527 were connected in any way with the Avars. The latter do not appear in central Europe until more than thirty years later. All the evidence suggests that the relations between the Slavonic peoples and the Avars were very similar to the relations between the eastern Teutonic peoples

---

[1] For the evidence see *The Origin of the English Nation*, pp. 111 ff. and the map facing p. 112.

[2] Archbishop John of Thessalonica in the 'Miracles of St Demetrios', quoted by Zeuss, *Die Deutschen u. die Nachbarstämme*, p. 623, note.

and the Huns nearly two centuries before. In both cases a number of peoples settled between the Dnjepr and the Danube have begun to expand westwards and south-westwards when they are struck in the back by an enemy from the steppe. Some of them accelerate their westward movements and seek homes in the lands they have been raiding, while others are reduced to various degrees of dependence by the new enemy and are carried forward by them in the impetus of their movements, or follow in their wake.

The Slavonic peoples beyond the Oder and the Carpathians are hardly mentioned before the end of the ninth century; for they were beyond the horizon of writers both in Constantinople and in the west. Alfred speaks of the Horithi, who are clearly identical with the Belo-Chrovatoi, or 'White Croatians', mentioned more than once by Constantine Porphyrogenitus. The latter locates this 'Great Croatia' vaguely between the lands of the Franks and Bavarians and Bohemia on one side and the land of the 'Turks'[1] on the other. He says also that these Croatians were neighbours of the Serbloi— by which term he seems to mean the Sorabi—and that they extended to 'the mountains', apparently the Carpathians. After the eleventh century their name disappears; but it was long preserved in the names of districts on the borders of Bohemia and Silesia. It would seem too that they must have occupied at least part of Galicia; for the ancient Russian Chronicle[2] represents them as at war with Vladimir the Great. At an earlier date they had fought under Oleg.

The Poles are apparently first mentioned by Constantine Porphyrogenitus (c. 950). Down to the eleventh century they are generally known by their old national name,[3] which is still regularly used in Lithuanian (Lenkai). The name 'Pole' (Poljak, properly a 'man of the field or plain') belonged originally to one district only. Other districts were Pomerania, Masovia, Silesia,[4] etc. Authentic history seems to begin with the acceptance of Christianity in 967. The kingdom was already of considerable size. The dominions of Boleslav I, at the beginning of the eleventh century, extended from the Baltic coast to Bohemia.

It is in the Ukraine that we first meet with the name Sclavenoi.

---

[1] This name is regularly applied to the Hungarians (Magyars) by Constantine.

[2] Ann. 992; cf. 904. No details are given in either case; but these Croatians cannot have been those of Yugoslavia, who were too far away from the kingdom of Kiev.

[3] Lench-, Lens-, e.g. Russ. Ljachove, Gk. Lenzanenoi (Const. Porph.), Norse Læsir (in a poem dating from c. 1050, quoted in Haralds S. Harðr, cap. 2).

[4] Pomerania from Pomorjane, 'people of the coast'; Silesia (pagus Silensis) and Lausitz from the names of two Vandal peoples (Silingai, Lugii), who had formerly occupied these districts.

Writers of the sixth century, Jordanes and Procopios, speak of two
neighbouring and closely related peoples, the Antai (Antes) and
Sclavenoi, threatening the Danube borders of the empire from this
region. At first the former seem to have been almost as great a
danger as the latter. But later in the century we hear of them only
in the Roman service; and after the beginning of the seventh century
their name disappears altogether. Their power seems to have been
completely broken by the Avars[1]—probably between 558 and 561.

After this time we hear little of the Slavonic peoples of Russia
until the tenth century, when they were already under Varangian
rule. Constantine[2] mentions several names; but a much longer list
is given by the ancient Russian Chronicle. Some of these names
have an obvious meaning. The people of the Kiev district are called
Poljane, 'people of the plain' (the same term as the Poles), while
others are called *Drevljane*, 'people of the forest'. But there are others
which are less obvious, and probably older. The peoples included in
the Russian list extend to Lake Ilmen and Novgorod, and even
Constantine's list includes the Kriviči, who in the Chronicle are
said to occupy the upper parts of (the basins of) the Dnjepr, the
Dvina and the Volga and to inhabit Smolensk. In the Chronicle
most of the peoples are said to be of 'Slovenian' stock (*ot roda
Slovenska*); but two peoples, the Radimiči and the Vjatiči, as distinct
from the rest, are stated to be of Polish origin (*ot Ljachov*). These two
peoples are represented as living on the Sož and the Oka—doubtless
the upper Oka—i.e. in the east of White Russia and in the Great
Russian provinces of Bryansk and Kaluga. The origin of the Kriviči
is not stated.

In later times there was a vast expansion of the Russian language
to the north and north-east, chiefly at the expense of the Finnish
peoples; but it is difficult to determine when these movements
began. The presence in districts east of the Dnjepr of peoples who
were believed to be Polish is noteworthy. Since Constantine[3] speaks
of Poles (*Lenzeninoi*) beside Drevljane (*Dervleninoi*) in tributary
districts of the Russian land, it would seem that their settlement in
this region took place at least before the tenth century. Indeed, it
is not easy to see how such a settlement can have come about after
the Russian expansion up the Dnjepr, in the direction of Lake Ilmen.
The evidence of place-names is said[4] to show that down to the sixth

[1] Menandros, fragm. 284.
[2] 'On the Administration of the Empire', cap. 9 (*ad fin*), 37.
[3] *Op. cit.* cap. 37.
[4] Cf. Buga in the *Streitberg Festgabe*, pp. 24, 33 f. and the two accompanying maps.

century White Russia and the Smolensk region were Lithuanian, and that between then and the end of the seventh both these regions were Slavonicised by movements partly from Poland, partly up the Dnjepr from the Ukraine. Unfortunately, hardly any evidence is available, apart from place-names; but, so far as it goes, this seems to indicate that the northern and north-eastern expansion in Russia began about the same time as the expansion in the west.

The recurrence of identical names of peoples in different parts of the Slavonic world should not be overlooked. No significance of course need be attached to names descriptive of districts, such as Poljane; but there are others which cannot be explained so easily. First, the Sclavenoi are found in the Ukraine, the Balkans and the eastern Alps.[1] Writers of the sixth century make it clear that those of the Balkans came from the Ukraine, chiefly across the lower Danube; but the frequent references to raids in Illyricum show that a route across the middle Danube, through the plain of Hungary, was also used. There is no need therefore to question that the Sclavenoi of all three districts had a common origin. But the application of this name to the Serbians and Croatians, and also to the Slavonic peoples north of the (upper) Danube[2] seems to be of literary (Latin and Greek) origin, without vernacular foundation either in their own or in neighbouring languages. In the Teutonic languages—German, English, Norse—the old collective term *Winid-* long continued in use. Alfred applies it to the Slavonic peoples of the Baltic coast; he seems not to have known the name *Slav-* (*Slov-*).

Again, the emperor Constantine (cap. 30–32) states that the Croatians and Serbians (of Yugoslavia) were sprung from the 'White' Croatians and Serbians who dwelt between the Franks, the Bavarians and the Hungarians. By 'White Serbians'[3] he clearly means the Sorabi, who lived between the Saale and the Oder. There is no doubt that the names are identical. *Chrovatoi* (*Horithi*) and *Sorabi* (*Surbi*, etc.) are attempts to represent *Hrvati* and *Srbi*, which are the true names of the (Yugoslav) Croatians and Serbians. Some scholars have rejected Constantine's statement on the ground that the western Slavonic languages, to which the Sorbian language belongs—and presumably this was true also of the 'White Croatian' —differ (collectively) from the southern Slavonic languages. But there is no reason for supposing that these linguistic differences are

---

[1] A similar name was applied to a dying language which half a century ago was known to a few score of people in the neighbourhood of the Leba See in eastern Pomerania, near the coast.

[2] I.e., its use as a collective term for all Slavonic peoples (and languages).

[3] οἱ Σέρβλοι ἄσπροι ἐπονομαζόμενοι.

as old as the sixth century, when the southern sections of the two peoples broke away. An analogy may be found in the Poles who settled in White Russia and to the east of the Dnjepr, apparently about the same time; their language seems to have developed in general conformity with that of the neighbouring (Russian) population.

If Constantine's statements are correct, the Croatian and Serbian movements to Yugoslavia must have crossed the track of the Alpine Slovenians, whose expansion would seem to have followed a more or less due westerly course. We cannot of course be certain as to the exact starting point of the former movements, since the White Croatians disappear at an early date. Their descendants, however, are probably to be found among the southern Poles, the Czechs of Moravia and the Slovaks[1]—perhaps chiefly among the last-named, though these may also contain a considerable Slovenian element. It was doubtless the rents in the Slavonic world made by the Avars, and reopened later by the Hungarians, which were responsible for the development of linguistic differences between the northern and the southern peoples.

The Slovenians, Croatians and Serbians are not the only Slavonic peoples which we find broken up and settled in distant regions. Apart from these the most striking case is perhaps that of a people called Obotriti or Abotriti, who occupied the province of Mecklenburg and are frequently mentioned in Frankish records. Alfred gives their name as Afdrede. But there was another people of the same name in 'the part of Dacia which adjoins the Danube' and not far from the Bulgarians—i.e. probably in the Banat. They are frequently mentioned in records of the reign of Louis (Ludwig) I, c. 818–24. In the list of Slavonic peoples contained in the Regensburg MS. (cf. p. 58) they are called Osterábtrezi, while the people of Mecklenburg are called Nordabtrezi. From their position it would seem likely that they had accompanied the southward movement of the Serbians, and that both branches of the people had set out from an earlier home in Silesia or western Galicia.

From all that has been said above it is clear enough that the expansion of the Slavonic peoples followed much the same course and was due to the same causes as that of the Teutonic peoples, though it began at a somewhat later date. It may, indeed, be regarded as a continuation of the latter. There were two chief causes. The first

---

[1] It has been suggested that the name Hrvati (Chrovatoi, etc.) may be derived from the early Teutonic name of the Carpathians, which is preserved in Norse traditional poetry as Harvaða fjöll; cf. Kershaw, Anglo-Saxon and Norse Poems, p. 145. The correspondence of sounds is of course not exact, but hardly impossible in a borrowed name. The Carpathians indicated by the evidence would presumably be the White Carpathians (between Moravia and Slovakia) or the Tatra.

was the presence in both groups of peoples of a numerous restless and adventurous element which was attracted by reports of the greater wealth and superior culture of the lands to the south and west. Movements due to this cause were usually preceded by a long period of raiding and plundering expeditions; settlement in the plundered lands seems not to have been contemplated at first. In the Balkans this period began in 527, and lasted over half a century. In the north of Europe we may infer from the reference to the 'waste' land in Procopios's story cited above (p. 59) that the period of raiding began rather earlier; and it may well have lasted quite as long. The second cause was the sudden and terrifying appearance from time to time of hordes of mounted nomads from the steppe, who scattered in all directions the inhabitants of the lands which they invaded, or incorporated them in their own armies and carried them along with them. It was the invasion of the Huns, c. 370, which produced these effects upon the Teutonic peoples; and it must also have affected the Slavs to some extent. But the horde which was chiefly responsible for the dispersion of the latter was that of the Avars, c. 550. The disruption of the Serbians and other peoples, noted above, is exactly parallel to that of the Goths, the Suebi (Swæfe) and other Teutonic peoples in the time of the Huns.

In regard to the expansion of the Slavonic peoples two strange misconceptions are widely prevalent. One is that the Slavs, unlike the Teutonic peoples, were no warriors, and that the Teutonic lands which they came to occupy had been evacuated before their arrival and were then without inhabitants. This notion, which has attained great popularity through national prejudices, seems to be due partly to Procopios's reference to the 'waste' land, which has been discussed above, and partly to a remark by the contemporary (sixth-century) Gothic historian Jordanes (cap. 23), who, speaking of a victory of the Gothic king Eormenric, two centuries before his time, describes the Slavs (*Venethi*) as contemptible in fighting (*armis despecti*), though strong in numbers. Immediately afterwards, however, he adds that 'now as a result of our sins, they are raging everywhere'. The inferiority of the Slavs as warriors is fully explained by another passage in Procopios (*Goth.* iii, 14), where he states that they were usually unmounted, that they had no body-armour, and that their equipment was limited to a shield and javelins. This outfit is substantially the same as that of the Germani of the first century, as described by Tacitus, *Germ.* 6. In other words, the armature of the Slavonic peoples in the sixth century was four or five hundred years behind the times—owing doubtless to the remoteness and backwardness of the region from which they came. Against the well-armed and mounted forces of the Romans and the Goths they had obviously no chance, except by numerical superiority. But there is no ground for regarding them as either cowardly or peaceful. Even in Tacitus's time (*Germ.* 46) they were a fighting people, famous for their devotion to brigandage—a description which points to a heroic society of a somewhat primitive type.

The assumption that the lands of the eastern Teutonic peoples had been evacuated long before the arrival of the Slavs is equally groundless. I know of no evidence for believing that whole peoples evacuate their old homes except under strong pressure. Examples of something like wholesale evacuation do occur in the history of the fifth and sixth centuries, e.g. in the movements of the Visigoths and the Vandals. But these were armies, rather than peoples; and they had left their old homes long before. In the 'old homes' change of occupancy involves two distinct processes: first, the draining off of the younger and more enterprising elements in the population by plundering expeditions, followed by conquest and settlement in richer and more desirable regions, and later, the devastation and conquest of the old homes themselves by newcomers, inspired by similar motives, from still poorer regions. The 'waste' land referred to in Procopios's story may reasonably be taken as indicating that the Slavonic peoples had already—very early in the sixth century—made their presence felt to the west of the Oder, though they had not yet occupied the country.

The other misconception to which we would call attention is concerned with the form of government prevailing among the early Slavonic peoples. It is commonly stated that this was of a purely democratic character, and that kingship was unknown. Good authority can indeed be produced for this statement. Procopios, who was alive when the first Slavonic raids upon the empire took place, says (*Goth.* iii, 14) the Sclavenoi and Antai are not ruled by one man, but have lived from ancient times 'in democracy' (ἐν δημοκρατίᾳ); and consequently all their (political) affairs are settled by public discussion. Four centuries later the emperor Constantine (*On the Administration of the Empire*, cap. 29) states that the Croatians, Serbians and neighbouring peoples 'have no rulers (ἄρχοντες), as they say, except župan[1] elders (πλὴν ζουπάνους

---

[1] A župan was the governor of a district (županja). According to Constantine (cap. 30) there were eleven such districts in Dalmatia. The word is of Turkish (perhaps originally Iranian) derivation, and was probably acquired by the Slavs from the Avars.

γέροντας), in accordance with the fashion of the other Slavonic peoples'. Whatever may be the exact meaning of this sentence, it must certainly be taken in connection with the following chapters (30 ff.), which contain a short account of these peoples. Each of them is said to have had a hereditary ruler (ἄρχων) of its own from the time when their possession of the lands which they occupy was sanctioned by the emperor Heraclios—early in the seventh century. The most detailed account is that of the Serbians (cap. 32). Succession here, as also among the Croatians and elsewhere, is usually from father to son; but there are instances of division between brothers and also of disputed succession, leading to war, between brothers and cousins. This chapter also records what seems to be a native tradition as to the origin of the dynasty. The first ruler—who obtained possession of the country from Heraclios—is said to have been one of two sons of the ruler of 'White Serbia' in the north. On their father's death they divide their people; and one of them sets out to the south with the half which follows him. A somewhat similar tradition is recorded of the Croatians (cap. 30); here the southward movement from 'White Croatia' is led by one family—five brothers and two sisters.

It may be observed that Constantine speaks of rulers and ruling families among the White Croatians and White Serbians, as well as in Moravia and elsewhere; and there can be little doubt that he regarded the existence of such rulers as a normal characteristic of the Slavonic peoples. The statement therefore quoted above from cap. 29, apparently denying the existence of such rulers, can hardly mean more than that—owing presumably to the absence of any elaborate administrative machinery, like that of the Romans—the Slavs knew of no effective rule beyond that of the župan, or chief of the district. Procopios's statement would seem to be still wider of the mark; but it is to be remembered that the only Slavs known in his time were roving bands of raiders. Taking the evidence as a whole, we are again brought back to Tacitus's description of the Germani, especially in *Germ.* 7 and 11, passages which leave us in doubt as to whether kingship was a normal or an exceptional institution. And this comparison will bring out the essential difference between the Teutonic and the Slavonic invasions of the empire. The Teutonic peoples had been affected by the influence of Graeco-Roman civilisation for over four centuries—an influence which penetrated in some degree even to so remote a people as the English, as may be seen from the Roman weapons and armour found at Thorsbjærg. But the Slavonic peoples in the sixth century had as yet been little affected by this influence. We have no early native records; but apparently their civilisation and institutions were in general similar to those of the Teutonic peoples in the first century.

It is often said that kingship cannot have been known to the early Slavonic peoples because their languages had no word for 'king' before the ninth century, when the foreign names *Car* (*Tsar*) and *Kralj* were borrowed for this purpose—from *Caesar* and *Karl* (i.e. Charlemagne) respectively. In Greek works the head of a Slavonic people is usually called ἄρχων (i.e. 'ruler'), while in Latin the usual terms are *princeps* and *dux*. But the native word everywhere seems to be *knez*—in the old ecclesiastical language *kŭnęzĭ*—which is identical with our word *king* (Ang.-Sax. *cyning*), and must have been borrowed from some Teutonic language. It is commonly assumed that the word has declined in value; but this is far from certain. Was the average Teutonic king before the fifth century more powerful than the average *knez* of the sixth or seventh century? Or was the realm, of which he was the head, on the average greater than a Slavonic realm in the later period? I think not. It is more likely that the term 'king' had risen in value, and that the non-recognition of the *knez* as a king was due to the increase in the size and wealth of the Teutonic kingdoms. On the Continent all of them, except those of the Danes and the Lombards, had been incorporated in the Frankish dominions before the end of the sixth century.

The word 'king' must have been borrowed by the Slavonic peoples at a time when the small (Teutonic) peoples were still in existence, but apparently after the word had come to mean '(in-dependent) ruler'.[1] Before that the Teutonic languages had used other words for 'king';[2] and the same may be true of the Slavonic languages also. It is of interest, however, to note that the oldest surviving Slavonic word is borrowed from Teutonic, especially in view of the fact that the earliest word which we can trace in the Teutonic languages is borrowed from Celtic.[3] Such borrowings suggest that the growth of political institutions tended to follow the course of civilisation in general, from west to east.

By the end of the sixth century the linguistic map of western and west central Europe had assumed more or less its present form, so

[1] Cf. p. 55, note. It is likely enough that a member of a Slavonic royal family was called *knez*, if he possessed an armed following (*družina*); but the linguistic evidence shows that the word had also come to mean a sovereign ruler.

[2] Goth. *þiudans, reiks*, etc., cf. p. 55, note.

[3] Goth. *reiks*, with the derivatives in other Teutonic languages; cf. Irish *rí*, O. Welsh *ri(g)*, 'king'.

far as the Continent is concerned. The same remark is true of a broad belt of country stretching from the southern border of Austria to the Aegean. But in eastern Europe and central Europe eastwards from the basin of the Elbe and the Upper Danube great changes have taken place since that date. With these we shall have to deal in the next chapter.

Something must be said here, however, about the distribution of peoples in the eastern half of Europe within the period which we have been discussing. Slavonic peoples, as we have seen, occupied the greater part of the basin of the Dnjepr, and in the sixth century expanded westwards on a vast scale. The upper part of the Dnjepr basin is believed to have been occupied by the Lithuanians until about the close of our period, when they were displaced by Slavonic peoples coming from the south and south-west. East Prussia was held by the Prusai, who spoke a related (Baltic) language, while the greater part of what is now Lithuania was divided among peoples of the same linguistic group. Latvia, however, at this time probably belonged to the Livonians and possibly also other peoples of Finnish stock. Moreover, peoples with Finnish languages seem to have occupied not only Finland and northern Russia, but also the basin of the Volga for about two-thirds of its course—i.e. as far as the forest region extended.

It is only in the steppe region of the lower Volga and the Don basin that we can trace important changes of population. This was the home of the nomad peoples, of whom there are records of a long succession, reaching back to the earliest times. All of them seem to have come, one after another, from the eastern steppes, north and north-east of the Caspian Sea. The first of whom we have any detailed knowledge were the Scythians, who possessed the region north of the Black Sea in the sixth century B.C., and had been known to the Greek world for perhaps two centuries before this time. In the fifth century Herodotos gives a fairly detailed description of them. It is not known how far they penetrated westwards; but Scythian gold objects have been found in Germany. In course of time—not later than the first century B.C.—their place was taken by the Sauromatai or Sarmatae, a similar people, who in Herodotos's time lived to the east of the Scythians. These newcomers extended their conquests as far as the mouth of the Danube, while the Iazyges, who seem to have been a part of them, settled in the plain of Hungary. There they remained until the fourth century (A.D.). From the plains of south Russia, however, they were cut off by the southward expansion of the Goths in the third century; and in the following century the Goths themselves had for a time possession of the Ukraine. In the meanwhile the Sarmatae had been displaced in the Don steppe by the Alani, a new wave of nomads from the east, who had occupied the lands between the Don and the Volga in the first century. Some of them would seem to have penetrated a good deal farther to the west, presumably before the Gothic conquests. According to Ammianus Marcellinus (xxxi, 2, 12, etc.) they were identical with the ancient Massagetae—a people of Turkestan, by whom the Persian king Cyrus was defeated and slain in 529 B.C.

Down to *c.* 370 (A.D.) all the nomadic peoples of the steppe in Europe seem to have been Iranians. In earlier times Iranians had doubtless also occupied the Asiatic steppe, perhaps as far as the western slopes of the Altai and Tien-Shan mountains. But from this region they had already been driven by Turkish (Altaic) nomads, coming from the Altai and Mongolia. The first of the latter to arrive in Europe, so far as we know, were the Huns, who reached the Volga about the date mentioned above. The Alani were overthrown and dispersed. Some of them attached themselves to the Vandals,[1] others to the Huns, while others again eventually withdrew towards the Caucasus (cf. p. 39). Then the Gothic king Eormenric, who held a supremacy over many peoples—Teutonic, Slavonic, Baltic and Finnish—took his own life in despair; and his successors retired westwards. The Huns subsequently made their way to the plain of the Danube, and fixed their capital between the rivers Tisa and Körös. Seventy years later their king Attila had about half of Europe under his sway; but after his death, in 453, their power collapsed almost immediately; and they disappear from history. They were doubtless dispersed and incorporated in other peoples; but one or more groups may have survived in south Russia under a new name.

The next to appear were the Bulgars, who occupied the steppe to the north of the Black Sea and round the Sea of Azov from the latter part of the fifth century. Some very early authorities identify them with the Huns; and it is the prevailing view that they were a portion of the latter who had attached themselves to one of Attila's sons. Before the end of the fifth century they are found raiding in the empire across the lower Danube; and these raids continued at intervals until *c.* 560, when they seem to have been conquered by the Avars. They recovered their independence in 634, and again began to raid the empire *c.* 670. In 680 they conquered and settled the

[1] After 418 the kings of the Vandals are said to have used the title *reges Vandalorum et Alanorum.*

lands between the Danube and the Balkans[1]—territories which were extended later both to the west and south. Rumania was also included in their dominions until the ninth century. By this time they had lost their own (Altaic) language, and adopted that of the Slovenians whom they had conquered. A portion of them, however, remained in the neighbourhood of the Sea of Azov, from whence later they moved northwards up the Volga, perhaps under pressure from the Chazars. The ruins of Bulgar, their old capital, are still to be seen near the confluence of the Volga and the Kama.

The Avars seem to have been a new wave of nomads from the east, though contemporary writers in western Europe usually call them Huns, not distinguishing them from the previous invaders. According to Greek writers they came from a land where they had been in subjection to the 'Turks'—apparently in the Altai region or Jungaria. They arrived at the lower Volga in 558, and sent an embassy to Justinian, offering their services as allies against his enemies. He paid them a subsidy; and very soon afterwards they attacked and subjugated the Bulgars, or a portion of them, and then shattered the Antai, the easternmost of the Slavonic peoples. After this they seem to have made a swift movement to the north-west, arriving finally in Thuringia, where they defeated the Frankish king Sigiberht in 561, or not much later. In 567, in alliance with the Lombards, they overthrew and virtually destroyed the Gepidae, whose dominions lay to the east of the Danube; and immediately afterwards, when the Lombards set out for Italy, they took possession of their territories on the west of the Danube (cf. p. 60 f.). They now held probably the whole of the plain of the Danube, and soon extended their conquests to the Adriatic. For the next half-century they were at the height of their power; their dominions reached from Thuringia to the Adriatic and the Black Sea. The Bulgars and many of the Slavonic peoples were, at least to some extent, subject to their authority, though it is uncertain whether, or in what way, they were responsible for the great Slavonic invasion of the empire in 582 (cf. p. 55) and the westward and southward movements of the Slovenians, the Croatians and the Serbians (cf. p. 64 f.). In any case they had now become the chief danger to the empire, which they were constantly threatening and raiding. But in 623 their power in the north was broken by the Czechs; and three years later they failed in a great attack upon Constantinople. About the same time their power in the Alps and in the region between the Danube and the Adriatic

---

[1] The early history of the Bulgars, before 680, is discussed by Runciman, *A History of the First Bulgarian Empire*, pp. 1–26.

was overthrown by the Croatians and Serbians; and in 634, or not much later, they were deserted by the Bulgars. From these blows they seem never to have recovered; but they retained possession of the plain of the Danube until the end of the eighth century, when— between 791 and 796—they were conquered by Charlemagne's armies. After this they lingered as a vassal state for some thirty years or more.

The ancient Russian Chronicle quotes a current proverb: 'They perished like the Avars; and there survives of them neither progeny nor heir.' But there can be little doubt that they influenced the map of Europe. They seem to have been for a time as formidable as any of the nomad hordes who came from the east. This was due partly to the speed of their movements, and partly to the great numbers of the forces which they raised from subject peoples, and which they posted in the forefront of their battles, as well as to their own ferocity and brutality. It is of interest to note that they fixed their capital not far from the place where Attila had resided (cf. p. 71), but on the west side of the Tisa. It is called Hringus by German Latin writers; and it is said to have been surrounded by nine concentric rings of fortification, made of tree trunks, stones and earth.

While they were still on the Asiatic steppe, the Avars seem to have been followed at first by the Chazars or 'Turks',[1] who sent an embassy to Constantinople in 568. The latter· are next heard of— apparently from the direction of the lower Volga—in 626, when they sent a force to help the emperor Heraclios against the Persians. Soon after this they seem to have come into possession of the south Russian steppe, and to have reduced to subjection the peoples who now remained there—a portion of the Bulgars, the Goths in the Crimea and some of the Slavonic peoples on the lower Dnjepr. Of the Avars we hear no more in this region. The Chazars themselves gave up military for commercial activities; and the period of their rule was a time of prosperity. Eventually they adopted Judaism as their religion.

All the nomad peoples of the steppe, whether Iranian or Turkish (Altaic), seem to have had certain common characteristics, which indeed were necessarily imposed upon them by the conditions of life in this region. They were primarily sheep-farmers and horse-breeders. Their dwellings were covered wagons instead of houses, owing to the need of moving from one pasturage to another at different seasons. They lived chiefly on mares' milk, which they not

---

[1] This name is applied to the Chazars only by early Greek writers. The emperor Constantine (in the tenth century) uses 'Turk' for Magyar (Hungarian).

only drank, but also took in a solidified form—called *kumis* by the modern peoples of the steppe. This peculiarity—the use of mares' milk—is believed to have arisen from the unsuitability of some parts of the steppe for cattle-keeping. It was the first thing which attracted the attention of the ancient Greeks. 'Mare-milkers' (Hippēmolgoi), 'who feed on milk', are mentioned even in the *Iliad* (xiii, 5f.) in connection with a reference to the 'horse-breeding' Thracians, while a fragment of poetry attributed to Hesiod[1] speaks of 'feeders on milk, who have their abodes on wagons'. So far as I am aware, the regular use of mares' milk is found only on the steppe and in communities which may be suspected of having come from the steppe. Among the latter may be included the kings and aristocracy of the Este—presumably the Prusai—as described in the account of Wulfstan's voyage, which King Alfred inserted in his translation of Orosius. It cannot of course be proved—for we have no information as to the northern movements of the nomads—but it seems at least a likely inference that the Este had had a ruling caste of this origin imposed upon them.[2] Indeed, I should myself be inclined to suspect influence, direct or indirect, from the steppe, wherever intensive horse-breeding is known to have been cultivated, as, for example, among the ancient Thracians or the Thuringians and the Swedes of the sixth century.[3]

Although the two groups of nomad peoples, Iranian and Turkish, had of necessity many common characteristics, it is clear from the accounts of ancient writers that in other respects they differed from one another greatly. This may be seen, for example, from the interesting comparative descriptions of the Huns and the Alani given by Ammianus Marcellinus, xxxi, 2, which must have been written within a few years of the first appearance of the former in Europe. He emphasises especially the physical differences between the two peoples. What he says of the Huns is an unsympathetic description —in fact a caricature—of a typical Mongoloid people, ugly, beardless and stunted, though very strong, and barely human in form.[4] The Alani, on the other hand, are tall, handsome, more or less fairhaired,[5] and with steadily flashing eyes. Both live in wagons; but the Huns are filthy and squalid, while the Alani are more civilised

[1] Fragm. 221 (Kinkel).
[2] According to a legend current in later times the Prusai acquired their devotion to horsemanship from the Mazuri of northern Poland, a district which can hardly have lain very far out of the course of the Huns and Avars.
[3] *Iliad*, xiii, 4, etc.; Jordanes, cap. 3.
[4] Cf. the descriptions of the Huns and of Attila given by Jordanes, cap. 24, 34.
[5] *Proceri autem Halani paene sunt omnes et pulchri, crinibus mediocriter flauis*, etc.

in their food and their manner of life. Both are warrior peoples, and swift in their movements, especially the Huns; but the warfare of the Alani is evidently of the 'heroic' type, whereas the Huns act more in concert. Both are devoted to horses—the Huns to such an extent that they even sleep on horseback. Finally, he says that the Huns are wholly without religion, treacherous, and ignorant of right and wrong. Of the Alani in these respects he notes only that they worship 'Mars' and are much given to forecasting the future. It may be added that his account of the Huns is not only prejudiced but also defective—e.g. he says they have no kings.

The Iranian languages have disappeared from Europe, as we have seen, except in the Caucasus; but they have left many traces of themselves in the Slavonic, Finnish and Hungarian languages. Several Altaic (Turkish) languages survive (cf. p. 46 f.). Except in the south of the Crimea, where the language is Ottoman Turkish, introduced by the Turkish conquest in the fifteenth century, all these languages seem to be due to movements of nomads coming along the steppe from the east; but it is difficult to determine which of the movements were responsible for the various languages. The differences between all these languages, except Čuvaš, are comparatively slight. The old Bulgarian language was spoken in the past at the ruined city of Bulgar; and something is known of it from inscriptions. But this region (the Tatar A.S.S.) has been occupied since the thirteenth century by Tatars from the Golden Horde, whose language has apparently displaced that of their predecessors. It is thought that the Čuvaš language may be that of the old Bulgars; and the fact that it differs considerably from the other languages suggests that it broke away from the rest at an early date—i.e. that it is a relic of an early invasion. If, however, the Bulgars formed only one section of the Huns ruled by Attila (cf. p. 71), Čuvaš may perhaps also represent the language of other sections. There is no reason for supposing that the language of the Avars has survived anywhere. As for that of the Chazars the evidence is uncertain. In their region —the south-east corner of Russia—several later movements of nomads have to be taken into account, as will be seen in the next chapter.

CHAPTER IV

THE FORMATION OF THE LINGUISTIC MAP OF EUROPE. II

I т was noted in the last chapter that by the beginning of the seventh century the linguistic map of western (Continental) Europe had assumed more or less its present form. In the eastern—and larger —half of the Continent, however, important linguistic movements have taken place since that time. It is to these that we shall now have to give our attention.

But first we may observe briefly that movements of languages have not been altogether unknown even in the west. They have taken place indeed on a great scale; but they have been transitory, and have left the distribution of languages much the same as it was before.

Such was the case with the Arabic invasions from Africa. In Spain Arabic was introduced by conquest in 710, and quickly spread over the peninsula and into France. It was not finally expelled until the deportations early in the seventeenth century—after a period of over nine hundred years. In Sicily the rule of the Arabs lasted from 827 to *c.* 1090, in Italy and France for much shorter periods; and in no case, apparently, did their language long survive the end of their rule. Their culture, especially in Spain, had a wide influence; but they seem nowhere to have become wholly amalgamated with the native populations, nor to have obliterated the native languages. In Europe the Arabic language now survives only in Malta; but here it has long been combined with the Catholic culture of the west.

The other languages which have gained a temporary expansion during our period are those of the north. This expansion was acquired by conquest and settlement on many different coasts, usually on a small scale, between the ninth and the eleventh centuries. Norse rule in Dublin lasted from 840 to 1170, and in the western islands of Scotland for more than a century longer. But the native languages, whether Gaelic or English, were hardly ever extinguished; on the cessation of Norse or Danish rule they reasserted themselves. Apart from Iceland and the Færoes, which previously had been uninhabited, it was only in Orkney and Shetland that the Norse language was able to maintain itself down to modern times—when it was gradually displaced by English. On the Continent the chief Scandinavian conquest was the Norse earldom of Normandy, formally recognised in 911. But the settlers did not retain their own language for much more than a century; the Normans who conquered England and those who established themselves in Italy and Sicily were virtually French. The Danish settlements established in the Netherlands in the ninth century had only a short life. Later in this chapter we shall have to notice Scandinavian conquests and settlements in the eastern half of Europe.

The chief changes in the linguistic geography of the Continent which have taken place since the sixth century may be assigned to the following movements:

(1) The eastward expansion of the Germans.
(2) The northward and eastward expansion of the Russians.
(3) A series of westward movements from the steppe.

To these we may perhaps add (4) the expansion of the Ottoman Turks, from Asia Minor, although, owing to subsequent collapses, the area in Europe within which Ottoman Turkish is now spoken is comparatively small.

(1) In the eighth century all the German peoples came to be politically united. The process had begun with the conquests of the Frankish kings early in the sixth century; but it was not completed until the time of Charlemagne, who conquered the Lombards in 774 and the Saxons in 785, while in 788 he definitely incorporated in his kingdom the Bavarians, who had hitherto been at least semi-independent.

By this time most of the non-German Teutonic peoples of the Continent seem to have been moribund, or at least on the down grade. Remnants of the Goths survived in the Crimea, and of the Gepidae apparently in the Banat. In Spain the Visigoths seem to have been Latinised to a great extent even before they were conquered by the Arabs. The Frisians were conquered in part by Charles Martel, and finally by Charlemagne; and their language in some districts began gradually to give way to German. Some remnants of peoples from the northern coasts had been planted in Thuringia by the Frankish kings c. 560–5. These were no doubt military bodies, intended to guard the frontier against the Avars; but they were sufficiently numerous for their descendants to retain traces of their own (Anglo-Frisian) languages for some centuries. The Baltic coasts themselves, including eastern Holstein, were now occupied by Slavonic peoples. In western Holstein the native languages probably still survived; but farther north they were being pressed by a southward expansion of the Danes. The overseas expansion from Scandinavian lands had as yet hardly begun, at least in the region of the North Sea.

It is to be remembered that the dominions of Charlemagne and his family were partly German and partly Latin—which was becoming French, Provençal or Italian. In the fifth and sixth centuries a German—or rather Dutch—ruling class had been imposed by conquest upon nearly the whole of Gaul. But this class had now become Latinised and absorbed; and a linguistic boundary now ran through the dominions, corresponding in general to the present linguistic boundary between French and German or Dutch, though in some districts it lay slightly more to the west or south. It was not, however, until the days of Charlemagne's grandsons that the dominions were divided. After various transitory arrangements, a division between the French and German portions was established in 870, though it did not follow the linguistic boundary at all closely. In the meantime the Lombards were adopting Italian in place of their own language. Politically they were usually separate from the two northern kingdoms from 840 down to 961.

In Charlemagne's time the German linguistic area included the whole basin of the Rhine, except the upper waters of the Meuse and the Moselle, the whole of the basins of the Ems and the Weser, and the upper part of the basin of the Danube. To the south it may be said to have included the territories of the Lombards in Italy, though here the language was dying out. To the east it extended to the lower Elbe, and bordered on the Saale perhaps throughout the whole length of its course. To the north and north-west it bordered on the Frisian dialects, upon which it was gradually encroaching. Within this area a number of well-marked dialects had already developed. The most distinctive of these were the Low German dialects, which differed from the rest not only in many regular phonological and morphological features, but also in the fact that they usually possessed many aberrant forms, which were not German at all, but Anglo-Frisian. They showed, in varying degree, a mixture of languages. In some districts, of course, this mixture might be accounted for by the encroachment of German upon Frisian. In the Saxon districts, however, where these aberrant forms occur most frequently in the oldest poetry, a different explanation is more likely. The earliest known reference to the Saxons[1] states that they lived on 'the neck of the (Cimbric) peninsula', i.e. the peninsula of Jutland. They belonged therefore originally to the Anglo-Frisian area. Their

---

[1] Ptolemy's *Geography* (ii, xi, 11), dating from the second century.

language must have been Germanised through their conquest and occupation of German districts; and it would seem that the forms to which we have referred were survivals from their original language. Such mixed languages must have served to facilitate communication between the Teutonic peoples of the Continent. English had long been unintelligible, except perhaps to Frisians; and the same is doubtless true of Danish and the other Scandinavian languages.

Charlemagne's policy was to unify, i.e. to bring within his own dominions, all the German peoples, and indeed all the Teutonic peoples, of the Continent. But he also extended his authority, partly by wars and partly by diplomacy, over many of the Slavonic peoples, who bordered on his dominions throughout the whole length of their eastern frontier, except in the valley of the Danube. The peoples mentioned by Einhard[1] as submitting to him were the Abodriti, Wilzi, Sorabi and Bohemians. The Slovenians seem to have been already—before 788—subject to the Bavarians, to whom they had appealed for protection against the Avars. The lands beyond them, between the Danube and the Adriatic, including Croatia and Dalmatia, were conquered by Charlemagne's general, Eric, duke of Friuli.[2] But the greatest war was that in which his generals, between 791 and 799, conquered the Avars. Not only Lower Austria, but also the whole plain of the Danube, seem now to have come under his power.

Charlemagne's eastern conquests were retained for a time by his son, Louis I; but most of them had apparently been lost by the middle of the ninth century. Only Lower Austria and Slovenia remained within the dominions of the family. The former was settled by Germans, and was called the Ostmark; the latter at first retained its native rulers, but later—perhaps after 870—was under German dukes, one of whom, Arnulf, became emperor in 887. It is possible that the curious installation ceremony noted on p. 27 may have originated in some agreement by which this change was effected. But elsewhere there seems to have been a return to the frontiers and the political conditions which existed before Charlemagne's conquests. The Croatians are said to have revolted and expelled the Franks owing to the atrocities which they perpetrated.[3]

About the middle of the ninth century the chief power in east

---

[1] *Vita Karoli Magni*, cap. 12, 15.
[2] A list of Eric's conquests and victories is given in the elegy on his death (in 799) by Paulinus (published in Waitz' edition of Einhard, p. 44).
[3] Constantine Porph., *Administration of the Empire*, cap. 30.

central Europe was in the hands of Rastislav, ruler[1] of the eastern Czechs in Moravia. He had revolted from the Germans and taken possession of a large part of the plain of the Danube—the former territories of the Avars. He was a Christian; but he wished to free himself from the German bishops at Salzburg and Passau, and also to protect himself from the German king Ludwig II. He therefore sent an embassy to Constantinople to ask for a bishop who would instruct his people in their own language, and also apparently for diplomatic support. In reply to this appeal the two brothers, Cyril and Methodios, the 'Apostles of the Slavs', were sent in 863. Cyril was a great scholar and linguist, and had had considerable diplomatic experience. In Moravia they were well received, except by the German clergy; and they were also welcomed by the Slovenian ruler Kocel. Cyril devoted himself with great energy to translating the Bible and liturgical works; and they attracted numerous disciples. Unfortunately, they could not ordain priests, for neither of them was a bishop; and they decided to go to Rome for consecration, apparently because it was nearer than Constantinople. At first they were favourably received. Cyril died in 869; but Methodios returned to Moravia as archbishop. In the meantime, however, Rastislav was dethroned by his nephew Svatopluk, who was more under German influence. The new Church encountered great difficulties; and after Methodios' death, in 885, it was suppressed and persecuted.[2] Many of the disciples fled to Bulgaria, where the ruler, Boris, had recently been converted, and there they were welcomed gladly.

Svatopluk's action has had a most disastrous effect upon the Slavonic world. The community which he suppressed flourished exceedingly in Bulgaria, and was soon established as the national Church. From thence the new organisation and liturgy spread to the Serbs, and in the course of the following century to the Russians, when they were converted. A large amount of literary work was produced. But all the more western Slavonic peoples, including the Croats, remained attached to the Church of Rome; and for the most part they adhered to the Latin liturgy. The northern peoples were still heathen at the time of which we are speaking; but when they came to be converted, it was the Roman hierarchy and the Latin

---

[1] At this time the term *künęzĭ* (*knez*) probably still retained its original meaning, 'king'; but in view of the translations noted on p. 69, above, this title is perhaps better avoided.

[2] It was apparently suppressed also in Slovenia, which came under direct German rule about this time (cf. p. 79). In some parts of Croatia, however, the liturgy was allowed to continue; and in a few districts it is still in use.

liturgy which they also received. The result then was a complete cleavage between east and west—a cleavage which has had the effect of preventing any common action and even any common feeling.

For over a century after Charlemagne's death nothing more seems to be recorded of any German expansion towards the east. The chief power in Germany eventually came into the hands of the duke of the Saxons, Henry the Fowler, who in 919 was elected king. He initiated a systematic conquest of the Slavonic peoples in the basin of the Elbe, and as far east as the Oder—a policy which was continued by his son Otto I (936–73). The lands temporarily acquired by these conquests were afterwards called (from north to south) the Marks of Brandenburg (or Nordmark), Lausitz (Lusatia) and Meissen. The lands between the Brandenburg region and the Baltic coasts— Holstein and Mecklenburg—were conquered by Billung, a vassal of Otto, from whom they were later known as 'Mark der Billunger'. Fortified towns were built, and bishoprics founded for the conversion of the Slavs who were still heathen. But nearly the whole of these conquests, except the Mark of Meissen, was lost in 983. The greater part of them came into the hands of the Polish king Mieszko I, whose son Boleslav I (992–1025) united under his sway nearly all the Slavonic peoples from the Baltic to Bohemia (inclusive).

More important and lasting was the second conquest of the same regions, which was carried out in the twelfth century. In 1134 the emperor Lothair II granted what was left of the Nordmark—the part west of the Elbe—to Albert the Bear, of 'Ascania' (Aschersleben). He reconquered most of the Brandenburg district; and his descendants extended their dominions, so as to include a large area (the Neumark) beyond the Oder, and also the Mark of Lausitz. Contemporary with Albert's conquests were those of Henry the Lion, duke of Saxony, who regained the 'Mark der Billunger', i.e. Holstein and Mecklenburg. All these conquests were due in the main to the weakness of Poland after the death of Boleslav III (in 1138), whose territories were divided among his family. In the northern region the newly conquered lands were given to settlers, from the west, especially the Netherlands and Westphalia. But towards the end of the century the conquests made by Henry the Lion came for a time into the hands of the Danes.

In the thirteenth century the conquest of the Brandenburg region was extended by the descendants of Albert the Bear. About the same time (c. 1227) Holstein and Mecklenburg were recovered from the Danes; and they were also deprived of Pomerania, which they had acquired some time previously. This brought a considerable stretch of the southern shore of the Baltic into German hands. Further conquests in this direction were carried out at the expense, not of Slavonic, but of Baltic and Finnish peoples, between Pomerania and the Gulf of Finland. These conquests were effected by two religious orders, the 'Brothers of the Sword', founded in 1202, and the 'Teutonic Knights', who began their ghastly 'conversion' of the Prusai, or native Prussians, about 1230. To these events we have already referred (p. 37); but it may be added here that the invitation to the Knights came from a Polish prince, Conrad of Masovia, whose territories had been raided by the Prusai. In the end the Knights succeeded in destroying the latter. But the Brothers, in the more northern region, were less successful, though they introduced a numerous German population. Their territories in 1561 were divided between the Poles and the Swedes.

Apart from these conquests a considerable German expansion towards the east and south took place on more peaceful lines. It seems to have begun soon after 1150, but the chief movement was in the thirteenth century. German colonists were encouraged by foreign rulers to settle in their territories. Many of them were merchants and craftsmen, who gave a great impetus to town life, which at that time was but little developed among the Slavonic and neighbouring peoples. But the movement was not confined to towns. The colonists would seem to have included many farmers and also, in some districts, a not inconsiderable mining population. The region most affected was Silesia, which was ruled by princes of the Polish royal family, but before 1300 had already become predominantly German. Bohemia,[1] Hungary and Transylvania were also affected; and though the colonists were never more than a relatively small minority of the population, their descendants still preserve their language and customs.

By the end of the thirteenth century the linguistic map of north central Europe was assuming more or less its present form. Further conquests by the Germans were prevented by the revival of the Polish kingdom, the various parts of which were reunited by Vladislav I (Lokietek) early in the following century. By this time the linguistic frontier had been pushed forward some distance beyond the Oder throughout the greater part of its course. Apart

---

[1] If the colonists here were largely miners, it is of interest to note that in the first century, according to Tacitus, *Germ.* 43, mines in the same region were worked by the Cotini, a Celtic people, who paid tribute to the surrounding Teutonic and Sarmatian peoples. Presumably the more advanced peoples had better appliances in both the first and the twelfth centuries.

from a few small linguistic islands, the only Slavonic peoples who maintained their positions in the west were the Czechs and the Slovenians. The latter had been reduced by half, and even the surviving half were under German rule; but they succeeded in retaining their language. The Czechs also were generally included in the Empire; but as a rule they were practically independent, under 'grand princes'—later kings—of their own. Early in the fourteenth century the kingdom passed by marriage into the Luxemburg family —to John, son of the emperor Henry VII; and from 1347 for over sixty years Prague was the capital of the empire. After this the Czechs again had kings of their own, who after 1490 also ruled Hungary. In 1526 both kingdoms chose the Hapsburg prince Ferdinand, who in 1558 became emperor. From this time the Czechs remained under the Hapsburgs; but their freedom was lost in 1620, during the Thirty Years' War.

(2) The expansion of the Russians—or, more properly, the Slavs in what is now Russia—is believed to have begun not much later than the Slavonic expansion in the west. Definite historical evidence is lacking; but some more or less safe inferences can be drawn from phonetic changes in place-names. From these it is thought that in the sixth century the upper part of the basin of the Dnjepr was inhabited by Lithuanians, who were adjoined, in the basin of the Desna, by the (Finnish) Mordwins. In the fourth century all this region is said to have been conquered by the Goths, whose rule was probably succeeded, in the fifth century, by that of the Huns. But the Slavs are thought to have forced their way to the north—the neighbourhood of Leningrad—between this time and the eighth century, the Lithuanians being driven westward and the Mordwins eastward.

The date suggested may be slightly too early; but there can be little doubt that a considerable expansion of the Slavs had taken place before the ninth century. By the middle of this century Scandinavian adventurers had established themselves at Novgorod and Kiev; and it seems clear that most of their subjects were Slavs, in the north as well as in the south of this region.[1] Scandinavian personal names begin to be displaced by Slavonic before 950; and we have no record or hint of any change of population during this period.

From the tenth century onwards a further expansion must have taken place, not only northwards but also, and more especially, to

[1] See N. K. Chadwick, *The Beginnings of Russian History* (to be published early in 1945).

the north-east, into the basin of the Volga. Moscow seems not to be mentioned before 1147; but its rise was preceded by that of other cities in the same region, especially Vladimir, Suzdal and Rostov. The Scandinavian dynasty which was established at Kiev before 900 had all the Russian Slavs under its authority; but the family themselves became Slavicised in the tenth century, though they retained connections with Scandinavia until 1050 at least. Kiev remained the capital and the residence of the head of the family down to c. 1170, while junior members of the family ruled over other cities. But after 1150 the district of Kiev became depopulated owing to the ravages of the Polovci, which were aggravated by endless strife among the Russian princes themselves; and the capital was moved to the basin of the Volga—first to Vladimir, then to Suzdal, and finally to Moscow. All this contributed to the northern and north-eastern expansion of the Slavs.

It is clear, however, from the enormous numbers of the Russian Slavs, as compared with those of the other Slavonic peoples, that this expansion must have been in the nature of a conquest, rather than a mere colonisation. The Slavs evidently absorbed and assimilated the native (Finnish) inhabitants of these regions. Even now there are still one or two millions of peoples, chiefly Mordvins, to the west of the Volga, who retain their original language. But these can be no more than a fragment of the peoples who lived there a thousand years ago—some of which seem to have wholly or almost wholly disappeared. The same process of expansion and absorption was repeated subsequently after every conquest made by the rulers of Moscow towards the north and east—e.g. those by Dimitri Donskoi in the latter part of the fourteenth century, by Ivan III a century later, and by Ivan IV a century later still. The conquests of the last, however, were more from the Tatars than from the Finnish peoples.

But long before this later expansion Kiev and the other principalities in the south had been overthrown by the invasion of the Mongols and Tatars (1236–9). The northern and eastern principalities (Novgorod and Moscow) were merely made tributary; but in the southern and western regions Russian government was entirely destroyed. The Tatars were soon expelled from the west by the Lithuanians, who nearly a century later also conquered the Kiev district from them. The Russian language (White Russian and Little Russian) survived through all these changes. But Russian government was not restored for four or five centuries—at Kiev in 1683, but elsewhere not until the partition of Poland in 1772 and 1795.

A new era of eastward expansion, on a far greater scale, began with the overthrow of the Tatars of Kazan by Ivan IV in 1552. Later, in 1581, the exile Ermak, who was acting for the Tsar's agents, succeeded in obtaining possession of Siberia—originally the region round Tobolsk. Eventually Russian power was extended as far as the Pacific, and was followed, especially during the last century, by a great wave of colonisation. In the eighteenth century the Russians advanced their frontiers in all directions; but the greatest and most important expansion was towards the south—the Black Sea and the Caucasus.

(3) In the last chapter mention was made of a long series of movements westward over the steppe, the last of which was that of the Chazars, early in the seventh century. For more than two centuries the Chazars seem to have retained possession of the European steppe, north of the Black Sea and eastwards as far as the Caspian. It is not until the ninth century that we hear of new peoples in this region.

The Magyars are first mentioned[1] during the reign of the emperor Theophilos (829–42), at which time they would seem to have acquired possession of the steppe west of the Don. They must have come from the north-east between the territories of the Chazars and those of the northern Bulgars on the middle Volga (cf. p. 72). Their original home can be determined with reasonable probability from the fact that the nearest affinities of their language are with Vogul, a dying language in the central Urals, east of Perm, and with Ostiak, which is spoken by a few small communities between the Urals and Tobolsk. It is likely therefore that they came from what was formerly the province of Ufa; but now it is the Baškir Autonomous Republic.

The Magyar (Hungarian) language and its cognates do not belong to the Altaic (Turco-Tataric) family, but are distantly related to the Finnish group. Yet the descriptions of the Magyars given by early writers clearly represent them as typical steppe nomads, like the Turco-Tataric peoples. In explanation of this it is generally thought that they must have been conquered and assimilated by a people of the latter stock, perhaps an offshoot of the Baškirs, which subsequently lost its own language. From about the middle of the ninth century they became a source of terror to the peoples of central

---

[1] They are usually called Ungri (Hungri) or Ungari, but sometimes Hunni or Turci. By Constantine Porph. 'Turk' is regularly used for Magyar. 'Magyar' was perhaps originally the name of one section of them.

Europe, owing to their mobility and the prowess of their fierce horse-men. In 894 they were appealed to by the emperor Leo VI, who was at war with the Bulgars on the Danube; but as soon as they had set out to attack the Bulgars they were themselves attacked in the rear by the Pečenegs, who had been called in by the Bulgars. In the following year, perhaps partly through fear of the Pečenegs, they crossed the Carpathians, and conquered and settled the great plain of the middle Danube, as the Huns and the Avars had done in earlier times. The plain was at this time occupied by Slavonic peoples, most of whom had been under the Moravian king Svato-pluk, the nephew and successor of Rastislav, who had invited Cyril and Methodios to his court in 863. After Svatopluk's death in 894 and the subsequent quarrels among his sons, the kingdom soon collapsed before the Magyars. The inhabitants of the plain were destroyed or absorbed, while the Slovaks and Rumanians and the other peoples of the surrounding hill-country were reduced to sub-jection. Raiding expeditions on a great scale were continued for the next fifty or sixty years; but the Magyars were severely defeated by the Germans near Merseburg in 933 and at the Lechfeld in Bavaria in 955. It was only during the latter part of the tenth century that they began to settle down to more peaceful conditions. They were converted to Christianity about 985-97.

In 1102, when the Croatian royal family died out in the direct male line, Koloman, king of Hungary, who claimed through a female line, was accepted by the Croatians; and the two crowns thenceforth remained united, though the Magyars tended to treat Croatia as a dependency. In the fourteenth and fifteenth centuries, again through marriage connections, Hungary was united at one time with Poland, at another with Bohemia; and the latter union lasted to the end. Then, in 1526, after the battle of Mohacs, in which the king (Louis II) perished with all his army, the greater part of the kingdom was conquered by the Turks; and this included nearly all the part occupied by the Magyars themselves. Those who remained independent, together with the Czechs, chose as their king the Arch-duke Ferdinand, the late king's brother-in-law, and were sub-sequently incorporated in the Hapsburg dominions. In the seven-teenth century Austrian tyranny is said to have been as bad as that of the Turks. But after the Turks had been expelled from the country (in 1699 and 1716), conditions improved until 1780, when Joseph II issued his edict for the Germanisation of his dominions. The result was a great outburst of national feeling among the Magyars—the beginning of modern nationalism. The movement soon spread to the other non-German peoples in the emperor's dominions; but among the subject peoples in Hungary it was directed more against the Magyars than against the Austrians. For later events we may refer to p. 44.

The settlement of the Magyars in the plain of the Danube has been a misfortune for central Europe, especially in modern times. Unlike their predecessors, the Huns and the Avars, they have succeeded in maintaining their position in the great plain of the Danube for nearly a thousand years. But they have always remained an alien element in central Europe; they have never been able to come to a lasting agreement either with their own subject peoples or with the independent peoples which border upon them. In their own kingdom they formed a minority of the population; but they never allowed the other elements a voice in the government. Their relations with the neighbouring peoples present a problem to which it is not easy to see any satisfactory solution. The most difficult element in the situation is the presence of a million and a half of Magyars (Szeklers) in the heart of Transylvania, where they are cut off from the rest of their people by a large stretch of country inhabited almost exclusively by Rumanians.

The peoples who came westward over the steppe after the Magyars seem all to have been nomads of Altaic (Turco-Tataric) stock. On the departure of the Magyars from the steppe their place was taken by the Pečenegs or Patzinaks, who have been mentioned above as threatening them from behind in 894. They are believed to have come from central Asia. They are said to have attacked Kiev for the first time in 915; from 968 for nearly a century references to their raids are frequent.

The Baškirs[1] are seldom if ever mentioned in European records before the thirteenth century; but it is clear from Arabic writers that they were already in the Volga regions early in the tenth century. Medieval travellers give the name 'Great Hungary' to the land of the Baškirs—which may have been more or less the territory of the present Baškir Autonomous Republic—and one of them (Rubruquis) states that the language was identical with Hungarian. But the language now is Turco-Tataric; and early Arabic writers represent the Baškirs as typical Turks of the steppe. The explanation may be that the Baškir conquest of the region was effected by stages—that the first wave of invaders adopted the language of the native

---

[1] The relationship of the Baškirs to the Magyars is discussed by Macartney, *The Magyars in the Ninth Century*, pp. 33 ff., with quotations (translated) from the Arabic authorities.

(Magyar) inhabitants and were driven westward by subsequent waves, which kept their own language.

The Polovci or Cumani seem to have displaced the Pečenegs on the western steppe—between the Don and the Dnjepr—about the middle of the eleventh century. The latter may have been dispersed and absorbed by the newcomers; both peoples are said to have had the same language. In the Russian Chronicle they are said to have attacked Kiev for the first time in 1068. Not many years later a large force of them—under the name Cumani—invaded Hungary. They were defeated, but allowed to settle in the land, where before long they seem to have been absorbed by the Magyars. In Russia for more than a century and a half the attacks of the Polovci were a constant source of danger to the southern cities. Very often they took part in the quarrels of the Russian princes.

The last important invasion from the east came in the early part of the thirteenth century. In 1224 an army belonging to the Mongol emperor Genghiz Khan appeared suddenly from beyond the Volga and overthrew the combined forces of the Polovci and the Russians. After a delay of thirteen years this army, which seems to have consisted almost wholly of Tatars, proceeded to devastate nearly all the eastern half of Europe. The leader now was Batu Khan, a grandson of Genghiz. All the northern Russian cities, except Novgorod, were ravaged, but maintained their existence as tributaries of the invaders. The southern cities, however, were practically destroyed—Kiev in 1240. In 1241 Hungary and Poland were devastated; but the invaders were defeated by the Czechs, and later by the Lithuanians, who succeeded in conquering White Russia from them. Within the next century they were driven by the Lithuanians from Kiev and from all the lands west of the Dnjepr down to its mouth. But to the east of that river the 'Golden Horde' long continued to maintain imperial power. Their capital was at Sarai, about thirty miles east of Stalingrad. Later there were separate governments at Kazan and in the Crimea (cf. p. 47 f.). In the fifteenth century, perhaps even earlier, the power of the Golden Horde began to decline; but it was not until 1480 that their suzerainty was finally repudiated by the ruler of Moscow. The conquest of most of the territories of the Tatars (in Europe) was effected in the following century by Ivan IV, though some regions retained their independence as late as the eighteenth century.

The collapse of the Golden Horde put an end to the ghastly series of devastations which the nomads of the steppe had carried out for two thousand years or more; and it is impossible to overestimate the debt which Europe owes to the Russians for bringing this about. In the reign of Ivan IV began the Russian expansion into Asia, to which we have referred above.

The Ottoman or Osmanli Turks belonged originally to the same stock as the Turco-Tataric peoples mentioned above. But they have had a different history from the latter; and they entered Europe by a different route.

In the ninth century the Caliphs at Baghdad began to employ Turks in their bodyguards to such an extent that eventually they are said to have become the strongest and most numerous class of fighting men in their empire. At first slaves had been employed; but soon these were augmented and displaced by recruits from the considerable Turkish population which at this time was pushing its way southwards into Persia from the steppe of Turkestan. Towards the end of the tenth century the chief power among these Turks was gained by the family of Seljuk, which seems to have come from the region of the Oxus. In 1055 they occupied Baghdad, at the invitation of the Caliph; and soon afterwards their empire extended from the Oxus to the Mediterranean. A century later their dominions were divided, and parts of them passed into the hands of other Turkish families. During the period of the Mongol invasions, which began c. 1214, the Seljuks lost all their power, except in Asia Minor, to which they had penetrated shortly before they acquired Baghdad. In Asia Minor their rule was brought to an end in 1299 by Osman (or Othman), the leader of another Turkish family, which had come from Persia and entered their service.

In 1356 the Turks crossed the Hellespont under Murad, grandson of Osman; and in the following year they established their capital at Adrianople. Bulgaria was conquered before the end of the century. In the reign of Mohammed II (1451–81) their territories in Europe were greatly increased. Constantinople was taken in 1453, Serbia conquered in 1459, Bosnia in 1463, and the Crimea with the region round the Sea of Azov in 1475. The greater part of Greece was conquered during the same period; and the Rumanian principalities were made tributary, though they frequently asserted their independence. The battle of Mohacs, in 1526, was followed by the conquest of the greater part of Hungary; and Vienna was attacked, though unsuccessfully, in 1529.

After this date the expansion of the Turkish dominions in Europe was at an end, apart from the transitory occupation of a part of Poland in 1672. In 1683 another unsuccessful attack was made upon

Vienna; but after this their power was obviously on the wane. Before the end of the century they had been expelled from Hungary by the Austrians. Indeed, if their enemies had been able to agree to any common action, it is not unlikely that they would have been expelled from Europe soon afterwards. As it was, all their territories north of the Black Sea were taken by the Russians in the course of the eighteenth century, while their power was further curtailed by the Serbian and Greek wars of independence in the early part of last century. Practically all the northern half of the peninsula was lost after the Russo-Turkish war of 1878; the southern half, except eastern Thrace, was lost in the Balkan war of 1912.

Apart from eastern Thrace, where the population is said to be mainly Turkish, there are now only a few districts in Europe in which Turkish of the Ottoman (Osmanli) type is spoken by any considerable number of people. The most important of these perhaps are the Dobrudža and the southern part of the Crimea. The 'Turks' of Bosnia are in reality native Yugoslavs whose ancestors embraced Islam after the Turkish conquest; and the Moslems of Albania also are no doubt for the most part of native origin. In Hungary few remains of the Turks seem to be left; and it would seem that the Turkish population introduced there by the conquest consisted mainly of garrisons and officials.

CHAPTER V

NATION AND KINGDOM

I T will be seen that the linguistic map discussed in Chapter II bears
on the whole a fairly close resemblance to the political map of Europe
which resulted from the Treaties of 1919–20. In nearly every independent state there is one language which is spoken by the over-
whelming majority of the population; so that one commonly connects the French language with France, the German with Germany,
the Italian with Italy. At the same time, however, it is to be remembered that the correspondence between the linguistic and the
political areas is seldom complete. Thus, for example, all these three
languages are spoken in Switzerland. Sometimes a political frontier
does not coincide with the linguistic one. Sometimes a state possesses
one or more languages in addition to the one which is spoken by the
majority of the population—as in this country, where English is not
the only native language. Sometimes again a language which is that
of the majority in one state is also that of a minority in another state
—as in the case of Hungarian in Rumania.

Before the Treaties of 1919–20 the resemblance between the
political and linguistic maps was much less close than it is now; and
before the Balkan Wars of 1912–13 it was still less close. In the early
years of this century eleven, or perhaps twelve, languages were
spoken within the territories of the Austro-Hungarian Monarchy.
In the Austrian half of the Monarchy German was the dominant
language; but it was spoken only by a minority of the population.
In Hungary the dominant language was Hungarian; but this also
was spoken only by a minority. Poland did not then exist as an
independent state; the Poles with their language were divided
between Russia, Germany and Austria. The Yugoslav (Serbo-
Croatian) language was spoken in the two small independent
kingdoms of Serbia and Montenegro and by fairly large populations
in Austria-Hungary and Turkey. Yugoslavia as a whole did not
exist.

Two or three centuries earlier there was, I think, still less resemblance. And the same is probably true of the Middle Ages, at
least in some periods.

The question then may be raised whether there was ever a time,
still farther back, when political and linguistic geography coincided
more closely, or whether the 'national state'—i.e. the state which is

co-extensive with nationality and language—is a modern invention. In order to answer this question two considerations must be borne in mind.

First, some fifteen or sixteen centuries ago there was but one Latin language, from which all the Latin languages now spoken are descended. At the same time there was also probably but one Slavonic language; for none of the differences which now exist between the various Slavonic languages seem to go so far back. Again at the same time the differences between the various Teutonic languages seem to have been extremely slight, except in the case of Gothic—no doubt with its neighbouring languages—where the differences from the rest must date from a period some two or three centuries earlier. On the other hand, the Teutonic peoples consisted of a large number of states, which were normally independent, whereas the Latin peoples all belonged to one political unit—the Roman Empire. For the Slavonic peoples we have no information for this period; but it is most unlikely that they formed one political unit. The state then was co-extensive with the language among the Latin peoples, but not among the Teutonic, and probably not among the Slavonic peoples.

Secondly, when we speak of the Latin language as co-extensive with the Roman Empire, we mean of course that it was everywhere the dominant and official language. The native languages could not have died out at once; some of them, e.g. Greek, Albanian, Basque and British (Welsh), still survive. So also after the collapse of Roman power in the west, in the fifth century, various Teutonic states—or perhaps we should say 'kings'—had under their rule large populations who spoke Latin or other (non-Teutonic) languages. In the fourth century the Gothic king Eormenric is said to have ruled over many peoples—Teutonic, Slavonic, Baltic and Finnish. And in much earlier times—perhaps the first century—there is reason for believing that the Teutonic states in the region between the Rhine and the Elbe had a not inconsiderable Celtic population under their rule. If we had more information relating to the Slavonic peoples, we should probably find analogous conditions with them. Here again therefore the idea that in early times state and language were co-extensive would seem to require some qualification.

The use of the Latin language seems everywhere to have been accompanied by a definite feeling for Roman nationality. This may be seen for example by the constant loyalty of the army, which after the first century was recruited from all provinces, and also by the fact that even rebellious provincial generals, who proclaimed themselves emperors at Trèves or in Britain, adhered to Roman traditions and ideas. Roman culture spread and was copied throughout the western provinces of the empire. Among the Teutonic peoples, on the other hand, there is no trace of any attempts or aspirations in the direction of a political union based on a feeling for common (Teutonic) nationality, though we do hear from time to time of leagues which comprised a limited number of states or kingdoms. It is quite correct, however, within certain limits to speak of a common Teutonic culture, which found expression, for example, in religion and in poetic forms, and more especially in the common possession of a body of heroic poetry relating to persons and events between the fourth and the sixth centuries. For the Slavonic peoples early records convey no suggestion of common action or common political aspirations. These records are too scanty to prove the existence of common cultural features which are distinctively Slavonic; but in general they give the impression that the civilisation was more or less uniform. For the Baltic peoples there is a good deal of evidence, though most of it is late, for a distinctive and fairly wide-spread culture, especially in religion; but we hear nothing of common action or of common political aspirations. For the Celtic peoples the evidence, which is earlier and more abundant, is to the same effect.

It would seem therefore that most, if not all, of the groups of peoples in the north of Europe corresponding to the linguistic groups which we are considering possessed in early (heathen) times certain common cultural features, especially in religion, but that these groups had no sense of common nationality such as would lead them to common political action or to common political aspirations. We do hear from time to time of alliances and associations of states, usually under a powerful king; but these generally collapsed soon after the king's death. There were others, it is true, which had a longer life and sometimes perhaps might be regarded as semi-permanent; but these normally consisted of only a few states. There was no analogy in the north of Europe to the Roman Empire, where the state itself and the feeling for nationality, both political and cultural, were co-extensive with the Latin language.

The states of modern Europe are comparable with the Roman Empire, in spite of its great size, rather than with the small states belonging to the northern peoples. Very few of the latter were larger than Wales. Yet it is from their history—their amalgamations and expansions, through conquest and otherwise—that the modern political map of Europe has been produced. We must therefore consider briefly how this has come about.

Among the northern peoples in early times there was in each state one family which formed its nucleus and backbone. Sometimes the rule of the whole state was in the hands of one member of this family, sometimes it was divided among several members. Most commonly these were brothers, who succeeded collectively at their father's death. Typical examples may be found among the Franks, e.g. in 511, when Clovis was succeeded by his four sons, and again in 561, when the last survivor of these, Hlothhari, was in turn succeeded by his four sons. But instances are to be found everywhere. Not seldom also we find divisions between cousins and even second cousins. The term 'king' was no doubt applied to all these persons; originally it may have meant no more than a member of the (ruling) family.[1] But Roman writers tend to regard states which possessed a number of kings as kingless, though they occasionally recognise the existence of a *stirps regia* in such states.

It is probable that before the times of written records every royal family preserved, together with its genealogy, a traditional account of its origin and early history. The two together may be regarded as a kind of title-deed. A number of such accounts have survived in Ireland, though mostly in an abridged form. For the Teutonic peoples the best examples come from the Goths, the Lombards and the Swedes. In this country the best is for the Picts, and there are others for Dalriada, Gwynedd, Kent and Wessex; but none of them are completely preserved. Among the Slavonic peoples the best is that of the Rus—a foreign dynasty—at Kiev; elsewhere we have only allusions to such stories, e.g. for the Croats and the Serbs. Among the Baltic peoples I know only the story of the Prusai, and that only in a very late form. These stories are seldom preserved in their entirety in any single work which has come down to us; but they can often be reconstructed to a considerable extent with more or less confidence. They belong to a world-wide genre of oral literature. They always contain, in varying degree, both historical and fictitious elements; one extreme may be seen in the story of the Scottish Dalriada, the other in that of Wessex. Royal genealogies and stories of the older dynasties frequently begin with deities or with (heathen) religious associations. The royal family thus had their authority fortified by the sanction of religion, which was no doubt concentrated in the state sanctuary.

When one king had the whole state under his authority it was often, if not usually, the custom for him to commit portions of it to

---

[1] Cf. p. 55, note. It should be borne in mind that Slav. *knez* (*knjaz*) is derived from 'king', and must originally have had the same meaning.

his relatives for government; and these also in early times commonly bore the title of 'king'. A good example of the system may be seen in Russia during the eleventh and twelfth centuries. The head of the family held Kiev—down to 1170—while the junior members each ruled one of the dependent cities and territories. Each of these dependent rulers bore the title *knjaz'* (*knęz'*)—which ought properly to be translated by 'king' rather than 'prince'—while the head of the family was called *veliki knjaz'*, which is commonly translated by 'grand duke', but should rather be 'great king'. There was a general tendency for these sub-kingdoms to become hereditary and semi-independent, if they consisted of solid blocks of territory; even in Russia this tendency appears in the twelfth century. Not unfrequently indeed they became wholly independent; but in early times some feeling for unity was generally preserved for a considerable period, in spite of wars between different branches of the family.

In the fifth and following centuries great changes were brought about by the collapse of Roman power in western and central Europe. Many of the northern peoples, or sections of them, were transformed into armies of occupation, vast alien territories were conquered, the native religions were discarded, the old sanctuaries desecrated or forgotten. One result of these changes was the appearance of kings who did not belong to the royal family—an innovation which shows that the kingdom had come to be regarded as something more than family property. The earliest examples seem to occur among the Goths, as might be expected from the fact that they were apparently the first people to undergo the process which we have noted. At times they were hardly more than armies on the march. When the first kings of non-royal family appear is uncertain, for the Romans had not a very intimate knowledge of the Goths before their invasions of Italy. But at all events there seem to be clear cases among the Visigoths in 531 and among the Ostrogoths in 536. Among the Franks the first example was Pippin (the father of Charlemagne), who was proclaimed king in 752, and founded a new royal line. His family had already been virtual rulers for some time. In this country the earliest examples are for Northumbria in 863, for Mercia (probably) in 874, and for England as a whole in 1066 (Harold II). It may be significant that none of these was able to keep his throne for more than a few years. The Welsh and Scottish examples are also late, and at least the former are far from certain. For the Slavonic peoples our information is defective; but Samo, who became king of Bohemia in 623, is said to have been a French merchant. On the other hand, in the ancient Russian Chronicle (*c.* 900) two rulers of Kiev, though they belong to the Rus (i.e. Scandinavians), are deposed and put to death by Oleg, apparently because they are not of royal family, but yet have assumed royal authority.

Another change was the growth of the power of officials who were not of royal birth. This may be seen best in the Frankish kingdom, though it can be traced also in this country and elsewhere. Owing to the great expansion of the Frankish dominions it became customary to give large provinces to officials—counts and dukes—who were not of the royal family. These appointments tended to become hereditary, and from the ninth century—877 in France—the practice was regularised. At the death of Louis I, in 840, his dominions were divided among his sons; but after their deaths a further division was made (in 887) by the governors of provinces, most of whom were not of royal birth. Among them was Eudes (Odo), duke of France, who now became king of that province, though Charlemagne's descendants recovered the throne a few years later, and held it until 987. In Italy, however, they disappeared after 887, and in Germany after 911.

After this time we find in both France and Germany a number of powerful dukes and counts, who often were practically independent. In France the kingship remained attached to one region (Paris); and after 987 it was hereditary in the family of Hugh Capet, a greatgrandson of the Eudes mentioned above. But in Germany it became 'elective'; and it was not permanently attached to any special region. The dukes and counts—with whom were associated some high ecclesiastics[1]—'elected' one of their number;[2] but in practice the kingship usually remained in one family for about four generations. Even children were allowed to succeed. From 919 to 1002 the kingship was held by the dukes of the Saxons, whose territories corresponded approximately to those of the kingdom of Hanover before 1866. To this dynasty belonged Otto I, who in 962 conquered Italy and took the title of emperor, which had fallen into abeyance before his time, but was borne by all subsequent German kings. Then from 1024[3] to 1125 the throne belonged to the counts of Franconia,

[1] The composition of the electoral council in early times seems not to be exactly known; perhaps it varied from time to time. As determined by the Golden Bull of Charles IV in 1356 it consisted of the king of Bohemia, the duke of Saxony, the Count Palatine of the Rhine, the Margràve of Brandenburg, and the archbishops of Cologne, Mainz and Trèves. Some of these dignitaries had been electors for a very long time. Charles IV (of Luxemburg) was king of Bohemia.

[2] Down to the great interregnum (1254) the new king seems almost always to have belonged to the late king's family circle; but he was apparently not always of royal descent.

[3] From 1002 to 1024 the king-emperor (Henry II) was a member of the Saxon family, but duke of Bavaria.

the region of the middle Rhine. After them, from 1138 to 1254,[1] it belonged to the dukes of Swabia—in Württemberg and western Bavaria. After 1254 no emperor or king was elected for nearly twenty years.

Long before the interregnum the old dukedoms had been broken up into numerous small principalities, many of which belonged to bishops. All of them were more or less independent. The emperors who reigned after 1273 were therefore drawn from families which had not been of great importance previously. Most of them belonged to the Hapsburg and Luxemburg families. The former, whose home was in Switzerland, acquired the dukedom of Austria soon after this date, while the latter became kings of Bohemia c. 1308, by marriage. In 1437, however, the Luxemburg line came to an end; and after this date all the emperors, except one, belonged to the Hapsburg family. In 1526 they acquired also the thrones of Hungary and Bohemia. From the beginning (i.e. 1273) they were always more concerned with their own hereditary territories than with Germany or the Empire as a whole—over which indeed they had little effective authority. The imperial title was changed to 'Emperor of Austria' in 1806.

The feudal system, which prevailed under the Empire, gave little scope for the growth of a feeling for nationality. The governing principle throughout was that of personal allegiance; but the influence of the Church also was as a rule extremely strong. It was only in frontier regions, e.g. in Spain and in the German-Slavonic borderlands—especially while the Slavonic peoples were still heathen or semi-heathen—that any feeling for nationality can be traced. But in these regions the feeling was bound up with, and subsidiary to, religion and the different cultural associations of Christianity and Islam or heathenism. Later, when the Slavonic peoples had accepted Christianity, their rulers and nobility became permeated by German influence, as may be seen, e.g. by the term *szlachta*,[2] which is regularly applied to the Polish nobility, and by the frequent use of German personal names by Slavonic princes. The Scandinavian kingdoms were affected by the same influence, though in varying degree. In Denmark German is said to have been the usual language of the nobility for some centuries.

Again, medieval German culture was very largely derived from

---

[1] Except for the reign of Otto IV, which may perhaps be dated 1208–14.
[2] Said to be derived from early Germ. *slahta*, 'family' (connected with *geschlecht*).

late Roman—especially French and Provençal[1]—culture, while
England after 1066 was hardly more than a province of French
culture. We may therefore speak of a more or less uniform culture
throughout the Catholic part of Europe, differing only in the degree
to which the peoples of Germany and of England[2] were permeated
by late Roman influence, and the Slavonic and Scandinavian
peoples by Romano-German influence. No doubt these influences
in the main affected only the upper classes. But it is to be borne in
mind that the whole Catholic world had one sacred language, which
was also the language of serious literature and the chief, if not the
only, vehicle of education. The poorer classes were entirely illiterate
everywhere. There was little opportunity therefore for the development of national feeling.

In the east of Europe, within the sphere of the Orthodox Church,
conditions were somewhat different. Late Roman or Romano-
German influence was slight or non-existent. The Russian royal
family were of Scandinavian origin; but they had left their native
land before these influences began to be felt there, while the ruling
families of the Balkans were either native or—in the case of the Bulgarians—derived from the nomads of the steppe. Cultural influence,
both religious and secular, came from Constantinople. But the
Greek language had not the privileged position which Latin possessed
in the west. Its use was never enforced in Russia, and only occasionally among the Slavonic peoples of the Balkans. For both religious and literary purposes these peoples, both in Russia and in
the Balkans, had the language of Cyril and Methodios, which for
some centuries must have been intelligible to them without great
difficulty. Yet education seems to have been at least as limited as
in the west; the poorer classes were apparently quite illiterate. It
is to be remembered that the Orthodox peoples suffered far more
from external pressure than those of the west. They had to bear the
brunt of the invasions of the Magyars and Pečenegs, the Polovci and
the Tatars, and in later times that of the Ottoman Turks. The
Russian kingdom was broken up, and most of it conquered in the
thirteenth century; the Bulgarians were conquered by the Greeks
in 1018, and again by the Turks in 1393–8; and the other Orthodox
peoples in the fifteenth century. As the conquerors—except in 1018
—were always either heathens or Mohammedans, any feelings for
nationality which the Slavonic peoples retained were necessarily
bound up with religion.

[1] Italian influence also was sometimes very strong, especially at the imperial
court. The later Swabian (Hohenstaufen) emperors lived in Italy and were virtually
Italians. So also was the earlier emperor Otto III (983–1002).
[2] The Celtic peoples also, but later, and hardly to the same extent.

We have next to notice a factor which modern historians tend to minimise, but which has in fact influenced the political map and the political history of Europe at least as much as any of the political changes which we have been considering. This is the royal marriage.

An example from our own country will serve to illustrate the extent to which this factor may influence the course of history. Cynan Tindaethwy, king of Anglesey (*c.* 754–816), had a daughter —perhaps his only child—who was married to an obscure prince named Gwriad, apparently in the Isle of Man. Their son Merfyn, probably in 816, succeeded his grandfather, who had been much harassed in his old age by the attacks of a neighbouring king from over the Straits. Later—apparently in 825—Merfyn obtained possession of the enemy's kingdom, which probably included the whole of Gwynedd, i.e. north-west Wales. In the meantime he married a sister of Cynghen, the last king of Powys, i.e. north-east Wales. His son Rhodri succeeded to both kingdoms and married a sister of the last king of Cardigan, which included Ystrad Tywi, the central part of South Wales. In 871 this realm too was added to the dominions of the family. Finally Howell the Good, son of Rhodri's son Cadell, married a daughter of the last king of Dyfed (i.e. south-west Wales), who died in 904. The family now possessed about three-quarters of Wales, including four kingdoms which had always before been independent. Indeed Howell himself during his last years (942–50) had all these territories under his rule; but after his death they were again separated to some extent by quarrels among the descendants of Rhodri.

In Continental history royal marriages with heiresses were of the greatest possible importance. I doubt if they ever occurred in quite so continuous a series as the one we have just considered; but they affected far greater areas and populations. Most of the examples belong to the period between the thirteenth and the seventeenth centuries.

In Spain the larger Christian kingdoms were united more than once by marriage before the thirteenth century. On one occasion —*c.* 1100, or very soon afterwards—all the three kingdoms, Castile, Leon and Aragon, came to be united in this way. But the unions soon broke down through quarrels, either between husband and wife or among members of the royal family. At last, however, Castile and Leon were finally united by the marriage of Alfonso IX of Leon with Berengaria, daughter of Alfonso VIII of Castile. Their son Fernando succeeded his mother in 1217 and his father in 1230. But the complete unification of Spain had to wait for another two centuries and a half, until the marriage of Isabel of Castile with Fernando (Ferdinand) of Aragon in 1469. The former succeeded to her throne in 1474, and the latter to his in 1479. Their daughter Joanna was queen of all Spain, since the last Moorish kingdom (Granada) had been conquered in 1492.

In central Europe royal marriages had quite as important results. As in Spain, the unions which followed sometimes soon collapsed, sometimes proved more or less permanent. A group of such unions arose from the marriage of Charles Robert of Anjou, king of Hungary (1309–42), with a sister of Casimir III, king of Poland, who left no children of his own. Louis I succeeded his father in Hungary (1342) and his uncle in Poland (1370). At his death (1382) he left both his kingdoms to his elder daughter, Maria, who was betrothed to Sigismund, son of the emperor Charles IV, and himself afterwards emperor (1411–37). The Poles, however, would not accept Sigismund; but they agreed to an offer by the queen-mother to give them Louis' younger daughter Jadviga (Hedwig), for whom they chose as husband the Lithuanian prince Jogaila, although she was betrothed to an Austrian prince. Jogaila was a heathen, but was baptised at his marriage, and reigned over both nations (as Vladislav II) from 1386 to 1434. This union, to which we have already referred (p. 38), lasted down to the partition of Poland at the end of the eighteenth century. But the separation between the two branches of the Polish-Hungarian royal family seems not to have been regarded as quite complete; for Jogaila's son, Vladislav III, who reigned in Poland from 1434 to 1444, was also king of Hungary (Vladislav IV) during the last four years of his life.

The history of Central Europe in the fifteenth century is made very complicated by the frequency of succession through marriage. John of Luxemburg, son of the emperor Henry VII, obtained the kingdom of Bohemia in 1310 by marriage with a princess of the native royal family, which had just died out in the direct male line. Their son was the emperor Charles IV (1346–78), who was also king of Bohemia. He was succeeded by his son Wenceslaus, who was deposed from the imperial throne in 1400, but continued to rule Bohemia until his death in 1419. The Sigismund mentioned above, who had obtained Hungary through his wife Maria, was a younger son of Charles IV. He became emperor in 1411, and in 1419 succeeded his brother on the throne of Bohemia. He and Maria left only one child, Elizabeth, who was married to Albert of Hapsburg. The latter succeeded his father-in-law in 1437 both as emperor and as king of Hungary and Bohemia, but died two years later. He left one infant son, who succeeded to his Austrian dominions and (nominally) to Bohemia, and five years later was recognised as king in Hungary (as Vladislav V); but in the imperial throne he was succeeded by his cousin Frederic III (1439–93), who also strove to obtain Bohemia, though without success. The Czechs eventually elected as their king one of their own nobles, George Podjebrad (1458–71), who had been acting as regent. His daughter Ludomilla was married to Vladislav, son of Casimir IV of Poland and nephew of Vladislav III of Poland (i.e. Vladislav IV of Hungary). This Vladislav was never king of Poland, but reigned in Bohemia (1471–1516) in succession to his father-in-law; and in 1490 he was recognised also as king of Hungary (Vladislav VI), owing to his relationship to Vladislav IV. Thus Bohemia and Hungary were now again united. Vladislav VI left a son Louis II, who succeeded him, but was killed at the battle of Mohacs in 1526, and a daughter, who was married to the archduke Ferdinand of Hapsburg, grandson of the emperor Maximilian I. Ferdinand succeeded to both Bohemia and Hungary, which thus came again into the hands of the Hapsburgs.

The emperor Maximilian I (1493–1519), son of Frederic III, married the daughter and heiress of Charles the Bold, duke of Burgundy. Charles' dominions were believed to be the richest in Europe; for they included not only Burgundy itself—most of which he lost—but also nearly the whole of Belgium and the Netherlands, which his ancestors had acquired through marriages. Philip, son of Maximilian, married Joanna, daughter and heiress of Ferdinand and Isabel (cf. p. 100). He died young, in 1506, but left two sons, Charles and Ferdinand. The former succeeded his mother as king of all Spain and his grandfather, Maximilian, as emperor, Charles V (1519–56). Maximilian's territorial dominions were divided: Charles received the Burgundy heritage, i.e. Belgium and the Netherlands; but Austria was given, a year or two later, to his younger brother, Ferdinand—who in 1526, by an unforeseen stroke of luck, inherited also Bohemia and Hungary. The two brothers now held between them a great part of Europe; but the two portions were never united. From Charles came the later kings of Spain, who also held Belgium and the title to the Netherlands—which revolted in 1572—while from Ferdinand, who later became emperor (1558–64) sprang the later emperors, who also held Austria, Bohemia and what was left of Hungary after the Turkish conquest.

This complicated story will serve to illustrate how between the fourteenth and sixteenth centuries large parts of Europe came to be united, shuffled and regrouped from time to time, without regard to

the nationality or language of the inhabitants. Most of Charles'
subjects spoke either Spanish or Dutch, while Ferdinand's subjects
spoke German, Hungarian, Czech and other Slavonic languages.
Some of the unions of which we have spoken were deliberately
planned and intended, e.g. the union of Poland and Lithuania in
1386; but others seem to be due to mere chance or to be the result
of merely personal considerations. In any case the process which
they illustrate was in no way confined to this group. Parallels are
in fact abundant; but one or two more examples must suffice here.

Sweden and Norway were first united by the marriage of the
Swedish prince Eric Magnusson with Ingibjörg, daughter of
Haakon V, king of Norway. Their son Magnus succeeded to the
throne of Norway in 1319 and to that of Sweden a year or two
earlier. In 1359 he arranged a marriage between his son Haakon
and Margaret, daughter of Valdimar III, king of Denmark, with
a view to the union of all the three northern kingdoms. But the
Swedes, dissatisfied with his treatment of them, banished both him
and his son in 1363, and offered the throne to a distant relative, Albrecht of Mecklenburg. In Norway Magnus was succeeded in 1374
by his son Haakon VI, who died in 1380, leaving one child Olaf, for
whom his mother, Margaret, acted as regent. Olaf himself died in
1387; but Margaret continued to rule—now as sovereign—in Norway, as well as in Denmark. A few years later she succeeded in
obtaining Sweden also, expelling Albrecht, whose rule had been
made unpopular by his German followers. In 1397 the union of the
three kingdoms was formally established at Kalmar. Margaret gave
up the triple throne to her nephew Eric of Pomerania, though apparently he had no more hereditary right than she had to either
Sweden or Norway. The Swedes practically regained their independence half a century later; but Norway remained under Denmark
till 1814.

In later times few marriages have had more far-reaching effects
than that of John Sigismund, who later (in 1608) became Elector of
Brandenburg, with Anne, daughter and heiress of Albert Frederic,
duke of Prussia. Albert Frederic had inherited the territories of the
Teutonic Knights, of whom his father Albert had been the last Grand
Master. John Sigismund succeeded to these territories—the greater
part of what was later called East Prussia—in 1618, at the death of
his father-in-law. He was now the possessor of two considerable
dominions which were separated from one another by a large part
of Poland; and the policy of his descendants—known from 1701 as
kings of Prussia—had as its aim the joining together of these two.

This object was achieved in 1772 by Frederic II, when he brought about the first partition of Poland; and the process was completed by his successor Frederic William II at the second and third partitions in 1793–5. Seldom has a union proved so disastrous to the peace and welfare of Europe.

Another long-lasting union, dating from much earlier times, was that of Croatia with Hungary. When the last king of the native Croatian dynasty died, in 1102, Koloman, king of Hungary, claimed the throne by marriage, and tried to enforce his claim by arms. In this he did not succeed; but eventually the Croatian leaders agreed to accept him. The union lasted until 1919, though Hungarian policy usually tended to treat Croatia as a dependency.

In our own country, apart from the Welsh examples noted on p. 99, royal marriages with heiresses seem to have been less frequent than on the Continent. Two outstanding cases, however, may be mentioned. One is a marriage of which we know nothing except that in 844 it brought Kenneth MacAlpin, king of Dalriada, to the throne of the Picts, and thereby led to the formation of the kingdom of Scotland. The other is the marriage of James IV with Margaret, daughter of Henry VII. This marriage, which took place in 1502, led to the union of the crowns more than a century later—a result which could hardly have been foreseen at the time, though it was the most important event in our history since the English invasion. It is true that there have been other marriages, which led to less beneficial results, e.g. the union with Hanover; but they have not been numerous, nor have their results been permanent.

Many more examples might be adduced; but what has been said above will be enough to show that for several centuries—especially from the thirteenth to the seventeenth—royal marriages were the most potent of all factors in the shaping and re-shaping of the political map of Europe. The map of the eighteenth century was very largely the result of such unions; and in a fair number of cases their effects remain even to-day.

In conclusion it may be remarked that royal marriages have sometimes led to results of quite a different character from the union of two kingdoms. It will be enough here to refer to the marriage of Malcolm III with the English princess Edith or Margaret. No union of territories resulted, for Edith was not an heiress. But under her sons, Edgar and his successors, Scotland was transformed from a Gaelic into an English country. In this direction also the influence—or possible influence—of royal marriages seems hardly to have received sufficient attention from modern historians. The historians

of last century gave their attention chiefly to constitutional and
ecclesiastical history, those of the present day to economic history.
In both cases, I think, there has been a tendency to overlook or under-
rate the part played, consciously or unconsciously, by women in
influencing history—except of course when women have been actual
rulers, like Catherine II.

What has been said above about royal families and royal marriages
will be sufficient to demonstrate the importance of the dynastic
principle in the history of Europe. Down to a later period in the
Middle Ages—sometimes indeed much later—the kingdom was
regarded as much like any other family property. It could be
divided between two or more members of the family, though this
gradually became less frequent; or two kingdoms could be united
by the marriage of a king or an heir to the throne with a queen or
heiress. Both processes have contributed greatly to the formation of
the political map of Europe; but neither of them was calculated to
promote the growth of national feeling.

It is true that we often hear of a form of election to the kingship.
Down to the later Middle Ages, however, this seems usually to have
amounted to no more than a recognition of the obvious heir, i.e. the
next of kin to the late king, at least if he was a male and not an infant.
Thus it has been noted above (p. 96 f.) that the German (imperial)
throne was occupied by three successive dynasties, Saxon, Franconian and Swabian, before the great interregnum (1254), and that
each of these held it for about a century. Within these dynasties the
succession was usually from father to son. But it may be observed
that the first Franconian emperor, Conrad II, was apparently next
of kin to the Saxon emperor Otto III,[1] though he was only his half-
cousin. Again, the first Swabian emperor, Conrad III, was nephew
(sister's son) to the last Franconian emperor, Henry V, who left no
children. The connections between the three dynasties were therefore
similar to those between the Plantagenet, Tudor and Stuart dynasties
in England. But there are a few cases which show that the election
was not always treated as a matter of course. The death of Henry V
(in 1125) was followed at first by an election—of Lothair II—which
was unexpected, and said to have been due to an intrigue by the
archbishop of Mainz. And the succession of the Swabian emperor

---

[1] Otto III was first succeeded by Henry II, whose relationship to him was more
remote than that of Conrad II, though he was of Saxon origin. Conrad was
descended from a daughter of Otto I, whereas Henry's descent was from Henry I,
the father of that king. Henry's descent, however, was in a purely male line.

Philip (in 1197) was disputed, with a long period of civil war as the result. But on the whole the imperial succession may be described as hereditary down to 1254. It is only after this date that the idea of a free and wide choice of candidates seems to have occurred to the electors; and even then their decisions sometimes brought about a good deal of fighting. A century and a half later the hereditary principle was restored, in the dynasty of Hapsburg.

Other kingdoms seem to have been somewhat slow to adopt the elective principle, or rather to elect kings from outside the royal family. Valdemar, who was elected king of Sweden in 1250,[1] is said to have been of non-royal family, though his father Birger had long ruled the kingdom as viceroy. Birger's family retained the throne down to 1389, and nominally until the Union of Kalmar (1397). The Union, however, brought into Sweden many Danish and German governors, who were very unpopular; and in 1434 a revolt took place, which was settled by the appointment of a native nobleman, Karl Knudson, as viceroy. In 1448 Knudson was elected king (as Charles VIII) and, though expelled in 1457, he recovered the throne in 1467. His family continued to act as regents—with some intervals—down to 1520, though only by more or less constant warfare with the Danes. In 1523 another native nobleman, Gustavus Vasa, connected with the previous family, was elected king, and finally secured the independence of the kingdom. His descendants reigned until 1818, when the French general Bernadotte, who had been adopted as heir in 1810, succeeded.

Both Bohemia and Hungary were under native dynasties of their own down to the fourteenth century. Then both, quite independently, came into the hands of foreign kings, who had inherited them through marriages. In 1458 both kingdoms elected native noblemen, George Podjebrad and Matthias Hunyadi, as their kings. It is difficult to resist the suspicion that this almost simultaneous action, in breaking with the past and raising native noblemen to the throne, must be connected in some way; and in both cases it may have been suggested by the similar action of the Swedes a few years before. We may note too that in 1448 the Danes elected a king, Christian I, belonging to a family which was only very remotely connected with their previous dynasty. Evidently therefore there was a widespread feeling for free election current about this time. But both the Czechs

---

[1] According to the Laws of Magnus Ericsson (c. 1347) the Swedish throne was elective and not hereditary; but the kings who reigned before 1250 seem to have claimed some connection, by marriage or descent through females, with the old royal family, which died out (in the male line) c. 1050. There seems to have been a great deal of family strife both among Earl Birger's descendants and before his time.

and the Hungarians soon reverted to the hereditary principle. In 1471, on the death of Podjebrad,[1] the former gave the throne to his daughter's husband, the Polish prince Vladislav, while in 1490, on Matthias' death, the Hungarians gave their throne to the same prince, whose uncle Vladislav IV (cf. p. 100) had been king of Hungary, as well as of Poland. From this time onwards, as we have seen, the kingdoms of Bohemia and Hungary remained united.

Early Polish history is complicated by constant divisions of the kingdom among brothers and other relatives, especially between 1138 and 1305, when it was reunited by Vladislav I. In 1386 it passed by marriage to the Lithuanian prince Jogaila (Vladislav II), but some form of election was involved (cf. p. 100). From this time the succession was of the normal hereditary type down to 1572, when the royal family died out. Recourse was then had to a national assembly, which was usually repeated whenever the throne became vacant, and sometimes attended by many thousands of people. The persons elected were sometimes Polish noblemen, though not on the ground of any hereditary claims, sometimes foreign princes—French, Rumanian, Swedish and German. The first Swedish king was followed by his two sons in succession, and the first Saxon king, after a short interval, by his son. Otherwise there was no near relationship between the successive kings. This system continued for over two centuries, down to the partitions of Poland. But the first part of this period was distracted by frequent civil wars, while later, under the Saxon kings, who were usually non-resident, the central government seems to have almost collapsed.

In Russia, after the southern cities had been conquered by the Tatars, c. 1237–8 (cf. p. 84), those of the north, in the upper basin of the Volga, continued to be governed by princes[2] of the old native —originally Scandinavian—dynasty, though they were at first usually tributary to the Tatars. From c. 1330 the supremacy among these cities passed to Moscow. The succession there followed normal lines—usually from father to son—until the dynasty came to an end with the death of Feodor, son of Ivan IV, in 1598. Then a national assembly was called, which elected to the throne Boris Godunov, a leading nobleman, who had virtually acted as regent for the last king. The next fifteen years, however, were a period of almost continuous

[1] Podjebrad had sons, whom he had wished to succeed him. But towards the end of his reign he recommended the appointment of Vladislav as his successor, because he thought that the Polish connection would strengthen the country against Hungarian attacks.
[2] In early times the term *knjaz'* ('prince') should properly be translated 'king', and the term *veliki knjaz'* ('grand duke') should be 'high-king'; cf. pp. 69, 95.

civil war; one pretender after another seized the throne by violence. Eventually, in 1613, another national assembly was held, and the throne was offered to Michael Romanov, who belonged to another noble family, which had intermarried with the previous dynasty. His descendants continued to reign until 1917, though in the eighteenth century two empresses, Catherine I and Catherine II, reigned without any claim to the throne, except that they had been the wives of Tsars. Catherine I, widow of Peter the Great, owed her election, at her husband's death, to the Guards; and Catherine II, although she was a foreigner, succeeded in deposing her husband, Peter III, and taking his place, likewise by a military revolution. It would seem therefore that the election of a sovereign has been a rare occurrence in Russian history.

In the west of Europe examples seem to be even more rare. In France there is apparently no clear case of election between the time of Hugh Capet in 987 and that of Louis Philippe in 1830, while in Spain the first occurrences are in the civil war of 1870–4. It is true that in this country a number of instances might be cited; but none of them are closely parallel to the Continental elections cited above. Some of them were ratifications by Parliament of the commands or requests made by deceased sovereigns, but in accordance with the regular law of succession, while others were recognitions of revolutions which had already been accomplished. The succession of George I was in accordance with the Act of Settlement, which had been passed many years before, in 1701. Perhaps the nearest analogy to the Continental type is to be seen in the invitation sent by Parliament to Charles II in 1660.

From what has been said above it will be clear that election to the throne in any true sense of the word, i.e. as opposed to mere formal acceptance of a new king, has not been a widespread custom in Europe. It prevailed for about a hundred and seventy years in the Empire—from 1273 to 1439—and for rather over two centuries in Poland—from 1572 to the end. Otherwise examples have been merely sporadic. Further, we may note that the imperial and Polish elections differed in one important respect: in the former the electors were only seven in number, or thereabouts, whereas the Polish elections were attended by vast concourses of people.

The question which concerns us is whether the adoption of election to the throne—in the unrestricted sense which we have been discussing—was due to national feeling. So far as the imperial throne is concerned, there is little doubt that the answer is 'No'. The electoral body as fixed by Charles IV was probably only a modified form of something which had existed for long ages.[1] Its members were all virtually monarchs of their own territories; and, when they were not overawed by the (Luxemburg or Hapsburg) king of Bohemia, it would seem to have been their chief concern to elect someone who would not have the power to interfere with them. Even foreigners—English and Spanish princes—were considered from time to time.

In Poland most of the kings who reigned during the 'elective' period (1572–1793) were foreigners. In the first part of the period there was little national feeling; the country was distracted by dissensions among the nobility and by intrigues in foreign courts. But in 1668, after a series of five foreign kings, the feeling is said to have been, at least for the moment, strongly national—or, perhaps one should say, anti-foreign. Yet less than thirty years later another foreigner was elected, the first Saxon Augustus, who reigned thirty-six years and had so little regard for his kingdom that he was willing to sell part of it to the Prussians. At his death, in 1733, Poland had no army left; and two years later the Poles were forced by the Russians to dismiss the native king whom they had elected, and to take the second Saxon Augustus, son of the preceding, in his place. This man reigned twenty-eight years, but was non-resident, and seldom visited his kingdom. The nobility in general seem to have been satisfied with the virtual absence of any central authority; and it was not until the partition period that any strong national feeling showed itself. This feeling began to take shape c. 1788, and led to the proclamation of a Constitution in 1791; but it was too late to save the country.

On the other hand, the elections of Swedish kings, referred to on p. 105, do seem to have been due to national feeling. The revolt of 1434 originated in the industrial districts of Dalarna, and the real leader was a mine-owner named Engelbrekt. The nobility were much divided in sympathies. Karl Knudson was an ambitious nobleman with nationalist leanings; and the Danish king preferred to accept him as regent, rather than Engelbrekt. Actually they were both appointed; but Engelbrekt was murdered soon afterwards. Much later, in 1521, it was again the miners of Dalarna who supported Gustavus Vasa in his revolt—which ended in his being elected king.

[1] The three archiepiscopates represented were those of the German part of the kingdom of the Franks, and all dated from the time of Charlemagne, or possibly earlier. Salzburg may have been as old, but did not originally belong to the Franks. Changes in the lay membership of the council must have been brought about by the disappearance of the old duchies.

The election of George Podjebrad to the Bohemian throne, in 1458, must likewise be attributed to national feeling, though here this feeli' g was combined with a religious movement. The official use of the Czech language had been authorised by Charles IV and his son Wenceslaus, but was resented by the German element in the population. At the same time the Reform doctrines preached by John Huss were generally accepted by the Czechs, including Queen Sophia, the wife of Wenceslaus, and most of the nobility; but almost all the Germans were opposed to them. Feelings were greatly embittered in 1415, when Huss was summoned to the Council of Constance, and was there betrayed by the emperor Sigismund and put to death. When Sigismund succeeded to the Bohemian throne, in 1419, civil war resulted, and lasted almost until his death. His son-in-law and successor, Albert of Hapsburg (1437–9), was accepted, though with reluctance; but after his death the Czechs demanded that his posthumous child (Vladislav) should be entrusted to them to bring up—a demand which the emperor Frederic, Albert's cousin and successor, who had got possession of the child, refused to concede until 1451. In the meantime the country seems to have had no properly authorised government; but Podjebrad, as leader of the national party, was the actual ruler. In 1451 Frederic recognised him as regent and as guardian of the child-king.

The election of Matthias Hunyadi at the age of fifteen was a remarkable event—so remarkable that in an old Yugoslav poem it is represented as due to a miracle. He was not of royal ancestry; but his father John Hunyadi, who had died not long before, had been the national hero for many years and the actual regent for about ten. After his death Vladislav or his advisers had been responsible for the death of his eldest son, Matthias' elder brother. I see no reason therefore for doubting that this election (in 1458) was due largely to a wave of national feeling, like that of Podjebrad in the same year, though I do not know whether there is any evidence for any similar religious influence—I mean, whether the Reformation had as yet made any headway in Hungary.

It would seem then that when an electoral body—whatever its character—has had before it a choice of kings not restricted to a special royal family, national feeling has sometimes led to the election of a native candidate. But instances seem to be very rare; and most of these were regents, or sons of regents, before they were kings. Usually, if not always, the national feeling seems to have been due to a reaction against foreign kings and their followers; but in Bohemia religion was a very important factor. It should be noted that as a rule, indeed perhaps everywhere, the chief opponents of these 'national' candidates were to be found among the chief nobles and the higher ecclesiastics.

It must of course be borne in mind that the large bodies to which we have referred above had many other functions besides the election of kings. Such bodies—Diets, Estates, Cortes, Parliaments—existed in most of the kingdoms of the Middle Ages, and were summoned by the kings from time to time for the discussion of important questions, both internal and foreign, especially perhaps taxation. They consisted usually of ecclesiastics, nobility and representatives of towns; but there were great differences in procedure—e.g. whether the various classes met together or separately—and in the frequency with which they met. We need not enter into these questions here; for an illustration it will be enough to refer to the differences in procedure between the English and Scottish parliaments.

The only question which concerns us here is how far these meetings affected national feeling. From the fourteenth century onwards both the English and the Scottish parliaments were strong enough to offer effective resistance to exactions and arbitrary government by their kings. That this was due to national feeling may be seen from the fact that it synchronised with the revival of English literature, and more especially with the restoration of English as the language of education (in England)—a restoration which was complete, though apparently recent, when Trevisa was writing, in 1385. England was beginning to recover sensibly from the effects of the alien domination to which it had been subject for the last three centuries—a domination which had even affected Scotland to some extent, owing to the influx of Norman noblemen. Yet it was not until the reign of James I (between 1424 and 1437) that Acts of Parliament were published in English; in England it was still later. Militant nationalism, directed against external enemies, is to be found in a few ballads and in the works of certain poets, e.g. Barbour and Minot. But in general the national awakening expressed itself in religious and social movements. The Reformation began, under Wycliffe, not long after the middle of the fourteenth century and found support even among members of the royal family; but it was accompanied, and apparently preceded, by a widespread popular movement against ecclesiastical abuses, which before long began to veer towards social, especially agrarian, revolution. The fifteenth century was in England a period of reaction and repression; but Scotland made a good deal of progress on the intellectual side.

Bohemia received the Reformation direct from England; but there it had much greater success. It was accepted not only by some members of the royal family, but also by a large proportion of the nobility. It soon came to be bound up with Czech national feeling in an acute form; for the German states—which constituted by far the greater part of the Empire—were all Catholic at that time, as were also the German elements in Bohemia itself. Frequent hostilities resulted; and on three occasions, in 1420, 1421 and 1431, a Crusade or Holy War was proclaimed against the Czechs. All these invasions were defeated; but two centuries later, in 1620, during the Thirty Years' War, the Hapsburg emperor Ferdinand II, with the Catholic League, succeeded in destroying both the Reformed faith and the independence of the kingdom.

There can be no doubt that other countries besides England and Bohemia were affected by the Reform movement in the fifteenth century or earlier, though it seldom came to the surface, owing to the absence of support from persons in high position. The sixteenth century is of course commonly regarded as the Reformation period, because it was now widely adopted by kings and princes—so widely indeed that in general it has little or no significance for the question which concerns us. In one or two regions, however, especially the Netherlands, circumstances brought about an acute outburst of national feeling in connection with the religious dispute. The emperor Charles V inherited this region, together with a large part of Belgium, as heir to the dukes of Burgundy. The Dutch had adopted the Reformed faith; but he attached them to Spain, which he had inherited from another source (cf. p. 101), and introduced the Spanish Inquisition in order to crush the new religion. The effects of the ruthless policy pursued by him and his son Philip II and the resistance offered by the States General are too well known to need discussion here.

We have been speaking of national feeling in connection with religion. But it was not wholly confined to this sphere, even in the Middle Ages. In records relating to estates or parliaments we very frequently meet with an antagonism between the great lords, secular and ecclesiastical, and the representatives of towns and industrial communities. The former seem commonly to have set the interests of their families and domains above those of the kingdom as a whole. The election of foreign and non-resident kings in Poland during the period of its decline is believed to have been due to the great nobles, who wished to have no ruler who could interfere with them. The principle is the same as in the later Empire, when weak and poor emperors sometimes seem to have been preferred by the electors. In Sweden and sometimes even in Bohemia the chief opponents of national and patriotic movements apparently belonged to the same class. In Scotland during the fifteenth century we often find the king and the representatives of the towns allied against the chief magnates. The principle which is involved in these movements may perhaps be patriotism rather than any feeling for nationality. But in any case it is worth noting that the leaders seem regularly to have derived their chief support from towns, industrial or commercial communities, and from the lesser nobility. This is said to have been the case with Engelbrekt and Gustavus Vasa, Podjebrad, Matthias Hunyadi (in his own country) and William of Orange.

CHAPTER VI

THE FEELING FOR KINSHIP BETWEEN PEOPLES: PAN-SLAVISM, PAN-LATINISM AND PAN-GERMANISM

To what extent is a feeling of kinship recognised by peoples of different nationality? I am not using the term 'nationality' here in the legal sense, but in the sense pointed out and discussed in Chapter I—the sense in which nationality is determined by language. Such questions as Anglo-American relations or the relations between Spain and the Spanish-American republics may therefore be left out of account.

It can hardly be doubted that a feeling of kinship is sometimes found between peoples who speak closely related languages. We may instance the peoples of the three Scandinavian kingdoms. As between Denmark and Norway the question is of course complicated by the 'Riksmål'. But I think that most Swedes would feel that Danes and Norwegians were more akin, or less foreign, to them than persons belonging to other nations; and that Danes and Norwegians would feel the same with regard to Swedes.

A far more distant linguistic relationship is involved in the Pan-Celtic movement which has from time to time held congresses attended by representatives of all the Celtic peoples—from the Gaelic communities of Ireland, Scotland and the Isle of Man, as well as from Wales, Brittany and even Cornwall. The Gaelic, Welsh and Breton languages have long been mutually unintelligible; indeed, the recognition of the relationship between them is largely due to the work of scholars. At the congresses communication between the delegates from different countries is doubtless carried on mainly in English and French. Yet the fact that such congresses have been held shows that the kinship involved is widely recognised.

It may be observed that the interests with which these congresses have been concerned are chiefly of a 'cultural' character—linguistic, historical, literary, artistic. I do not think that economic questions of a practical kind—e.g. the development of trade between the various Celtic communities—have occupied much attention. Nor have politics been very prominent, except in so far as they affect the preservation or encouragement of Celtic languages. Indeed the Celtic peoples differ from one another a good deal in the general trend of political thought, just as in religion. Attempts have been made from German sources to exploit Celtic studies for the purpose of injuring this country or France; but, except in Ireland, these attempts seem not to have met with much success.

It would seem, however, that under certain conditions the recognition of a remote linguistic kinship may lead not only to political, but even to military action. A remarkable case of this kind is said to have occurred during the Russo-Finnish war of 1939–40. It was reported in the newspapers that many Hungarian airmen had offered their services to the Finnish government. There is said to be a strong anti-Russian feeling in Hungary. But this by itself can hardly have been responsible for their action. And, indeed, the reports themselves were explicit enough that they were prompted by the kinship existing between the Finnish and Hungarian peoples—a kinship which is not shared by any other independent nation except the Estonians. Yet the relationship between the two languages, upon which this kinship is based, is very remote—at least as remote as the relationship between English and Sanskrit or Persian. It could never have been discovered except as a result of careful linguistic research.

The claims of kinship, however, with which we are chiefly concerned in this chapter are those of the Latin, Teutonic and Slavonic peoples. The terms applied to these claims, and to the movements arising from them, are Pan-Latinism, Pan-Germanism and Pan-Slavism. Of these the third has long had a certain limited currency in this country, whereas the two former were unfamiliar until very recently. We will therefore begin with Pan-Slavism.

The first Pan-Slavist of whom we have any record was apparently Jurij Križanić, a Croat and a Catholic priest, who was born in 1618.[1] The doctrine to which he devoted his life was 'One race, one language, one religion for all Slavs'. The uniformity in religion which he had in mind consisted of the recognition of the supremacy of the Pope, together with the use of the old Slavonic liturgy; and the dream of his life was to bring the Pope and the Russian emperor to agree to this. The Vatican gave him little encouragement; he did not even get permission to use the Slavonic liturgy in his own church, though it was still in use in a number of Catholic churches in Croatia. Eventually he found his way to Moscow, in 1659. His object there was to persuade the emperor, Alexei Mihailovič, to assume the headship of the Slavonic world, and to liberate the western Slavs from the

---

[1] An interesting account of Križanić and also of the (later) Pan-Slavistic movement is given by H. J. A. van Son, *Autour de Križanić*—to which I am much indebted.

German yoke. But, two years later, he was exiled to Siberia, from which he was not allowed to return until the Tsar's death in 1676. He spent his later years in Vilna, and perhaps died as a hospital chaplain in the army which John Sobieski led to Vienna in 1683. Apart from his political writings, he devoted a great part of his life to the composition of a kind of Slavonic Esperanto.

Many Russians seem to have been interested in Križanić's writings, especially those in which he advocated reforms in Russia itself, anticipating in some respects those which were effected later by Alexei's son, Peter the Great. But the Pan-Slavistic idea apparently never took root. In its place there grew up a feeling which in this country, I think, has been misinterpreted as Pan-Slavism— a recognition of kinship which was limited strictly to the Orthodox Slavonic peoples of the Balkans. Within a few years of Križanić's death the Serbian patriarch Arsen appealed to Peter the Great for protection against the Turks. Then, in 1711–15 bishop Danilo Petrović, who had won the independence of Montenegro, received subsidies and promises of support from the same Tsar. By this policy, and especially by extracting a promise from the Turks (in 1774) not to persecute, the Russian government came to be regarded as the protector of all Orthodox Christians. In the early years of last century the same policy led to material and even armed support for Kara-Gjorgje in the Serbian War of Independence; and it reached its culmination in 1876–8, when Russia intervened to save Serbia and Montenegro, and to secure independence for Bulgaria.

But this policy was of course far removed from the Pan-Slavism of Križanić, which had in view the union of all Slavonic peoples, and primarily the emancipation of the Catholic Slavs in Austria. Križanić's own scheme was never revived; but a new Pan-Slavistic movement arose out of the national movements which began towards the close of the eighteenth century. Its interests were at first mainly, if not exclusively, cultural. Its chief centre was Prague; and it was supported by most of the leaders of the Czech renaissance. Perhaps the most important figures were, at first the philologist J. Dobrovsky, and later—in the early part of last century—F. Palacky and P. J. Šafařyk, of whom the former was a historian, while the latter's interests were mainly linguistic and literary. But there were also many others, among whom mention may be made of the poet and classical scholar, J. Kollar. His view was that every educated Slav should acquire a reading knowledge of all Slavonic languages, and that books published in one Slavonic land should circulate in all Slavonic lands. The movement, however, was by no means limited to the Czechs. It had supporters in all Slavonic lands, e.g. in Russia the historian N. M. Karamzin and, at least to some extent, Puškin.

It was not until 1848 that the Pan-Slavist movement assumed a definitely political character, though a tendency in that direction had no doubt been growing for some time previously. That year was a time of great unrest in many parts of Europe; but the incentive to the change in the Pan-Slavistic movement came from the growth of German nationalism, which, as shown in the Diet at Frankfort, was felt to be fraught with danger to the Slavonic peoples, especially those which were under Austrian rule. A congress therefore was held at Prague, under the presidency of Palacky, for the purpose of considering certain questions, most of which were concerned with the relations of the Slavonic peoples to the Austrian government. No Russians were present; but delegates attended from most of the other Slavonic peoples. There is said to have been a good deal of disagreement between the representatives of the different nationalities; but the congress was cut short by the Austrian authorities.

After the accession of Alexander II, in 1855, the Pan-Slavist movement received a certain amount of support from Russia, though the Orthodox party were still dominant there; and in 1867 Czech representatives visited the Tsar with a view to bringing about an agreement between all the Slavonic nationalities. But the Poles, who were embittered by the reprisals taken for the rebellion of 1863–4, refused to support this mission; and the Russians themselves gave little or no encouragement to the proposals. And for the next forty years no further progress was made. The Russo-Polish animosity continued; and Russian sympathy was practically limited to the Orthodox Slavs of the Balkans. It may be said indeed that there were now two separate and quite independent 'Slavonic' movements in existence—one for the Orthodox Slavs against Turkish oppression, and the other for the Catholic Slavs against Austrian oppression. It is true that in Austria proper the conditions gradually improved during this period; but in Hungary, from the restoration of its independence (in 1867), they went steadily worse.

In Russia after the revolutionary movement of 1905–6 certain changes took place. A form of parliamentary government was established, which allowed the circulation of more liberal views. There was a growing desire to come to terms with the Poles, which led ultimately—though not until the beginning of the first World War, in 1914—to a promise of the restoration of independence. At the same time it began to be felt that the support given to the oppressed peoples should not be limited to the Orthodox. It had now come to be recognised that the troubles which afflicted the various Slavonic peoples were not so different as they appeared. In the Balkans Turkish misgovernment was less to be feared than the threat of German expansion; and the expropriations in German Poland and the failure of the Austrian Slavs to recover their autonomy were due to the same cause. Discussions now began again between representatives of the various Slavonic peoples; but they were cut short by the Balkan Wars, which were soon followed by the outbreak of the first World War.

By the treaties which followed the conclusion of the war several of the Slavonic peoples attained the fulfilment of their ambitions. But the trouble between Russia and Poland broke out again, in a new and acute form, while in other respects the policy of the new Russian government was guided by considerations which had nothing in common with Pan-Slavism or with specially Slavonic interests. It is only during the course of the present war that these interests have again come to require attention.

Before leaving this subject, it may be well to refer again to the misconception which has been widely prevalent in this country as to the character of Pan-Slavism. The term has often been applied to the hopes which Russians cherished from time to time of making Constantinople the capital of their empire, or of 'seeing the cross once more upon the dome of St Sophia'. These were of course purely Russian aspirations, which had little or nothing in common with the Pan-Slavistic movement. On the whole, Russian support for this movement has generally been rather lukewarm.

Pan-Latinism is still an unfamiliar term. There may be readers who will not be inclined to admit the existence of such a movement. But I think they are mistaken.

It is true that the movement has little or nothing in common with Pan-Slavism, apart from the formation of the name. Pan-Slavism may be defined as a movement undertaken by various Slavonic peoples, indeed by most of them, for the purpose of securing advantages and protection for all. It began with the encouragement of cultural relations, and only later developed political activities. Pan-Latinism, on the other hand, has emanated, I think, only from one nation, namely Italy; and its purpose apparently is to establish a kind of Italian hegemony over the other Latin nations, in order to secure advantages which would seem to be, at least primarily, in the interest of Italy. The movement has been political from the beginning. The only cultural interest involved, so far as I am aware, is the doctrine of 'realities'; and even this is concerned, mainly if not exclusively, with political affairs, especially international relations. In declared opposition to the 'Anglo-American' doctrine of moral law, Pan-Latinism recognises only the principle of power. If one nation—or at least if Italy—desires the territories of another nation, the only questions to be considered are when and by what means they may most easily be appropriated.

Pan-Latinism is a recent outgrowth from the national expansion movement which—as apart from colonial enterprise—began to take definite form about thirty years ago. The governing idea in the latter was that Italy should be regarded as the legitimate heir of ancient Rome, and as such should claim as much as possible of the Roman empire, including the control of the Mediterranean. An aggressive policy was of course involved; but this was welcomed by many as a means of uniting party factions and distracting attention from industrial and financial troubles. When Italy entered the first World War, maps were circulated, showing some of the territories claimed —many of which contained no Italian population. After the war a good deal of these territories was secured. This was only a beginning; but it was enough to gain a considerable amount of popular support for the policy of aggression, and to convince an ambitious politician that advancement was more likely to be gained by this policy than by championing Social Democracy. He might even attain to the rank of Caesar—which would be more difficult for a Social Democrat.

The change from this purely national policy to Pan-Latinism was due to the consideration that Italy could not proceed alone against all the states which owned Mediterranean territories. With the western basin securely held by a Latin league, the reduction of the countries on the shores of the eastern basin could be accomplished more easily. And it is obvious that Italy, with Rome, the ancient capital, has good historical claims to the headship of a Latin league. But in France[1] the Pan-Latin movement has evoked no great enthusiasm. There are no doubt a number of wealthy people who would prefer an Italian hegemony to a Communist or even a Socialist government. But in general the French, in spite of their language, would rather regard themselves as a Celtic people than as a colony or province of Italy, and would emphasise their possession of a very distinctive history and traditions of their own. Consequently the Italian overtures ended in disappointment, and were succeeded by a threatening attitude, which demanded the cession of Nice, Corsica

---

[1] I do not know how far Pan-Latinism has taken root in Spain. The question is complicated by the existence of a strong conservative and clerical party.

and Tunis—presumably as a first instalment, to be followed by some arrangement for securing control of the rest of the Mediterranean zones in France and Africa.

Pan-Latinism itself may have originated before the establishment of the Fascist regime.[1] At all events the policy which led up to it was inherited from earlier governments. The aggressions committed against Abyssinia and against Italy's maritime neighbours, Albania, Greece and Yugoslavia, the demands made upon France, the Arabic broadcasts from Bari, and the constant efforts to fabricate an 'Italia Irredenta' in Malta—all these betray a type of mentality which can be seen at an earlier stage in the destruction of the Austrian flagship —after the cessation of hostilities—in 1918 and in the 'unofficial' seizure of Fiume in 1919. They will, I fear, secure an unenviable fame for Italy in the future.

The term 'Pan-German' came into use among English writers as a translation of 'Alldeutsch', the term applied in all German-speaking lands to the (German) nationalistic movement. In 1894 this movement led to the founding of a Pan-German League ('Alldeutscher Verband'), the chief objects of which were to promote German national feeling among Germans living in all countries, to support German colonial policy, and to encourage German nationalism in schools. The leader of the movement was E. Hasse, who advocated the annexation of Holland, Belgium, certain districts in France, Bohemia, Moravia and parts of western Russia. 'We want territory, even if it be inhabited by foreign peoples, so that we may shape their future in accordance with our needs.'

It may be observed that the movement was definitely German, not Teutonic, in origin. The regions which it was desired to annex and exploit were only in part Teutonic. The majority were Slavonic and French. But the region most coveted of all consisted of the Netherlands and Belgium—which control the approaches to the Rhine. A saying which gained much currency at the time was: 'What is the use of a house which has no front door?' The Powers against which the movement was chiefly directed were Britain (as an obstacle to colonial expansion), France and Russia.

A somewhat new orientation was given to the movement in 1899–1901, at the time of the South African war. By enlisting sympathy

---

[1] At the beginning of September 1943, after the collapse of this regime, rumours were current that the idea of a Latin International Union had been revived by a leading anti-Fascist statesman. The rumours may have been ill-founded; but it is of interest to note that the idea was still alive, and that apparently it was regarded as non-Fascist.

for the Boers it was hoped to come to some agreement with the Netherlands, which would eventually lead to the incorporation of that country with the Reich. But about the same time, or not much later, still greater attention was paid to the development of German influence in the Balkans and the Turkish empire, especially by the Baghdad railway. The domain marked out for German domination now became enormously expanded. Now also the League began to make considerable headway in Austria, where many of the German population were already looking forward to union with the Reich.

The term 'Pangermanismus' seems to have come into common use (in German) about the same time, or not much later. In practice it denoted hardly more than the nationalistic policy professed from the beginning by the Alldeutscher Verband. But the word *German-*, which is of academic origin, means 'Teutonic', not 'German' in our sense; and, consequently, the term 'Pangermanismus' implied that the movement had come to include within its scope not only the Germans of the Reich and all the various German communities outside the Reich, but also the other Teutonic peoples.

The Dutch lands—the Netherlands and northern Belgium—had always been regarded as falling within the scope of the League's policy. It had not received very much support from these quarters. But that was not considered essential; for it is a characteristic of German nationalistic psychology that reciprocal action or feeling is not regarded as necessary in such movements. On the other hand, Scandinavian participation can hardly have been expected very seriously at this time, while the thought of English participation would have been absurd, since the movement was directed largely against this country. Actually therefore the 'Pangermanismus' did not amount to very much. But the employment of the term had the effect of bringing Germany forward as the head of the Teutonic peoples and, indeed, practically of identifying 'Germanisch' with 'Deutsch'.

In the first World War, when German armies were in occupation of Belgium, Pan-Germanism succeeded in gaining there a considerable number of adherents, who were attracted by the prospect of attaining political power or commercial advantages thereby. But the Peace of 1920 was unfavourable to its activities, except in Austria, where it made great progress among those who desired union with the Reich. Eventually the League was absorbed in the Nazi movement. The latter had of course a slightly different orientation; at first it seems to have paid less attention to colonial expansion. But it continued the policy of attracting recruits in other Teutonic (non-

German) countries—the effects of which were seen in the speed with which not only Belgium, but also the Netherlands, Denmark and Norway were seized in 1940.[1] Indeed the rapid success of the Nazi movement in Germany itself from its beginning was without doubt largely due to the work of the older organisation, especially its activities in the schools.

The use of the word 'Germanisch' in the sense of 'Deutsch', implied in the term 'Pangermanisch', as noted above, was not initiated by the Alldeutscher Verband, but borrowed from academic usage, in which it had long been current. What the Verband did was to apply it to purposes of political propaganda. Later we shall have to notice briefly the history of these words, which is in fact rather complicated and has led to much confusion both in this country and in Germany.

[1] From the way in which the peoples of the Netherlands and Norway have been treated since that time it would seem that German policy considered it no longer necessary to conciliate them.

CHAPTER VII

THE CLAIMS TO DOMINATION. I

FOR a considerable time past—perhaps since the beginning of this century, or even earlier—nationalist aspirations in Germany and Italy have included the establishment of domination over neighbouring but alien peoples, which have never been politically connected with these Powers. Sometimes the desire for annexation has been inspired by strategic considerations, sometimes by the idea of securing new fields for 'colonisation' or exploitation. But these motives have usually been associated with a certain ideology, based upon a feeling that the aggressor nation is entitled by its past history to the domination which is contemplated.

When power had come into the hands of the Fascists and the Nazis, these aspirations were seen embodied in schemes of practical policy, the realisation of which—after conflicting claims had been adjusted—has been carried out during the last few years. In the course of 1940–1, Germany and Italy came into military occupation of more than half of Europe.

From the historical point of view the Italian claims are the easier to understand. Nationalist Italy regards herself as the heir of the Roman Empire. She cannot claim the whole of the Empire; for, apart from other difficulties, a considerable part of it is claimed, or actually possessed, by Germany. But she regards herself as entitled to dominate, in one form or other, all the coasts of the Mediterranean. Some of the lands now occupied have of course been connected with Italian states more recently. Nice and Savoy were connected with Piedmont until 1860; and it is from Savoy that the Italian royal family takes its name. Corsica belonged to Genoa until 1768. In the Middle Ages Venice possessed large territories in Dalmatia and in Greece. But the Italian language has long disappeared from the eastern side of the Adriatic, excepting a few towns on the coast; and there is no evidence that it ever extended far from the sea. For the more inland regions, as well as Slovenia and Tyrol, the claim can be made only for Roman times. In the Franco-Italian borderlands the linguistic problem is more complex. French and Italian have displaced dialects of the Provençal type. Formerly there seems to have been no clear-cut linguistic border either to east or west. In Corsica, however, the Italian dialect which is now spoken was probably introduced by the Genoese.

The expansionist policy has of course included Africa, as well as Europe, in its scope. The occupation of Eritrea (in 1882) and the first conquest of Abyssinia (1889–96) took place in the period of colonial expansion, before the Roman idea took root. But the resumption of activities in this region in 1935 is to be connected with the development of Tripoli and Cyrenaica, which were acquired in 1911. It is clear enough that the intention was to overwhelm Egypt from both sides, and then gradually to 'recover' Roman Africa by expanding westwards. The key-point in the scheme is of course Tunisia, the possession of which, combined with Sicily, would ensure the command of the Mediterranean.

There is no reason for supposing that the Roman territories in Asia have been overlooked. The broadcasting campaign in Arabic would seem to have been addressed to that quarter—especially Palestine and Syria—as well as to Egypt. Indeed, the acquisition and fortification of Rhodes suggests that an eastward movement was contemplated even in pre-Fascist times.

The movement for the recovery of the empire of the Caesars has been accompanied by a praiseworthy zeal for the preservation of Roman monuments and sites, especially in Rome itself. Fascist Italy, as the resurrection of Imperial Rome—with a glorious past such as cannot be equalled by any other European state—presents an idea simple enough for anyone to grasp, and calculated to appeal as a unifying force to all classes of society.

The German claims to domination are more complex, and will require much fuller discussion. German ideology of to-day is not modelled upon the conditions of any one epoch of past history, like that of Imperial Rome; it is of composite origin, derived from the records of various epochs.

The records which have contributed most to the formation of modern German ideology are perhaps those which relate to the earliest times for which we have historical evidence—say the first six centuries of our era. And here we have to distinguish between an earlier period, during which the Teutonic peoples were confined to regions beyond the Roman frontiers, and a later period, beginning from c. 400—or somewhat earlier, on the lower Danube—during which all the western provinces of the empire were submerged by wave after wave of Teutonic conquest.

The earlier period is known to us only from Roman (Latin and Greek) authorities. The most interesting information comes from Tacitus, who wrote at the end of the first century and gives, especially in his *Germania*, an unusually detailed and vivid description of German[1] life. This work has had an immense amount of attention devoted to it by German scholars; but in this country it has been comparatively neglected, except—as regards certain chapters—in works on constitutional history. The descriptive chapters give what is in general an attractive picture of society. The Germans are represented as a courageous, warlike, frugal and freedom-loving people; and frequently a comparison is drawn, or rather implied, with Roman society, to the disadvantage of the latter. Scholars who are not Germans commonly regard these comparisons as the leading motive of the description—which they take to be inspired by the desire to expose the contemptibleness of the decadent city life of Rome by comparing it with that of the 'noble barbarian'. But German scholars are apt to accept the description in full seriousness, and to infer from it that even in Tacitus' time the Germans were superior to the Romans, and indeed to all other peoples known to the Romans.

In the later period the Teutonic peoples had become dominant. In the fifth and sixth centuries they had conquered and occupied all the western half of the Roman Empire. This of course did not mean the substitution of a Teutonic empire for the Roman. The conquests were effected at different times and by different peoples, each of which had an independent royal family of its own. Moreover, several of the conquests were transitory. Africa and much of Italy and of the Danube basin had ceased to be under Teutonic government before the close of the sixth century, while in other lands the conquerors were already beginning to lose their languages. But in spite of all this the Teutonic peoples—as a group, not a unity—on the whole still retained the dominant position which they had won.

It is this period too which produced the earliest Teutonic literature which has come down to us. The heroic poems are not concerned with nationalities, but with the deeds of individual heroes; but they had a currency throughout the Teutonic peoples which must have served as a unifying influence to some extent even in their own day. In modern times, where they are known, even in the very late German versions, they have given living reality to the period of Teutonic domination and thrown round it a glamour comparable

---

[1] The geographical part of the work embraces all the Teutonic peoples known to Tacitus; but the detailed description of society applies primarily in all probability to the Germans. The region between the Rhine and the Elbe seems to have been better known to the Romans than any other part of the Teutonic area.

with that which the Homeric poems have shed upon the Heroic Age of Greece.

It is to be observed that the domination of which we have been speaking was a domination of the Teutonic peoples collectively. The leading part in the period is played by the Goths; next after them perhaps come the Vandals. The German peoples do not figure very prominently, unless indeed the Salic Franks are counted among them. So also in the heroic poems; there are no Alamannic, Bavarian or Old Saxon heroes, while those of the Franks are few, though they include Siegfried, the hero *von Niderlant* (Xanten). Nevertheless it must be borne in mind (cf. p. 120 f.) that German writers very frequently fail to distinguish between 'Teutonic' (germanisch) and 'German' (deutsch); and consequently the domination of this period is claimed as a German domination. In the same way the heroic poems are often described as German, though almost all the early examples—which are by far the most valuable—are either English or Norse; only one short fragment of such poetry has survived in German. The claims therefore commonly made by Germans to a kind of proprietary right in this age are in themselves inadmissible. What, however, they can fairly claim is that their scholars and historians long ago discovered the significance of the age and caused it to be generally appreciated, whereas our scholars and historians, owing to the limitations of their knowledge, especially on the linguistic side, failed to make any independent study of it. In particular they neglected the poetic evidence; what little they knew of it was derived not from the early English and Scandinavian poems, but at second-hand from German sources, and consequently represents a purely German point of view.

The next period to be considered is that of the Holy Roman empire. And here we may take first the times of Charlemagne and his family. Charlemagne's empire was the greatest which any of the peoples in the northern half of Europe had yet possessed. It extended from the Atlantic to Dalmatia and the plain of the Danube, and from the North Sea to Rome. It was not wholly of a national character; for the Franks in Gaul—except in the most eastern districts—had now become denationalised, and may be regarded as French. The Teutonic population of the Empire, however, was almost wholly German; the only alien element were the Frisians, who had been recently conquered, and now counted for little. The Church too, as represented by the archbishoprics of Cologne, Trèves, Mainz and Salzburg, had become wholly German by this time.

Charlemagne's realm may be regarded as the first German empire. It had a certain cosmopolitan character, due partly to the French population in the west, partly to the various alien peoples—Frisians, Avars and Slavonic peoples—whom Charlemagne had conquered, and partly to Charlemagne's intimate relations with the Pope. But the German element was evidently dominant. It is not, however, until after the division of the Empire among Charlemagne's descendants that we meet with a more or less purely German kingdom. In 843 and 869 his grandson, Ludwig II ('the German'), secured all the German districts,[1] while France, Italy and the imperial throne fell to other members of the family. His territories were of course much less extensive than Charlemagne's. Most of the Slavonic peoples conquered by the latter now recovered their independence.

Next we may take the rule of the Saxon dynasty, from 919 to 1002. When Henry I, the first king of this dynasty, was elected, in 919, the boundaries of the German kingdom were almost the same as they had been at the death of Ludwig II, in 876. He set himself to the task of conquering the Slavonic peoples, which bordered his kingdom on the east, and which still consisted of a considerable number of small and politically independent states. His war of conquest was continued by his son and successor Otto I (936–73), who extended his territories as far as the Oder, and enforced his suzerainty upon large tracts of country beyond, including Poland. The conquest was accompanied by forced conversion; and German bishoprics, dependent on an archbishop at Magdeburg, were established throughout the conquered lands. Otto also intervened in the affairs of Italy, and acquired possession of the greater part of the country. In 963 he took the imperial title, which had fallen into abeyance for some time previously, but after this was borne by all subsequent kings of Germany.

These conquests again placed the Germans in a dominant position over large alien populations. Indeed, the new domination was more thoroughly German than that of Charlemagne's time. To a large extent, however, it was soon lost. Otto at his death in 973 was succeeded by his son Otto II, who spent most of his time in Italy, and married a Greek princess. In 982, just before his death, the conquered Slavonic peoples revolted, and recovered their independence as far as the Elbe, except in the Mark (and diocese) of

[1] The western frontier of medieval Germany was finally fixed (*c.* 880) a little further west; but the strip of country then added, including Toul and Verdun, was French-speaking. The difference of language between the two parts of the empire is brought out in an earlier agreement made between Ludwig and his brother Charles at Strasbourg in 841.

Meissen (in what is now Saxony). The new king, Otto III, who succeeded as a child, was brought up by his Greek mother, and seems to have been more Italian than German in sympathies. At all events he grew up with decided cosmopolitan ideas, probably through the influence of Pope Sylvester II (Gerbert of Aurillac), an ecclesiastic who was far in advance of his times. He worked for the conversion of the Slavonic and other heathen peoples; but he made no attempt at reconquest. He held that the newly converted peoples should be independent ecclesiastically, as well as politically; and consequently, in 1000—much against the feelings of the German bishops—he supported the petition of King Boleslav I for the independence of the Polish Church, under an archbishop of its own at Gniezno. Very soon afterwards the Hungarian Church obtained a similar independent status. This Otto is not esteemed by German historians; but it is of interest that so liberal a policy should be even initiated in his times. Unfortunately he died in 1002, at the age of twenty-two; and the Pope did not long survive him.

Italy remained in the possession of the subsequent emperors; and they were usually much occupied with its affairs. But the next epoch of conquest on a large scale came in the twelfth century under the Hohenstaufen dynasty. During the reign of Conrad III (1138–52), the first of these emperors, the conquest of the northern Slavonic peoples was again undertaken, and continued under his successor, Frederic I (Barbarossa); but it was not by these emperors themselves that the war was carried on, but by vassal princes, Henry the Lion, duke of Saxony, and the margrave Albert the Bear. The struggle was long and deadly, but in the end it brought about the destruction or Germanisation of all the peoples as far as the Oder, and to some extent even beyond (cf. p. 81). Then, early in the next century, the same desperate kind of warfare was begun by the Crusading Orders against the Baltic peoples in East Prussia and the coastlands farther to the north. In East Prussia the conquest is said to have been even more destructive than that of the Slavonic peoples (cf. p. 82).

The history of the Hohenstaufen dynasty itself bears a curious resemblance to that of the Saxon. The first two emperors were vigorous rulers, whose primary interests lay in Germany, though Frederic I ended his life in Asia, during the Third Crusade. Frederic's son Henry VI (1190–7) married a Sicilian wife, by whom he obtained possession of the south of Italy. Before his death he made his home in Sicily, and received homage and tribute from various foreign kingdoms round the Mediterranean. He was succeeded in Sicily and southern Italy by his infant son Frederic II, who eventually was recognised also as emperor—partially in 1212, and completely in 1218. This Frederic was wholly Italian or cosmopolitan in his sympathies. He lived in Sicily, and the greater part of his reign was occupied by a struggle with the Papacy. He seldom visited Germany—once after an interval of fifteen years—and he granted privileges to the great lords, including ecclesiastics, which made them practically independent rulers. At his death in 1250 his son, Conrad IV, obtained some recognition as emperor; but he soon returned to Italy, where he died in 1254.

For both the Saxon and the Hohenstaufen dynasties Italy seems to have had an irresistible attraction. In each case the second generation becomes involved in the affairs of that country, the third marries and makes his home there, the fourth is wholly denationalised and become Italian or cosmopolitan in feeling. Both dynasties had won for Germany a paramount position and a widespread domination over subject peoples; but their later history was in neither case such as to satisfy modern German ideology.

Germany itself had now become little more than a loose confederation of virtually independent rulers; and the domination over subject peoples now belonged to these rulers alone. Italy, however, passed into the hands of native or other non-German families. As for the imperial throne, no election was made for some time after the extinction of the Hohenstaufen. It would seem indeed that cosmopolitan ideas had for the moment penetrated even into Germany; for an English prince and a Spanish king were among the candidates who were considered. In 1273 a new emperor, Rudolf of Hapsburg, was at last elected; but from this time onwards the emperors had—as emperors—very little power.

Next we may take the history of the Hapsburg dynasty. This family obtained the imperial throne for the first time in 1273, as noted above, and frequently during the following centuries—indeed regularly from 1437. It is not as emperors, however, that we have to consider their history here, but as the owners of vast territories, some of which lay within, and others beyond, the borders of the Empire.

The original domains of the Hapsburgs lay mostly in Switzerland, and were not very extensive. But a few years after Rudolf's election he gained possession of the duchies of Austria, Styria and Carniola, which lay just within the eastern border of the Empire. They had been occupied a few years before by Ottakar II, king of Bohemia, who was the most powerful prince in the Empire and had been strongly opposed to the election of Rudolf. The war which soon broke out between them was eventually brought to an end by the defeat and death of Ottakar at the Marchfeld in 1278.

It would probably be a mistake to attribute much significance to the nationalistic aspect of this war. Rudolf was purely German, whereas Ottakar was a Czech; but the latter had become Germanised to a great extent both in his family connections and in his sympathies. Indeed, he is said to have introduced many Germans into Bohemia. As for the provinces in dispute, Austria was doubtless wholly German before this time, while the others were largely or wholly Slovenian,[1] though they had been under German rule for some four centuries. The real importance of the war is that it produced a large new hereditary domain within the empire—a domain which remained under the Hapsburgs down to our own times, and which always contained a considerable (non-German) subject population. Austria was the centre, and Vienna the capital, of the new dominion from the beginning.

The expansion of the Austrian (Hapsburg) territories took place chiefly through peaceful processes, and especially through royal marriages. The imperial throne was occupied in the fourteenth and early fifteenth centuries chiefly by the Luxemburg dynasty, who in 1346 inherited also Bohemia with its dependencies Moravia and Silesia. But Albert II of Hapsburg married the daughter and heiress of the last of the Luxemburg line, Sigismund, and succeeded his father-in-law in both positions. At his death, two years later, he was himself succeeded as emperor by his cousin Frederic III; but the latter could not maintain his position in Bohemia.

In 1526, however, the Hapsburgs regained Bohemia, together with Hungary, through the marriage of the Archduke Ferdinand, brother of the emperor Charles V, with a sister of King Louis, who had inherited both these kingdoms, and who was killed in that year by the Turks. Ferdinand himself became emperor in 1558. From that time until the end of the first World War (1918) Austria, Hungary and Bohemia had the same ruler, who almost always was also emperor.[2] But in 1526 the Turks conquered by far the greater part of Hungary. Ferdinand and his successors actually possessed only a rather narrow strip of country along the northern and western borders, together with the north-western part of Croatia. It was not

[1] Carinthia, which was acquired by the Hapsburgs c. 1333, was also partly Slovenian. On the other hand Tyrol, which was acquired somewhat later, was probably already wholly German.

[2] The title was changed to 'Emperor of Austria' in 1806.

until nearly the end of the seventeenth century that the rest of the kingdom, including Transylvania and south-eastern Croatia, was recovered. Not much later, in 1713, part of Lombardy (Milan) was acquired from Spain. On the other hand, nearly the whole of Silesia, which for several centuries had been attached to Bohemia, was annexed by the Prussians under Frederic the Great in 1740–2.

At the partition of Poland in 1772 Austria obtained Galicia, the southern part of that kingdom. Again, when the republic of Venice was destroyed by Napoleon in 1797, its territories in Italy and its possessions in Istria and Dalmatia were assigned to Austria—first in that year itself, and later in 1814. In the latter year Austria obtained also the territories of the republic of Ragusa (Dubrovnik) and the bishopric of Trent. Lastly, Bosnia and Hercegovina were occupied in 1878, after the Russo-Turkish war, and annexed in 1908. All these acquisitions served to increase the non-German population in Austrian territories. Lombardy, however, was lost in 1859, and Venetia in 1866.

The Hapsburg emperors have earned a bad name for religious persecution. In the Thirty Years' War (c. 1620) this led to the complete destruction of Bohemian independence, and the kingdom was reduced to the position of an Austrian province. Even Czech literature ceased to exist. In Hungary, which also was largely Protestant, the same persecution was carried on, though not quite so far; that kingdom did not wholly lose its freedom, except for a short period (c. 1673).

The eighteenth century saw the gradual adoption of a more liberal policy, which culminated under Joseph II (1780–90) in drastic reforms—including the abolition of serfdom and the provision of schools. Complete religious toleration was now established. But the reforms were accompanied by an attempt to enforce the use of German everywhere as the official language and the language of education. This attempt aroused bitter opposition, especially in Hungary, and was abandoned shortly before Joseph's death. Not many years later, however, there was a return to the repressive policy of earlier times—which led ultimately to revolutionary movements, culminating in 1848 in a great revolt in Hungary. This was crushed with the help of a Russian army. But in 1867 independence was restored to Hungary, and parliamentary government established both there and in Austria. Bohemia, however, failed to recover its independence, though Czech was recognised as the official language there. A similar recognition was given to Polish in Galicia.

Austrian history since the reign of Joseph II has been of the greatest importance for the development of national feeling. English histories have tended to concentrate attention upon the Hungarian struggle for independence. But the other repressed nationalities had also recovered consciousness, and were striving for their own freedom—in some cases against Hungary rather than Austria. When the Hungarians revolted, in 1848, the Austrian government had a Croatian army ready to hand against them. And after the establishment of parliamentary government, in 1867, it was found that neither of the privileged nationalities—German and Hungarian—had a majority in its own half of the dual monarchy. The Czechs were eager for the restoration of their own independence, the Poles for that of Poland, the Italians, Rumanians and Croatians for union with Italy, Rumania and Serbia respectively. The Slovenians desired freedom from Austria, the Slovaks from Hungary, the Ruthenians from the Poles of Galicia. All these movements provoked counter movements in some degree.

Austrian history as a whole has failed to rouse much enthusiasm or sympathy either in Germany or in this country—but for different reasons. In Germany less value is attached to personal freedom than here; there is no strong feeling against coercion, or even persecution, as such. The Thirty Years' War is deplored, not as an outrage against religious freedom, and of course still less for the disasters which it brought upon the Czechs, but solely because of the disunion and ruin which it caused to the purely German states. Coming to more modern times Joseph's attempt to enforce the use of the German language is applauded, perhaps more than anything else in Austrian history. But Austrian policy in the latter part of last century is regarded as weak-kneed, especially in respect of the concessions made to various nationalities. In point of fact there was a rather widespread drift towards a more liberal policy at this time—even in the German-speaking provinces of Austria—which deserves notice all the more because Germany was then moving in an opposite direction. The influence of the Church too tended to favour the repressed nationalities, among whom it was especially strong; and, although Pan-Germanism made considerable headway among the professional classes, it seems on the whole not to have met with any great encouragement in official circles. It may be doubted, however, whether any further concessions, e.g. in the direction of federalism, could have been carried out without forfeiting the alliance with Germany; for Germany regarded Austria as a stepping-stone for German expansion towards the south-east, and consequently would not have allowed the position of the non-German nationalities to be strengthened.

The Hohenzollern dynasty came into possession of the Mark of Brandenburg in 1415. The hereditary ('Ascanian') ruling family of this Mark (cf. p. 81) had died out in 1320; and soon afterwards it was acquired by the family of Wittelsbach, to whom belonged Ludwig IV, who was then emperor. From them it was bought in 1373 by the (Luxemburg) emperor Charles IV; and it was his son, the emperor Sigismund, who granted it to Frederic of Hohenzollern, margrave of Nürnberg. It was now a principality of great importance. Since 1356 its ruler had been one of the electors to the imperial throne. Its territories were now very extensive, and included both the Altmark (to the west of the Elbe) and the Neumark (to the east of the Oder), as well as the lands between these rivers. They had no natural frontiers.

The kingdom of Prussia arose eventually out of the union of the 'Electorate' (electoral principality) of Brandenburg with the Duchy of Prussia, which contained by far the greater part of what is now East Prussia. This duchy was also a state of considerable size and importance, though by no means equal to Brandenburg; but it was subject to Poland. It had belonged to the Teutonic Order (cf. p. 102), which at the Reformation, in 1525, had been secularised, and its territories converted into a duchy, hereditary in the family of the last Grand Master, who was sprung from a branch of the Hohenzollerns. In 1594 the daughter and heiress of the second duke was married to John Sigismund, son of the elector of Brandenburg; and from 1618 the two states were under one ruler, though one belonged to the Empire, while the other was a vassal state of Poland.

Frederic William, the 'Great Elector' (1640–88), raised Brandenburg into one of the chief Powers of Europe. He brought this about partly by astute diplomacy—changing sides in the disputes between Sweden and Poland, and between France and Austria—and partly by the extreme attention which he paid to his army. In order to meet the expenses required for the latter, which was a large professional force, he gave great encouragement to industry and commerce. In the course of the constant wars between Sweden and Poland he succeeded in obtaining eastern Pomerania from the former and the recognition of the independence of Prussia from the latter. The acquisition of Pomerania extended the territories of Brandenburg to the coast of the Baltic; and from now onwards the chief object of the family was to secure a geographical connection with

Prussia, which was separated from the rest of their dominions by a comparatively small part of Poland. Brandenburg had never possessed natural frontiers, and consequently had always borne a more military character than other states; but now, owing to this new ambition of its rulers, its military character became more pronounced than ever.

Frederic (1688–1713), son of Frederic William, supplied the emperor Leopold I with very large forces for his wars against the French, and by this means succeeded (in 1701) in obtaining his consent to acquiring the title of 'king'. He had, however, to take this title from Prussia, which lay outside the Empire, and not from Brandenburg.

King Frederic William I (1713–40), son of Frederic, devoted his whole attention to his army, which is said to have absorbed five-sevenths of the revenue of the state. He introduced compulsory military service.

His son Frederic II, 'the Great' (1740–86), followed closely the lines of policy adopted by the Great Elector. He made his army to be the best in Europe, and enlarged his territories by tortuous diplomatic dealings. Soon after his accession he seized the rich Austrian—properly Bohemian—province of Silesia from the Arch-duchess Maria Theresa, in violation of a guarantee and without declaration of war. Later, in 1772, he persuaded Maria Theresa and the Tsaritsa Catherine II to co-operate with him in annexing large parts of Poland. Poland was at this time very weak, after a long period of non-resident kings, and could offer no resistance. By this partition Frederic secured the part of Poland which separated Prussia from Pomerania and Brandenburg, and which had long been coveted by his family. This territory was known henceforth as 'West Prussia', and the old Prussia as 'East Prussia'.

Frederic the Great is regarded as a hero by modern nationalists; but he himself had no sympathy with nationalistic aspirations. Like all his dynasty, his aim was the aggrandisement of his own family and state. He was a fairly voluminous writer, but wrote wholly in French. He is also said to have spoken French habitually.

Further large portions of Poland were annexed by Frederic William II (1786–96), Frederic's nephew and successor, in the partitions of 1793 and 1795. These districts were now called 'South Prussia'. The territorial arrangements were subsequently dislocated in the Napoleonic wars; but Prussia retained the western part of Poland, which was known later as the province of Posen (Poznan).

The early part of the reign of Frederic William III (1796–1840), son of the last mentioned, was the time of the Napoleonic wars, which threw all Germany into confusion. At the Congress of Rad-stadt, which was held in 1803 under Napoleon's influence, the ecclesiastical principalities, which owned a large proportion of western Germany, were dispossessed, and most of their territories were acquired by Prussia, which was then in alliance with Napoleon. At the final peace, in 1815, these acquisitions were augmented by other territories, especially to the west of the Rhine, which had been annexed by Napoleon. All in all the new territories covered a very large area, though they were not connected geographically with the older parts of the kingdom.

The havoc caused in Germany by the French invasions gave rise to a desire for national unity and for reforms of various kinds. The old empire, which had long retained only a shadow of power, was abolished by Napoleon in 1806. After Napoleon's fall its place was taken by a loose Confederation of thirty-nine independent states, though Austria and Prussia far exceeded the rest in size and power. A Diet, consisting of representatives nominated by the various governments, was established in 1816 at Frankfort-on-Main; but it acquired very little power. Reforms of one kind or another, however, were carried out in most of the states. Some of them indeed adopted forms of constitutional government; and proposals for this purpose were put forward even in Prussia, though they were decisively re-jected by the king. But the most important result of this movement was the establishment of a Customs Union. At first there were at least three such Unions, i.e. combinations of states which allowed unrestricted free trade within their limits. Of these the one to which Prussia belonged was by far the largest; for Austria, as also some of the smaller states, did not enter into any of the Unions. The three Unions were amalgamated into one between 1831 and 1834; and the few states which still remained outside them, except Austria, joined this Union later—Hanover in 1854, Mecklenburg not until 1867. This German Customs Union proved to be of much greater importance than was expected at the time, owing to the increased facilities for trade and travel offered by the introduction of railways in the next few years.

Under Frederic William IV (1840–61) the demand for con-stitutional government flared up again in the 'revolutionary year' 1848. An elective house of representatives was secured in the Prussian Landtag. But it obtained very little power; for the king insisted on retaining in his own hands the appointment of ministers and all questions relating to the army and foreign affairs. About the same time the Diet authorised the summoning of an elected parliament at Frankfort. This body seemed to be unable to come to an agreement on any definite proposals; but it set itself to the task of drawing up something in the nature of a democratic constitution. The awakening of national feeling was shown also in its readiness to champion the cause of Sleswick and Holstein, which were in revolt against Denmark. Then the parliament decided to re-establish a German empire; but difficulties arose through the conflicting claims of Austria and Prussia. Eventually it decided to exclude Austria and to offer the imperial throne to the king of Prussia, to be hereditary in his family. But Frederic William refused the offer; and the parliament, now hopelessly torn by dissensions, collapsed. The Diet, which had been in abeyance while the parliament lasted, now resumed its functions.

William I, brother of the last king, acted as regent from 1857, and succeeded him as king in 1861. He was an extreme conservative, and entrusted his policy throughout his reign to his minister Bismarck. Now it was clear to Bismarck that the movement which had failed in 1848 was inspired partly by liberal ideas and partly by nationalism. With the former he had no sympathy; but he saw that the latter could be exploited for the aggrandisement of Prussia. He therefore took up the cause of Sleswick and Holstein again; but his intention was to annex these duchies to Prussia—which was not what they themselves desired. At the same time he laid his plans for attacking Austria—which was actually taking part in the war against Denmark—as soon as might be convenient, and then for dealing with the other German states in such a manner as would best serve the interests of Prussia. His plans were entirely successful. Austria was defeated in 1866, and expelled from the Reich; and Hanover and Cassel—which separated the western territories of Prussia from the rest of the kingdom—were annexed. Then, in 1866-7, the North German Confederation was formed—consisting of the states north of the Main, which were now entirely under Prussian influence. The south German states were excluded; but a secret alliance was made with them, which brought them into the war with France in 1870. This was followed by the establishment of the new German empire.

The gradual method by which Bismarck built up the empire enabled him to mould its constitution—more or less on the lines of the Prussian—with little opposition, and to prevent liberal or democratic elements from obtaining control. National unity was achieved, but not in the form which had been the object of the parliament of 1848. What had now actually taken place was that Germany had been annexed or absorbed by Prussia.[1]

In carrying out his schemes Bismarck followed the traditional lines of Prussian diplomacy. Thus he is said to have promised the Danes to defend them at the very time that he was preparing for the invasion of their country. More famous is the device by which he forced the French emperor into war by publishing a garbled account of an interview. He was of course true to Prussian tradition also in the assiduous care which he devoted to the army. The efficiency of the army and its unbroken success in his time gave rise to a feeling towards it which was virtually religious. The deity seems to have assumed an essentially military character, which was hardly more than a reflection or replica of the king of Prussia in his military capacity. It is true that not all Germans regarded this conception as a beneficent deity; but no one doubted his omnipotence—a feeling which still prevails, in spite of the collapse in 1918. On the other hand, the pose of semi-divinity which William II (1888–1918) adopted, though it struck people in this country as absurd, was in reality a not unnatural outgrowth from a conception which had long been prevalent.

After Bismarck's retirement, in 1890, the chief characteristics which the new German empire had inherited from the kingdom of Prussia showed no sign of disappearing or fading. But nationalism tended steadily to increase. William II personified Prussianised Germany rather than Prussia itself. Expansion was provided for by the development of colonial policy—which had begun under Bismarck—and more especially by promoting movement towards the south-east. This was effected partly by means of the close alliance with Austria-Hungary, and partly by the infiltration and exploitation of Turkey and neighbouring lands. But the worst side of this expansion policy was the attempt—during the first decade of this century—to displace the Polish inhabitants of Posen and West Prussia by the importation of German farmers and landworkers.

After the collapse of 1918 a reversion took place to the liberal and democratic ideas of 1848. But this was temporary and superficial, and due to the exigencies of the time. It was soon felt that the

---

[1] Cf. Treitschke, *Politics*, II, 368f. (Engl. transl.): 'Against the will of all Germany the Prussian state carved out with its good sword a Constitution which...could naturally be nothing but a complete subordination of the smaller States, a submission of the vanquished to the victor. Here was no realisation of the dream of 1848, of a German nation elevating Prussia almost against her own will to become part of a united Germany...Prussia was not swallowed up in Germany....Prussia extended her own institutions over the rest of Germany.'

military deity had fallen, not through any inherent fault of his own, but because the cult had taken too narrow, and not sufficiently national, a form. Prussian militarism and autocracy—which had now become German—were in the ascendant again before long, as shown by the election of Hindenburg in 1925 and the reintroduction of conscription in 1935. The reaction has been accompanied by an accentuated nationalism, fortified more than ever by the belief that the Germans are superior to all other peoples, and therefore entitled to rule over the rest of the world.

The belief of the Germans in their superiority to all other nations is due perhaps above all else to the apparent invincibility of their army, which, after being the object of assiduous care by successive Prussian rulers for more than two centuries, enabled Bismarck's diplomacy to secure for them a commanding position in Europe. Other considerations, however, must not be left out of account.

First, mention must be made of their great achievements in industry and trade during the last century. I am not qualified to speak on this subject; but the facts are well known.

Their intellectual achievements have perhaps not been so widely recognised. Yet in this sphere, and in particular through their discovery of the value of a University, they have actually succeeded in establishing a world domination.

Germany was far behind this country in the establishment of Universities. The first University in central Europe was that of Prague, founded by the emperor Charles IV in 1348. But this was only partly German, and partly Czech; and the latter element soon became predominant. The establishment of purely German Universities began only towards the end of the fourteenth century. Vienna and Heidelberg seem to have been the earliest. Some German Universities, like that of Prague, and our own Universities played an important part in the Reformation. But it was not until c. 1750 that the activities began which have placed them ahead of all the other Universities of the world. By this time practically every German state of any importance had a University of its own. Prussia had several; but some of them had been founded before the provinces in which they were situated had come into Prussian hands.

The activities of which I am speaking began c. 1750 and continued down to our own days. It was in those subjects which were formerly known as 'the Arts' in this country, and more especially in what are best described as 'humanistic' subjects, that German ascendancy was most marked. I do not know how far this ascendancy prevailed in 'scientific' subjects; but at any rate it can hardly have been acquired to the same degree. The effect of these activities was to introduce very many new subjects of study, as well as to provide new approaches to the old subjects. It meant the pursuit of knowledge for its own sake. In order to appreciate the importance of the movement it must be borne in mind that in English Universities, down to 1850, study in 'humanistic' subjects was virtually limited to the Latin and Greek Classics; and hardly any research was carried on in any other such subject. At Cambridge there were at this time only five or six[1] Professorships in these subjects; none of them had been founded within the last 125 years. Practically all the teaching was given by the Colleges; and its object was to enable students to obtain a degree, which would serve as a professional qualification—at that time most frequently for the Church. I doubt whether in other European Universities, except in Scandinavia, the pursuit of knowledge was any more advanced.

It would not be true of course to describe this country as lying in an intellectual backwater during the period 1750–1850. A great deal of valuable work was done in historical, linguistic and antiquarian subjects. But nearly all the authors were ecclesiastics, barristers, bankers, government officials or people of private means. Very few of them were in direct contact with the Universities.

Since 1850 the interests of our Universities have gradually become wider. But this was due very largely to German influence; frequently it was effected by the introduction of German teachers. Now, if we require full information about any country in Europe or elsewhere— even about the early laws and institutions of our own country—we turn instinctively to German authorities. As a result we have learned to see everything through German glasses. Even the faults and shortcomings of the German models—and they are by no means inconsiderable—are slavishly copied. So great is the ascendancy which German learning has won.

This ascendancy may be interpreted by Germans themselves as a proof of their intellectual superiority over other peoples. But the valuable work done by British authors who were not connected with Universities shows that the true explanation is to be found in the Universities themselves. Both the German Universities and the rulers of the states to which they belonged took a more enlightened view of knowledge than was—or is now—to be found in the corresponding classes in this country. At the beginning of this century over 70 per cent of the expenses of the Universities are said to have

---

[1] Six with Music. Divinity and Law are not included here.

been paid from government funds; and the proportion of teachers to students was very much higher—three or four times as high, according to some statistics—than in our Universities. Moreover both teachers and students were more or less free from the tyranny of examinations,[1] which in our Universities tends to absorb the energies of both classes and to restrict the scope of their activities.

To what extent has national feeling affected the German Universities, and how far are they responsible for the dissemination of this feeling? I do not know whether any trustworthy data are available for answering these questions. There has certainly been an influential element with a pronounced national feeling among the Professoriate since the early years of this century; in some quarters indeed it showed itself at a considerably earlier date. But I do not know whether the majority were affected by any such feelings. The Universities do not seem to have been regarded with any special favour by the present regime. All that I have seen suggests that the present rulers have failed to realise the advantages which they have inherited from the intellectual ascendancy of their Universities. Their propaganda, for instance, is stupid and tactless, and seldom uses any argument beyond intimidation. No doubt plausible propaganda—for external use—is difficult to produce for a policy of brigandage and piracy; but some effort in that direction might have been expected. The explanation, however, may be found in the fact that they attach supreme importance to swiftness of action and the element of surprise.

Whatever may be the truth about the Universities, there can be no doubt that schools have been largely responsible for the growth of a militant nationalism. Hitler says that he himself acquired his views on this subject from one of his teachers at school; the movement therefore must have taken root among teachers, at least in Austria, by the beginning of the century. This was no doubt due to the activities of the Alldeutscher Verband, which gave special attention to the dissemination of its views in schools (cf. p. 119 ff.).

Among Germans of to-day it is a commonplace that all that they value most in their national characteristics and ideology is inherited from their heathen ancestors of long ago. Many are said to desire the restoration of the old forest cults in place of Christianity. All this may be due indirectly to the influence of the Universities; but it has come through very popular channels and in a much distorted form.

---

[1] On the other hand, the rewards to be gained from the 'Abiturienten', or school-leaving, examination, especially the very substantial reduction in military service, had the effect of stimulating intellectual activity to a very great extent.

A good deal is derived ultimately from Tacitus' *Germania*. But what has the love of freedom, attributed there to the Germani, in common with the Nazism of to-day? How would they have felt towards the Gestapo? Almost as much, indeed possibly even more, has been built upon the great victories and conquests of the Teutonic peoples in the fifth and sixth centuries. These peoples are commonly identified with the Germans themselves; and their achievements are held up to admiration, as showing the dominant position which the Germans are entitled to occupy in the world. The principles of government and warfare which find favour to-day—autocracy, unquestioning obedience, speed in movement, the organisation of atrocities, and the custom of posting contingents from subject peoples in the forefront of the battle—all these, it is true, can be traced back to the period of which we are speaking; but they were characteristic, not of the Goths or any other Teutonic people, but of the Huns and Avars, the nomads of the Asiatic steppe.

It is of course a tribute to the influence of the Universities that interest in Teutonic (or 'German') antiquity has gained so firm a hold upon the public imagination, however distorted a shape it may have taken. The process has been long in operation; for much of the terminology now current in popular use is obsolete in the Universities. We may instance the term 'Aryan', which in its current sense had been discarded by the Universities long before the end of last century. There is, however, one doctrine, closely connected with this name, which is very widely current both in Universities and in popular circles, and which has had an important influence upon modern German ideology. This doctrine is, briefly, that the domination of the Teutonic peoples—interpreted as the Germans—did not begin for the first time with the fall of the Roman Empire in the fifth century, but that, on the contrary, owing to their innate superiority to other peoples, they have supplied the conquerors and the ruling classes of nearly all Europe and a great part of Asia from time immemorial. This doctrine will require notice in the next chapter.

CHAPTER VIII

THE CLAIMS TO DOMINATION. II

In the preceding chapter we have reviewed briefly the historical grounds upon which the Germans base their claim to domination and the processes which have led them to believe themselves superior to all other peoples. It is to be borne in mind, however, that, apart from the historical evidence, there is a widespread belief that this superiority is due to something innate in the people themselves—something which has been inherited from the most remote times. In particular it is very widely held that the Teutonic (or Germanic) area was the original home of the Indo-European languages—which in Germany are called Indo-Germanic—and that the great expansion of these languages, over nearly all Europe and a large part of Asia, was due to expeditions which set out from this area. Those who took part in the expeditions are believed to have established themselves as ruling classes in the various regions which they conquered, and to have imposed their own language upon the conquered peoples. The Teutonic peoples are therefore the true Indo-Europeans—the nucleus and purest stock of the great group of peoples which have dominated Europe and western Asia for thousands of years.

It is to be observed that this claim is made for the Teutonic peoples collectively, not for the Germans alone. Most of the leading authorities hold that the original Teutonic area included only a small part of Germany—the northernmost districts extending from the mouth of the Weser, or possibly the Ems, to that of the Oder—together with Denmark and its islands and the south of Sweden. But in practice it is customary for even serious writers to confuse 'German' (deutsch) with 'Teutonic' (germanisch) and to regard Germany as the homeland of the Teutonic peoples, while an undefined kind of headship is universally claimed. For the Scandinavian peoples are relatively insignificant in numbers, while the English are thought of as a 'colonial' people, only half Teutonic in origin.

The confusion in terminology to which we are referring is of course still worse in this country, owing to our use of the name 'German' for the language and people of the Reich. It will be necessary therefore to notice briefly the history of these terms before we enter upon any discussion of the German claims.

The names *Germani* and *Germania* date from Roman times. By early Latin and Greek writers, about the beginning of our era and for the next century, or rather more, they were used as a collective term for all the Teutonic peoples and for the whole of the area which they occupied. Later writers, however, restrict the former term to the Franks and neighbouring peoples in western Germany; they do not apply it to the Gothic or Scandinavian peoples. After the sixth century it seems to have gone out of living use, in both Latin and Greek, and to occur only in references to the past. It was never used in any of the vernaculars. The geographical name *Germania* had a longer life; but this also is known only from Latin and Greek records. It may be observed that in English the word 'German' first appears (in its modern sense) towards the end of the sixteenth century. Before that 'Dutch' was used for the people and language of Germany, as well as for those of the Netherlands. Still earlier the French term *Almaygnes* had been in use.

From the second to the seventeenth century no collective term for the Teutonic peoples and languages as a whole seems to have been current. The earliest, at least in this country, was 'Northern' (*Septentrionalis*), which was introduced by Bishop G. F. Hickes, shortly before 1700, and maintained itself for the greater part of a century. Before long, however, this term had to contend with—and was eventually displaced by—'Teutonic', which seems to have come from abroad. Originally—in the tenth century—*Teutonicus* meant the German- and Dutch-speaking populations of the Empire (*Franci Teutonici*) and their languages, etc. Apparently it was adopted as a Latinisation of *thiodisc*, 'national, native' (from *thioda*, 'people'), which was used to distinguish the German from the Roman population. The Goths perhaps used the same word for their own language and customs. But elsewhere—in Germany itself, Scandinavia, England and Italy—the word (Deutsch, Tysk, Dutch, Tedesco) has survived only in the sense of 'German' or 'Dutch'. Its use therefore in the extended sense found in the eighteenth century was an innovation.

Last century the word 'Germanic' was introduced—or, perhaps we should say, re-introduced—sometimes, like 'Teutonic', as a comprehensive term for the whole group of peoples and languages, sometimes as a subdivision of 'Teutonic'. On the Continent it soon displaced the latter. Attention was now concentrated chiefly upon language, and a classification of the languages was drawn up, as follows. The whole group, Teutonic or Germanic (germanisch), was divided into two: (*a*) Scandinavian, (*b*) the rest of the languages.

The second sub-group—Germanic or (more usually) German (Deutsch)—was then divided into (*a*) Low German and (*b*) High German. In the former of these were included not only Low German proper (Platt-deutsch) and Dutch, but also English, Frisian and even Gothic. Later, however, this system was modified, and a triple division adopted, by which the whole (Germanic) group was divided into (*a*) North Germanic or Scandinavian, (*b*) East Germanic, represented by Gothic, and (*c*) West Germanic, which included High and Low German, Dutch, Frisian and English. The two last were regarded as standing somewhat apart from the rest.

This system of classification, especially its later form, was of German origin; but it was generally accepted in this country. Many English philologists, however, have preferred to retain 'Teutonic' in place of 'Germanic', owing to the ambiguity of the latter and its liability to be confused with 'German'. These considerations seem to me to outweigh the fact that 'Germanic' has a superior antiquity in its favour. Both terms, however, are open to objection; and it is a misfortune that Hickes' 'Northern', which was more suitable than either of them, was discarded.

In Germany the introduction of the new terminology had a most stimulating effect. It served to bring out the antiquity of the German nation and to impress upon the Germans of the present day that they were the descendants and heirs of the Germani who fought successfully against the Romans more than eighteen centuries before. All records relating to Teutonic antiquity were eagerly studied, though Tacitus' 'Germania', owing no doubt largely to its laudatory tone, was the work which made the strongest appeal. Further, it was fully appreciated that, though Tacitus and his contemporaries applied the name *Germani* to all the Teutonic peoples, yet by far the greater part of what they had to say related properly to peoples who were German in the strict sense, the ancestors of those who speak German (deutsch) to-day. From this sprang, perhaps not unnaturally, the idea that Germany should be regarded as the head and source of all the Teutonic peoples. In any case it came to be realised now that Germany had had an ancient culture more purely native and—to many people—more attractive than that of the Holy Roman Empire.

The new learning soon permeated the Universities, and before long made its way into the schools. Eventually, in more or less popularised form, it had a wide influence throughout the country. It served to arouse a quite legitimate feeling of national pride in a nation which at the time had no political unity. Indeed, I doubt whether philological and antiquarian learning has ever produced such far-reaching effects.

At the time when the new learning reached its apex—in the second quarter of last century—German learning in general, at least in the Universities, had already succeeded in establishing its supremacy over that of all other nations. Our Universities have frequently found it advisable to follow their example in taking up a new subject; and such was the case with the subject we are now discussing. In the next half-century, gradually and without much intelligence, they began to copy their German models. The slavishness with which these were followed may be illustrated by one or two examples. Early German literature, before the eleventh or twelfth century, has seldom anything of interest to offer, except the language itself of the records—which are mostly translations or paraphrases of Latin religious works. Attention was therefore concentrated on the language. But in our Universities Anglo-Saxon literature, which is full of historical and antiquarian interest, was—and often still is— treated in the same way. The historical and antiquarian interests could not of course be wholly ignored. But they had to be studied out of connection with the language and by a different set of students. No student was encouraged to study the records in their original language. Consequently all serious study of our early history and antiquities had to be left to German students, who were better equipped for the purpose.

Our historians of last century seem to have been ignorant of the existence of any records or traditions relating to the English in their original home. In place of these they contented themselves with a claim to be descended from Tacitus' Germans. Indeed, quite frequently they spoke of our English ancestors as Germans—a practice which has not been completely discarded even yet. It is possible of course to defend such a usage by pleading that 'Germans' is to be understood, not in the ordinary (modern) sense of the word, but in the sense of Tacitus' *Germani*. But that is pedantry of a mis- leading kind. Presumably this usage is a relic of the old system of classification mentioned above, which treated the English language as a branch of German.

If our historians had had more knowledge and more independence, they would have seen not only that the old classification was in- correct, but also that the later system was far from satisfactory. It is to be remembered that both classifications were primarily lin- guistic. Now to determine the genealogical relationship of languages it is necessary of course to give special attention to the earliest evidence which is available. For times in which there was no native written literature we are dependent upon inscriptions, loan words from foreign (Celtic and Latin) languages and the forms of Teutonic words and names which are found in Latin and Greek authors. But to all such evidence comparatively little attention was paid until towards the close of the century, or even later. Thus, to take an example, the early inscriptions found in the old home of the English —the province of Sleswick and neighbouring districts—were generally regarded as Danish, though it was not believed that the population was Danish at that time.

The evidence which is now at our disposal points, I think, to the following conclusions. (i) Down to the fifth century the German, English and Scandinavian languages differed but slightly from one another. (ii) By this time, and for some considerable time previously, the Gothic language—and probably also the other eastern languages —had already come to differ from these languages in many important respects. (iii) We may therefore constitute an eastern and a north-western group at this time. (iv) In the fifth and following centuries differentiation took place very quickly within the north-western group. English developed in general on lines about midway between German and Scandinavian, but with many special features of its own. Frisian seems to have differed little from English for a long time; but, owing to the lateness of the records, its development is difficult to trace.

The differentiation of the languages was obviously governed by their geographical position. The position of English was intermediate; but both English and Frisian were essentially maritime, whereas German was for several centuries exclusively an inland language. English originated in Angel (in eastern Sleswick); but we do not know how far it extended. Kindred dialects may once have been spoken as far as the Great Belt, and possibly even up to the Skaw, while southwards they may have reached the mouth of the Elbe. But they have now disappeared from the whole region, except perhaps in Sylt and the neighbouring islands (cf. p. 18 f.). Early in the ninth century Danes and Germans had already met at the border of Sleswick and Holstein, though it would seem from names recorded by Danish (Latin) historians that English had not wholly died out in the twelfth century. Since then Low German has become the language of the southern part of Sleswick, and Danish of the northern part. Again, in the ninth century Frisians occupied the whole of the coast from the Scheldt to the Weser; but their language, or kindred dialects, must once have been conterminous with English.

The home of the German language—the area in which it developed its distinctive character—was the interior of western Germany, from the lower Elbe southwards to the Alps. In the fifth century it was probably spoken throughout the basin of the Elbe, except perhaps the estuary, whereas all the Teutonic languages of the region to the east of that basin may have been of the Gothic type. But in the sixth century all the east of Germany, including eastern Holstein and the greater part of the Elbe basin, was invaded and occupied by Slavonic peoples. Their western border ran (roughly) southwards from Kiel to the Harz, then back to the Elbe, below Magdeburg, then along the Saale, and southwards into eastern Bavaria. In the Altmark, between the Harz and the Elbe, Slavonic survived until the eighteenth century.

Before the eighth century the German language had developed considerable dialectal differences. The most important of these was the distinction between High German in the south and Low German in the north. The modern German language belongs to the former, the modern Dutch language to the latter. But the greater part of the Netherlands has changed its language. The western provinces, as well as the north, were formerly Frisian; and Dutch seems to have been much influenced by the older language. Some of the Low German dialects in Germany itself also have been affected by Frisian or English influence. Such influence is most apparent in the earliest (Old Saxon) poetry, dating from the ninth century, which contains numerous forms of English type. It was doubtless due to these forms that the older philologists connected Low German with English. But they are inconsistent with other forms in the same language, and are clearly intrusive. They are in all probability relics of the original language of the Saxons, which may well have been akin to English. The earliest reference to the Saxons—in Ptolemy's *Geography*, in the second century—locates them 'on the neck of the peninsula'; and in their native tradition, as recorded by their historian Widukind (1, 3), they are said to have come by sea and to have landed at Hadeln, in the neighbourhood of Cuxhaven. There was evidently a southward movement in this region about the fourth century. It may be remarked that certain cemeteries, dating from a slightly later period, on the heath of Lüneburg (south of Hamburg) show a close resemblance to heathen English cemeteries, and contain objects which would seem to have been acquired in this country.

After the Slavonic invasion, as mentioned above, the home of the German language lay to the west of the Elbe, or rather to the west of the Harz and the Saale. It may indeed be defined practically as the region between these districts and the Rhine; for the lands to the west of the Rhine had only recently been conquered. Now this region was the part of the Teutonic world which had been best known to the Romans, and about which Roman writers, especially Tacitus, give the most detailed information. Indeed, it was no doubt from this region that the name *Germani* was originally derived.

Tacitus (*Germ.* 2) gives us some information regarding the origin of the names *Germani* and *Germania*. He specifies certain names (*Suevi, Vandali*, etc.)—evidently those of groups of peoples—as genuine and ancient, and then adds that the name *Germania* was said to be modern and recently introduced, 'for those who were the first to cross the Rhine and expel the Gauls, and are now called Tungri, were then called Germani. So the name of a particular tribe (*natio*), not of the whole people (*gens*), came gradually into general use', etc. What follows is obscure;[1] but Tacitus seems to be trying to show, after the Roman fashion, how the name *Germani* came to be adopted by the Teutonic peoples as a collective term for themselves. There is no other evidence, however, that the name was ever used by any Teutonic people.

Caesar, in his *Gallic War* (II, 4, and elsewhere), states that most of the Belgae were said to be sprung from the Germani; and he adds that they were believed to have crossed the Rhine long ago (*antiquitus*) and expelled the Gauls from this region. Later in the same chapter he gives a list of the Belgic peoples and their forces, ending with four small peoples—the Condrusi, Eburones, Caeroesi and Paemani[2]—'who in common are called Germani'. It is not clear whether these peoples, or any one of them,[3] were identical with the people later called Tungri, whose name Caesar does not mention; but, if not, they must have been their near neighbours.

From what is said by Caesar and Tacitus it would seem that the name *Germani* belonged originally to a people or group of peoples whose territories lay to the west (south-west) of the lower Rhine—chiefly in the east of (modern) Belgium. The name of the Tungri is preserved at Tongres, not far from Liège. These peoples were believed to have come from beyond the Rhine long before Caesar's

---

[1] In the edition of the *Germania* (p. 42) by J. G. C. Anderson it is translated as follows: ... 'so that all (i.e. the whole people) were called Germani, first by the conquerors (i.e. the Tungri) from fear (or "to inspire fear") and subsequently by themselves as well, adopting the name which had been devised for them.'

[2] From VI, 32 it would seem that a people called Segni belonged to the same group.

[3] The Eburones have the most likely claim. Aduatuca is said to be their capital by Caesar, that of the Tungri by Ptolemy.

time. Moreover, most of the other Belgic peoples claimed a similar origin; and so also did the Treueri.[1]

Yet there is no evidence that these peoples, with one possible exception, spoke or ever had spoken a Teutonic language. Their names and those of persons belonging to them, recorded by Caesar, are all either definitely Celtic or at least non-Teutonic. It is to be inferred therefore that *Germani* was originally the name of a Celtic people, and that subsequently it came to be used in a wider sense, but with a geographical rather than an ethnic or linguistic significance—denoting any peoples whose home lay beyond the Rhine.

The one exception, to which I have referred, is formed by the Aduatuci, who according to Caesar, II, 29, were a remnant of the Cimbri and Teutoni, left behind by those peoples when they set out on their great expedition to the south, half a century before Caesar's time. Now the Cimbri, and probably also the Teutoni, belonged to Jutland, and are therefore generally regarded as Teutonic, though this may not be quite certain.[2] But this is a special case: the Aduatuci are not reckoned among the four peoples collectively called Germani, and in the list of Belgic peoples given in II, 4 they are entered separately from them—though they were evidently close neighbours of the Eburones (cf. V, 27).[3]

With this possible exception there is no evidence that any of the Belgic Germani were Teutonic. Nor is there any satisfactory reason for believing the name *Germani* itself to be Teutonic, though various attempts have been made to show that it is. It is clearly connected with *Paemani*, the name of one of the four peoples of the Belgic Germani, and probably also with *Cenomani*, the name of a people found both in central Gaul and in Cisalpine Gaul.

The question of course remains: How could the name of a Celtic people or group of peoples come to serve as a collective term for the Teutonic peoples? I have suggested above that the name *Germani* had acquired a geographical sense—denoting any peoples whose home lay, or had lain, beyond the Rhine. The Romans, however, used the name in an ethnic sense, i.e. as 'Teutonic'. A further change of meaning had therefore taken place—which must be due

[1] Cf. Tacitus, *Germ.* 28. The Treueri are reckoned among the Belgae by Mela, but apparently not by Caesar.
[2] In *The Origin of the English Nation*, pp. 210 ff., I discussed the geographical position of these peoples; and I did not then doubt the prevalent view, that they were Teutonic. Now I do not feel so confident. In Pliny's *Natural History*, IV, 27, there is a passage which may be interpreted as meaning that the Cimbri spoke a Celtic language; but unfortunately the sentence is ambiguous.
[3] The chief fortress of the Eburones was called Aduatuca. Had they captured it from the Aduatuci?

to the fact that by the time of the Roman conquest the lands beyond the Rhine had for the most part come into Teutonic hands. It may be added that the Romans may not have been able to distinguish clearly between Teutonic and backward Celtic peoples. They seldom took the trouble to learn native languages, and consequently were wholly dependent on interpreters. There were without doubt a number of non-Teutonic peoples within the limits of 'Germania'. Even the list of contingents to Ariovistus' army, recorded by Caesar (I, 51), contains names which can hardly be Teutonic; and other examples are to be found in Tacitus and Ptolemy. Yet only on two or three occasions does Tacitus mention that a people (in Germania) spoke a non-Teutonic language. Usually, when the question arises whether a given people is Teutonic or not, he bases his opinion upon cultural considerations. There is of course no doubt that in their interest in foreign peoples the literati of the Romans were far in advance of ours; but their linguistic knowledge seems to have been defective.

I think then that the use of the name *Germani* as a collective term for the Teutonic peoples was due to a misunderstanding on the part of the Romans, and that, when the Belgic peoples claimed to be Germani or sprung from Germani, what they meant was that their ancestors had come by conquest from beyond the Rhine. This explanation is of course not new. But it is rejected at present not only by German nationalists, but also by many archaeologists in other countries. It is not disputed—at least not by well-informed writers—that a very large part of western Germany had been occupied by Celtic peoples until within a few centuries before the beginning of our era. The evidence of place-names indeed leaves no room for doubt on this score. But there is a very widespread belief that the northern part of the area—extending southwards as far as the Lippe and to the lower Rhine, west of its junction with that river—had long been in Teutonic hands, perhaps even since the late Bronze Age.

The chief evidence on which this belief is based is the presence (in graves) of a certain type of bronze razors and of two types of pottery —found among other types—which are thought to have Nordic affinities. But such evidence is hardly sufficient by itself to bear the weight which has been laid upon it. Razors are known to have travelled—and to have been copied—over great distances. In this country we find a type which seems to have originated in Sicily, and also examples of another type which is not very remote from the Nordic type just mentioned, though not identical with it. Of the two types of pottery claimed as Nordic, at least one, the Harpstedt type, has been found at various places in this country, in associations which show that it was introduced here by invasion from the Netherlands, late in the seventh century. But there is no trace of any Teutonic element here in that period or indeed before Roman times.

It is a most serious—I think, fatal—objection to this theory that Britain is generally believed to have been invaded from the lower Rhine at least twice during the period under discussion—first about 1000 B.C. and again late in the seventh century, and that there is no ground for doubting that the invaders in both cases were Celtic. The earlier invasion, which affected the whole of the British Isles,[1] is commonly thought to have brought Celtic languages here for the first time, though some writers connect their first introduction with that of the 'Beaker' culture, some eight or nine centuries earlier. I do not see therefore how it can reasonably be questioned that the lower Rhine was a Celtic region, at least from the late Bronze Age onwards. Indeed, the districts to the south and south-west of the river were still Celtic down to Caesar's time; and he states that one Belgic people, the Menapii, occupied both banks. But in earlier times Celtic territory must have extended far to the north and east, as is shown by place-names. Even the Weser, the largest river of north-west Germany, has a Celtic name; and the same is probably true of the Ems and various smaller rivers. Note is also to be taken of place-names compounded with *Walh-*, which—like such names as Walton and Walcot in this country—indicate previous occupation by a Celtic population. They are to be found, e.g., throughout the whole of the basin of the Weser, with its tributaries, and extend to within a short distance of the Elbe. In the light of such evidence the theory that north-west Germany had been Teutonic since the Bronze Age seems to me untenable.

Those who held this theory maintain that the original home of the Celtic peoples and languages lay in the south-west of Germany and perhaps the adjacent parts of France. I know of no evidence for this view beyond the fact that it is an obvious corollary from the one we have just discussed; and it seems to me to be equally open to objection. The question, however, is complicated by a third language

---

[1] The case is well, though briefly, stated by A. Mahr, *Proc. Prehist. Soc.* 1937, pp. 399 ff. Those who dispute the occurrence of a great invasion *c.* 1000 B.C. must explain why the slashing sword and especially the riveted spearhead were not introduced before the socketed axe. Was Britain under a Protectionist government, which was not overthrown before this date? The scarcity of invasion pottery (from the Utrecht and Weert types) must be taken in connection with the facts that even in later times these people were rather sparing in their use of pottery for funeral purposes and that very many of the pots have been repaired.

—neither Celtic nor Teutonic—which is believed by many recent writers to have come from the east, about 1000 B.C., probably by way of the Danube, with the people who buried their dead in urn-fields. It is generally called 'Illyrian', because it has obvious affinities with what is known of ancient Illyrian; but it also had features in common with Celtic and Latin, so far as one can judge from place-names—for hardly anything else is left. Its chief differences from Celtic (Gaulish) were (i) the use of masculine river-names, such as *Danuuius, Rhenus, Licus, Moenus, Sarauus* (Saar); (ii) the preservation of the sound -*q*- (as in the name *Sequani*), which in Gaulish had regularly become -*p*-; (iii) the use of certain suffixes which are not found in Celtic, e.g. -*isko*- (*asko*-, -*usko*-) and -*inko*-.[1]

Extravagant claims have been made as to the wide distribution of this language in Germany. Actually I do not know of any certain examples north of the Main. In France, however, they are widespread, especially in the basins of the Moselle, the Seine, with all its tributaries, and the Loire. One of the chief directions taken by the urnfield culture was apparently through western Switzerland, where it became blended with the native ('West Alpine') culture. From there a great movement of invasion seems to have spread, through the basin of the Seine, down to the sea. There the invaders, whom we may call Sequani, developed a considerable maritime activity, apparently in the ninth and eighth centuries. Their distinctive (bronze) artefacts are found all along the French coasts, and also in the southern and eastern parts of England, though I cannot find any convincing evidence for an invasion of this country.

Other movements of invasion carried the same language over the Alps and down the valley of the Rhone, into north-west Italy and Provence, where the invaders acquired somewhat different cultural connections. Their descendants here were known to the Greeks as Ligyes (Ligurians); and there is some evidence that the same name was applied in early times to the people (Sequani)[2] of the same stock in the north of France. At all events the early Greeks recognised the Ligurians as one of the three great peoples of the west (with the Celts

---

[1] E.g. *Vibisci, Taurisci, Matisco, Agedincum, Abrincatui*. For names in -*asco*-, which are especially common in Piedmont, Liguria and Provence, but occur as far north as Trèves, see D'Arbois de Jubainville, *Premiers Habitants*, pp. 68 ff. Names in -*ontio*(*n*)- are extremely common; but they occur also, though less frequently, in Celtic.

[2] Avienus, *Ora Maritima*, 130 ff., seems to speak of Ligurians on the northern coasts, though the passage is much disputed. These would probably be the Sequani. We need not enter here into the question of the Sicanoi in Sicily and Spain. Thucydides (VI, 2) distinguished them from the Ligurians; but he seems to be recording a Greek speculation, not a native tradition.

and the Iberians); and therefore this name seems to me preferable to 'Illyrian' as a collective term for the invading peoples. I do not think that the Greeks ever speak of Illyrians in the west.

The place-names derived from Ligurian show a rather remarkable uniformity throughout the whole area, from the Channel and the Moselle to the Mediterranean. But they are of course interspersed almost everywhere with Celtic names which were introduced doubtless in a later period.

The Celtic peoples were apparently separated from the Ligurians by a broad belt of forest country running through the Ardennes and the Hunsrück, and continued to the east of the Rhine by the *Silva Hercynia* ('Oak-forest'), which was believed to extend for several hundred miles, probably along the mountain ranges which separate Bohemia from Saxony. But eventually—in the sixth century, according to archaeological data—they broke through these barriers, and conquered the whole of France, together with south Germany and a considerable part of Spain.[1] In the following century they conquered the Alpine lands, Bohemia and (*c.* 400) northern Italy. Still later their conquests extended to the Illyrian lands in the basin of the Danube, and to regions still farther east.

The first Celtic conquests in France[2] must have driven the Sequani back to their original home between the Saône and the Jura, where we find them in Caesar's time. But they left a trace of their former dominion in the name *Sequana* (Seine), which was given to their chief river, presumably by the Celtic conquerors. From this time the whole country was probably under Celtic rulers; and in Caesar's time the recorded names, which are usually those of princes, are mostly Celtic. Caesar says, however, that the language of the Belgae differed from that of the rest of the country. This statement cannot be verified; but the few inscriptions which survive are almost wholly unintelligible, and seem to contain hardly anything which is demonstrably Celtic, except the names.[3] Caesar therefore may not have been so much mistaken as he is generally supposed to have been.

[1] The Celtic hosts which invaded Spain about this time seem to have included contingents from Belgic peoples (e.g. the Paemani and Germani), though the evidence is indirect and slight; cf. Bosch-Gimpera, *Two Celtic Waves in Spain*, pp. 44 f., 101.

[2] Apparently referred to in Avienus' poem (133 ff.); see the last note.

[3] Some inscriptions in Greek characters found at Nîmes and at Orgon near Arles contain a word *dede*, which would seem to mean 'gave'—suggesting a language with Latin, rather than Celtic, affinities. And I think this is borne out by certain names of rivers, peoples, etc.; but unfortunately their meaning cannot be determined with any confidence. The calendar found at Coligny, Dep. Ain, which must have been near the southern end of the territory of the Sequani, preserves two words or names which contain -*q*-.

THE CLAIMS TO DOMINATION. II

There can be little doubt that the Teutonic conquest of western Germany was connected with the vast expansion of the Celtic peoples to which we have referred—just as the Slavonic conquest of eastern and central Germany, nearly a thousand years later, was connected with the expansion of the Teutonic peoples. But it is difficult to give even an approximate date; for there is no direct evidence earlier than Caesar's day. At this time there were still a number of Celtic peoples east of the Rhine—which might perhaps suggest that the conquest was recent. On the other hand, certain names seem to indicate that the Teutonic languages had no 'tenues' (or 'voiceless stops') when the conquest took place. What that means chronologically is not clear; but two or three centuries might perhaps be a reasonable estimate.

It is generally agreed that the Volcae were the Celtic people who were in closest contact with the Teutonic peoples in early times. Their name (*Walh-* in Teutonic form) came to be adopted by the latter as a generic term for the Celtic peoples of the Continent, and was later extended to include the Romans, when they had conquered and absorbed these peoples.[1] In this country it was applied by the English to the Britons,[2] though not to the Picts or the Scots. In historical times the Volcae had been much dispersed. In the south of France there were Volcae Tectosages centred at Toulouse and Volcae Arecomici centred at Nîmes. In the interior of Germany also, *circum Hercyniam silvam*, Caesar (*Gall.* VI, 24) speaks of Volcae Tectosages, whom he believed to have come from Gaul. Again, in Galatia we hear of Tectosages, who were centred at Ankara. These were believed to be connected with Toulouse. In the course of their expedition to Asia they sacked the Greek sanctuary at Delphoi (in 279 B.C.); and there was a story current, though not universally credited, that they had sent the loot to their own sanctuary at Toulouse.

The general opinion of modern writers is that the ancients were mistaken in believing that Toulouse was the original home of the Volcae. That belief can of course be supported by the interesting story told by Livy, v, 34—which seems to have suffered somewhat in transmission. But it is quite contrary to the general trend of the Celtic movements, which was southwards (south-eastwards) or westwards. And how could the Teutonic peoples come to take a generic

[1] Cf. Ang.-Sax. *Galwalas*, 'people of Gaul'; *Rumwalas*, 'Romans'; O. High Germ. *Walho lant*, O. Norse *Valland*, 'Gaul'. *Welsch* is still used for 'French' in Switzerland. The name *Walh-* for 'Roman' passed from Teutonic into Slavonic (sing. *Vlah*, pl. *Vlasi*), where it is applied especially to the Rumanians.

[2] Ang.-Sax. *Walh*, pl. *Walas* (whence 'Wales'). Adjective *Wel(h)isc*, 'Welsh'.

term for the Celtic peoples from such a distant region as Toulouse?
I think we need have no hesitation in following the now most
commonly accepted view, that the Volcae who lived 'round the
Hercynian Forest' were those who had remained nearest to the
original home. And this view is strengthened by the fact that Pliny
and Ptolemy mention a people called Hercuniates—obviously a
Celtic name—near Lake Balaton, in the west of Hungary. They
must have come by the same route, and possibly on the same expedition, as the Tectosages who penetrated to Delphoi and Ankara.
Unfortunately the limits of the Hercynian Forest cannot be fixed
precisely. The word—which is Celtic, but transmitted through
Greek—probably means no more than 'Oak-forest'. But the
ancients applied the name primarily to the wooded mountains which
form the northern borders of Bohemia[1]—yet without any clear idea
as to where the forest came to an end. Indeed, they seem to have
thought of it as extending indefinitely to the east and north. Here,
however, the place-names which contain *Walh-* (cf. p. 150) may
help us. They are distributed throughout the west and south-west
of Germany.[2] But if, as we are bound to assume, the original home
of the Volcae is to be sought in a frontier region, bordering upon the
Teutonic peoples, it must obviously be located in the easternmost
region in which these names are found, i.e. in the eastern part of the
basin of the Weser, extending eastwards nearly to the Elbe and
southwards as far as the Saale. The name *Elbe* seems to be Teutonic—
though not exclusively Teutonic[3]—from which we may perhaps
infer that it had been known to the Teutonic peoples, possibly as a
frontier, from earlier times.

In the place-names of this region therefore there is no need to
interpret *Walh-* as 'Celtic' (in the general sense). More probably its
original meaning was preserved here, i.e. (village, dwelling-place,
forest, etc.) 'of the Volcae'.

The movements of the Volcae become easily intelligible when the
area from which they started is rightly located. They are similar to

---

[1] On the south side of the range the Illyrian-Ligurian form of the same name
seems to be preserved still in *Krkonoške* Hory, the Czech name for the Riesen-
gebirge. Ptolemy locates a people called Korkontoi apparently in the same
district—which shows that the name goes back to ancient times.

[2] In the extreme west and south-west such names may mean 'Roman', i.e.
Latin-speaking. But this explanation of course would not hold good for the interior
regions—east of the Rhine and north of the Danube—since Latin was never
spoken there.

[3] Cf. Swed. *älf*, 'river', but also the French *Aube*, a tributary of the Seine, in
eastern France. The name therefore would seem to have been Celtic or Ligurian,
as well as Teutonic.

those of some of the Teutonic peoples in much later times—the fifth and sixth centuries of our era. One movement evidently took a south-westerly course across the Rhine and into the south of France, while the other must have followed the course of the Elbe, through the Silva Hercynia, into Bohemia, and thence to the middle basin of the Danube.

The Volcae are not the only people who may be traced with some probability in this ancient western frontier of the Teutonic peoples. Ptolemy mentions a people called Turonoi, apparently in the Thuringian region. The name, which is doubtless Celtic or Ligurian, is identical with that of the people of Tours.[1] Had the latter come from Thuringia? But a connection has also been suggested with the Teutonic (H)Ermunduri, who occupied Thuringia in Roman times, and with the Thuringi who possessed the same region in the fifth and following centuries (A.D.). It looks as if a Celtic or Ligurian people had been dispersed, part of them establishing themselves in the west of France, while the rest remained behind and were eventually Teutonised. Judging from the changes which took place in the name, this Teutonisation must have begun in very early times.

The process just noted is not without analogies. The Brigantes were perhaps the greatest of the Celtic peoples in this country at the time of the Roman conquest. About the same time we hear also of Brigantioi at Bregenz, on the Lake of Constance, offshoots from whom seem to have established themselves in Savoy (at Briançon) and perhaps in Spain (at Corunna). Again, the same name, in Teutonic form, is borne by the Burgundians, who are located by Ptolemy apparently in the neighbourhood of Berlin or a little farther east. This people seems to have colonised Bornholm; but they do not appear in western Germany before c. 290 (A.D.). I see no reason for doubting that this is another instance of dispersal. But it must have happened at a remote date; for *Brigantes* (*Brigantioi*) is a definitely Celtic name, not Ligurian or Illyrian, and consequently it carries a

---

[1] Some writers connect these names (*Turoni*, etc.) with certain *Teur-*, *Taur-* names. I prefer to leave this question to bolder spirits; but the latter names are interesting in themselves. We find the Ligurian Taurini or Tauriskoi at Turin and the Celtic Tauriskoi or Teuristai in the Julian or Carnic Alps. Moreover Ptolemy mentions a people called Teuriochaimai apparently somewhere in or near the kingdom of Saxony. The last name—which is Teutonic—should mean 'those who occupy the (old) home of the Teurioi' (like Bohemia, 'the (old) home of the Boii'). It would seem as if this region had twice changed its language, and that its people had sent out offshoots to the south-west in Ligurian times, and to the south or south-east in Celtic times. Names in *-isci* (*-iskoi*) are probably those of the Keltoligyes or Celticised Ligurian (or Illyrian) peoples. But the Taurisci or Taurini of Turin seem to have been regarded as Ligurian rather than Celtic.

Celtic people back far to the east of the Rhine. The Brigantes arrived here sometime between the sixth and the third centuries; but it is to be suspected that their journey across north-west Germany was not carried out in one march, and that they spent a while—perhaps many generations—in the Netherlands before embarking. I have not much faith in great overseas invasions carried out by inland peoples.[1] Such invasions are usually preceded by periods of raiding, which surely require maritime bases. The primary object of the war-bands was presumably plunder, rather than settlement.

The dating of the Teutonic invasions from across the Elbe seems to me not quite so desperate as in this case. The first Celtic invasion of Italy seems to have taken place c. 400 (B.C.); for Livy's story is now, I think, generally discredited. The Boii took part in this invasion; but there is no mention of the Volcae. I know of no Celtic movement towards the Balkans until c. 280 (B.C.);[2] and in this the Volcae (under the name Tectosages) did take part. The Hercuniates, whom we find later on the middle Danube, can hardly have arrived there except by a route along the Elbe and through Bohemia and Moravia; and they must have been connected in some way with the Volcae. Indeed, it is probable that all the Celtic peoples settled in the basin of the Danube came from the Elbe. Such evidence is of course not conclusive; but it at least suggests that the Volcae were still occupying their old homes on the Elbe about the beginning of the third century. If so, we may obtain a probable *terminus a quo* for the Teutonic invasions from the east of this river.

The Teutonic invaders from east of the Elbe must be regarded as Germans in the strict sense; it is only very seldom that we hear of possible exceptions.[3] They formed the nucleus of German nationality; and with them the German language had its origin. Apart from them the only Teutonic people in western Germany[4] were the Frisians, who had doubtless come by sea. They arrived probably much later than the Germans; in early Roman times they had ap-

[1] So it seems to me rash to assume that the Parisoi of the East Riding must have come from Paris, or the Catuellauni from Chalons-sur-Marne. Such pairs may more probably be offshoots from common ancestral homes within reach of the sea, perhaps in the Netherlands.

[2] If the Celts from the Adriatic, who interviewed Alexander the Great in 335 B.C., came from a Celtic community already established in the eastern Alps, this date would have to be put back rather over half a century. But they may have come from Cisalpine Gaul; and I think this is the view now generally held.

[3] E.g. the Harudes in Ariovistus' army. Elsewhere the name is known only in Denmark and Norway.

[4] Down to the late third century. Then we hear of the Burgundians, later of the Saxons, and later again of fragments of other peoples from north and east of the lower Elbe.

parently not penetrated to the south or west of the Zuyder Zee.[1] But, in spite of what Tacitus says, or rather implies, to the contrary, the population of western Germany must still have been very mixed. Gaulish seems to have been widely spoken, not only by slaves, but perhaps also by whole communities, who had attached themselves to successful German princes, and were gradually being Germanised. It must be repeated that the Romans were apparently unable to distinguish Gaulish from German. They might be expected to know something about the seeress of the Bructeri, who caused them great trouble in the war of A.D. 69–70. But they knew no name for her except the Gaulish word for 'seeress' (*veleda*). On the whole, so far as language is concerned, the conditions seem to have been similar to what they were in England during the earlier part of the Saxon period. The Germany—west Germany—known to Tacitus was by no means the ancient home of the Teutonic peoples, but a region which had been conquered and settled by Germans within comparatively recent times.

In any discussion as to the origin of the Teutonic (or Germanic) languages it must of course be borne in mind that these languages are merely a branch of the Indo-European languages (called Indo-Germanic in Germany), and consequently that their original home —as distinct from the area in which they acquired their special characteristics—was that of the whole Indo-European family. The same remark applies to the Celtic languages, Greek and other members of the family.

Languages of the Indo-European family are now spoken over nearly the whole of Europe and a considerable part of south-west Asia, together with India; and it is known that formerly they were widely current in other parts of Asia, north of the great mountain ranges. No one doubts that these languages, or rather the parent language from which they are derived, were once limited to a much smaller area than that of their present distribution. But it is a matter of much dispute where this area lay.

Last century it was generally thought that their original home was in Asia, chiefly because Sanskrit is the oldest known of them and preserves what seem to be the earliest forms. Many scholars at one time gave to the whole family the name 'Aryan', which properly belongs only to the peoples and languages of Ariana (Iran) and the peoples who from there invaded India in the second millennium (B.C.).

[1] Leyden (*Lugdunum Batavorum*) was a Celtic town belonging to a people who seem to have been German.

But about the middle of the century it was suggested—first by d'Omalius d'Halley and R. G. Latham—that the original home was rather to be sought in Europe. Latham argued that only one group in the family—as was then thought—belonged to Asia, as against seven groups belonging to Europe. The new view did not make much headway until *c.* 1880 when it was taken up by Linden-schmit and other archaeologists, who favoured northern Europe and more especially the Teutonic area. They were brought to this conclusion by the results of excavation, which seemed to show that no change had ever taken place in the physical characteristics of the inhabitants of Scandinavia and the adjacent parts of Germany, and that civilisation in the same region had had an organic and unbroken development from the Stone Age. The inference was that the Teutonic group of languages was the original stock, and that all the other groups, Greek, Italic, Indo-Iranian, etc., were offshoots from it, due to movements of population and conquests. And the original Indo-Europeans must have belonged to the Nordic race.

This view did not at first gain much acceptance among philo-logists. Many of them indeed were inclined to favour Europe; but the majority favoured a modification of the original view, locating the original homeland on the steppe north of the Black Sea, or perhaps somewhat farther east, on the borders of Europe and Asia. The evidence of linguistic palaeontology seemed especially favour-able to the steppe—the life of pastoral people, cattle-keepers and shepherds, who were familiar with the horse and the use of wheeled vehicles from the earliest times.

In the course of the last thirty years this question has passed beyond the bounds of purely academic controversy in Germany. The contention of the prehistoric archaeologists, that the Teutonic area was the original home of the Indo-European languages, has come to be a political doctrine, and has produced a considerable volume of popular literature. The term 'Aryan' has been revived for the people who spoke the original Indo-European language. They are identified with the original Teutonic people—though practically they are re-garded as Germans—and with the Nordic race. The other Indo-European languages arose out of expeditions which set out from this homeland in all directions, west, south and east, on a career of conquest; for they are held to have been an essentially warlike people. These bands of conquerors became ruling castes in the countries where they settled. They were everywhere a Herrenvolk or Herrscher-volk. Usually they became more or less assimilated in the course of time to the native populations. But their original character may be traced in the traditions of Rome, Greece and India, while their (Nordic) appearance is preserved in the traditional representations of deities and heroes in Greek art. Sometimes more extravagant claims have been advanced, to the effect that the most ancient civilisations of the East were derived from the same people; but these need not be taken too seriously.

There is no doubt that the present wide distribution of the Indo-European languages, from the Atlantic to India—formerly also to eastern Turkestan—implies great movements of population from very early times, perhaps from the third millennium (B.C.). It is also clear that these movements must often have been of a more or less military character and in the nature of conquests. We may cite (e.g.) the evidence of the Rgveda relating to the Aryan conquests in India. For such wars of conquest the pastoral peoples of the steppe were exceptionally well qualified, owing to their mobility and their wealth in horses. In Europe, too, evidence for the existence of such warrior peoples goes back to very early times—the centuries before and after 2000 B.C. It may be found especially in the battle-axes, stone and metal, which are widely distributed throughout the north of Europe, from the Atlantic to the Caucasus. The question, however, is whether the general trend of such movements was from west to east, or from east to west.

In their treatment of this question the early prehistoric archaeo-logists, such as Lindenschmit, were guilty of a serious historical mistake, to which their successors, especially in Germany have adhered. They recognised, correctly, that the usual trend of the movements of warrior peoples would naturally be in the direction of richer lands than those they were leaving. They knew also that such movements had taken place within historical times. But they made the mistake of supposing that these movements were all from west to east, or from north-west to south-east. They cited the case of the Gauls who invaded Anatolia c. 275 B.C., and that of the Goths who in the third century (A.D.) conquered Rumania and the Ukraine. But they overlooked the long series of invasions of Europe from Asia which came by way of the steppe. The last and best known of these was that led by Batu Khan in 1237–41, which ravaged Poland and Hungary, and in Russia nearly reached Novgorod. Similar invasions are recorded to have taken place every two or three centuries before that time. We may instance those of the Cumani or Polovci in the eleventh century, the Pečenegs and Magyars in the late ninth century, the Avars in the sixth century, the Huns in the fourth. Still earlier examples are those of the Iranian peoples—the Alani, the Sarmatians and the Scythians.

The south-eastward movements of the Gauls and the Goths were not the first of their kind. A similar movement had brought the Phrygians into Anatolia many centuries before the Gauls, and in all probability the Hittites had travelled along much the same route still earlier. But it must be observed that this series of movements is not the reverse of the movements from east to west. The course of the latter series was clearly along the steppe, north of the Caspian and the Black Sea, whereas this series either stopped at the Black Sea or proceeded across the straits into Anatolia. I do not know of any movement of population along the steppe from west to east.[1] The rich lands of the Ukraine and the cultivated regions west of it offered plenty of attraction to the nomads of the steppe. They were one of the earliest homes of civilisation in Europe. But there was nothing to the north of the Caspian or in the Aral region which could tempt the inhabitants of the Ukraine to traverse the steppe in that direction. How then are we to account for the former presence of Iranian peoples on the steppe or for the Tochari, who also spoke an Indo-European language, in Chinese Turkestan? It was presumably from the eastern steppe that the Aryans (Indo-Iranians) set out to conquer Iran and India. The historical evidence therefore, so far as it goes, is wholly in favour of a movement from east to west.

As regards the linguistic evidence it has been mentioned that philologists were rather slow to accept northern Europe as the home of the Indo-European languages. Attempts have been made during the last thirty years to show that the vocabulary points in this direction. Thus it has been urged that the original language had words for the eel and the salmon, which are said not to be found in the Black Sea area. But this statement seems to have been successfully refuted in the case of the eel; and indeed none of the evidence is of a convincing character.

On the other hand, the general trend of the movements of languages, so far as we can trace it, has been from east to west. In the fifth and sixth centuries the Teutonic and Slavonic languages moved westwards. Before the fifth century the steppe and even parts of Hungary and Russia were occupied by Iranian peoples, who must have come from farther east. After the fourth century these peoples

---

[1] Ermak's expedition, in 1580, was through the forest country far to the north of the steppe; and the number of his followers seems to have been very small. The Russian expansion eastward in more recent times can hardly be compared with the movements which we are considering.

were displaced by Turkish peoples, who had come from still farther east. An indication as to the boundary between the Teutonic and Slavonic languages at an early date—probably the early centuries of our era—is given by the word 'beech', which was borrowed by the latter from the former. The beech is said not to grow east of a line between Odessa and Königsberg; and consequently the boundary must have been to the east of this line down to the time of the borrowing. I suspect, however, that the encroachment of Slavonic upon Teutonic began long before this. Otherwise it is difficult to account for the origin of so many—apparently very early—loan words from Teutonic, e.g. the words for 'goose' and 'husband's mother'.

In central Europe evidence for a large-scale western movement is to be found in the expansion of the urnfield culture about, or shortly before, 1000 B.C. Reasons have been given above for regarding this expansion in the Alpine regions and in France as Ligurian, though in a later period—the sixth and fifth centuries—the Ligurians were in most regions conquered by the Celts. But the Celtic area itself was affected by the urnfield movement. Did the Celts themselves, or rather their language, also come into western Germany at this time? Or were they already settled there in the time of the 'tumulus' culture? I do not think that at present we are in a position to answer such questions. We can only point to the existence at some time of linguistic frontiers, which may have been due either to natural (or other) barriers which hindred communication, or to dislocations in the process of expansion. It is likely enough that the expansion had begun centuries before the urnfield movement. The Ligurian language too may have been current in the Alpine region before this movement. On the other hand, since movements into Italy must have taken place before this time, it is quite possible that the language in the earlier period may have been nearer to Latin. But I doubt if any of the differences between the Celtic, Ligurian and Italic (Latin) languages can be traced to much earlier times. I would prefer to describe all earlier movements of expansion in this region as 'West Indo-European'; and I would apply the same term to the Unjetice and Lausitz cultures.

It is very probable, if we may judge from the analogy of the great movements of peoples in historical times, that the expansion of the Indo-European languages was commonly due to conquest, and consequently that the peoples who brought these languages with them were warrior peoples. And there is a more or less general tendency to connect the expansion with those cultures which seem to have been of the most warlike character—those which are known as the 'battle-axe' cultures. The stone battle-axe is found throughout the northern half of Europe. In western Germany, as in this country, it overlaps with the 'beaker' culture, which came from the south-west. Its appearance in both areas may be dated very early in the second millennium, in the Elbe basin perhaps somewhat earlier. One special variety is of frequent occurrence in Saxony and Thuringia and also in Jutland. The graves in which it is found are individual graves, with contracted bodies: and it is regularly associated with the pottery known as 'corded ware'. The graves and their contents are so similar that there can be no doubt of an intimate connection between the two regions. The same pottery is found in Poland, again in individual graves; and its influence may be traced in one type of beaker pottery. Here too the graves are individual graves, with contracted bodies; but the battle-axes are of a somewhat different type.

It has been observed that in Jutland these individual graves first appear in the interior, at a time when the megalithic culture, with collective tombs and a different funerary furniture, still prevailed on the coasts. Later, they gradually superseded the megalithic culture on the coasts, and then in the islands. The battle-axe culture therefore, to which they belong, must have come into the country by land, i.e. from the south. The Elbe region would seem to be its earlier home.

About the same time a similar culture, likewise found in individual graves, appears in southern Sweden. Here the battle-axes are of a somewhat different type, generally known as 'boat-axes'; and in place of the corded ware there is found a globular type of pottery, with impressions of cord. Eventually this culture met the Jutland culture in the Danish islands. But its original connections were with Poland, where boat-axes are also found, and where the globular pottery seems to be more frequent than the corded ware. This culture extends also eastwards into Russia. It would seem to have made its way to Sweden through Pomerania.

Many archaeologists are now inclined to the view that these individual graves mark the appearance of a new people, whom some describe as Teutonic, others as Indo-European. No objection can be taken to the former description for the Swedish graves. But, if the Jutland culture came from Saxony and Thuringia, it can hardly have been Teutonic in origin; for this region would seem not to have come into Teutonic hands until a thousand or fifteen hundred years later. In any case the term Indo-European is much more appropriate for such remote times.

It may be argued that, if the individual graves mark the appearance of Indo-European invaders in Scandinavian lands, they ought to have the same significance in this country; and indeed there can be little doubt that the two sets of movements were connected. Yet many writers, both archaeologists and philologists, are unwilling to allow that an Indo-European, i.e. presumably Celtic, language was introduced into this country at such a remote date. They point out that beakers have very seldom been found in Ireland, and also that, if a Celtic language had been introduced so early, it would inevitably have come to differ from the Celtic languages of the Continent much more than our earliest linguistic evidence will allow. These arguments have without doubt considerable force; and hence it would seem probable either that the influence of the battle-axe culture was merely indirect or that the element derived from this culture among the invaders was too small to retain its own language. In Scandinavia, on the other hand, the invaders, at least in Sweden, may have belonged wholly to the battle-axe culture; and they may have been reinforced later—which seems not to have been the case in Britain.

It has been mentioned above that the boat-axes and the globular pottery found in Sweden appear also not only in Poland, but also farther to the east, in Russia. The evidence indeed seems to indicate that the battle-axe culture in general came from this quarter. Note may be taken of the fact that copper battle-axes are found occasionally even in Poland, and become more frequent farther east, as also in Hungary. In the Ukraine also both the copper and the stone battle-axe are found. The latter are thought originally to have been copies of the former, made by persons in remote districts who had no metal. The copper axes themselves can be traced to the Kuban region, north of the Caucasus, and are evidently derived from ancient Mesopotamia. It would seem then that the movement of the battle-axe culture was from east to west or north-west, starting from the steppe.

It may be observed here that very little metal seems to have been available in northern Europe down to *c.* 2000 B.C., or even for some three centuries later. It may also be observed that, to judge from the linguistic evidence, the civilisation of the original Indo-European period was clearly chalcolithic. Metal was known; but we cannot tell how abundant it was. The conditions shown by the battle-axe cultures would seem to be quite compatible with the linguistic evidence. If the steppe was the original home of the Indo-European languages, the portions of the population which expanded towards the Baltic would be those who would find most difficulty in obtaining metal.

Lastly, the identity of the Teutonic peoples with the Nordic race cannot seriously be maintained. No doubt these peoples, especially in the north, contain a large Nordic element. But the same is true of peoples to the east of the Baltic, and not only peoples who speak Indo-European languages—Baltic and Russian—but also peoples who speak languages of the Finnish family. Moreover it is said that the skeleton remains in the ochre graves of south Russia, dating from before and after 2000 B.C.—the battle-axe period—show much the same characteristics. The Nordic race then would seem to have occupied the steppe in prehistoric times; and this is borne out by the very striking description given by Ammianus Marcellinus, XXXI 2, 21, of the Alani, the last Iranian people in this region. When the Alani were driven from the steppe by the Huns, in the fourth century, the change was not one of language only, but also of race, as may be seen by a comparison with the same author's description of the Huns (XXXI, 2, 2; cf. Jordanes, cap. 24, 35). Before the coming of the Huns, the first Turkish people, the whole of the steppe would seem to have been occupied by Nordic peoples; for the Alani were said to be identical with the Massagetae, who in earlier times lived around the Aral Sea.

The theory that the Teutonic peoples were a Herrenvolk or Herrschervolk from the earliest times, owing to certain innate qualifications, was probably suggested by a consideration of their achievements in the fifth century, when they established themselves as possessors or rulers of the greater part of Europe. But it is to be remembered that this process of expansion involved the loss of their eastern territories. A very close analogy is to be found in the expansion of the Celtic peoples some eight or nine centuries earlier. The Celtic peoples were a great Herrenvolk in the age which preceded the rise of the Roman Empire; but their expansion too was followed by the loss of much of their original territories. A much earlier—prehistoric—analogy may be found in the expansion of the true Aryans or Indo-Iranians who, setting out doubtless from the eastern steppe, conquered great parts of south-western Asia and India in the second millennium (B.C.). They too were a great Herrenvolk, in Asia from the eighteenth century, in eastern Europe from the time of our earliest records—perhaps the seventh century B.C.—down to the third or fourth century A.D. And these vast conquests were by no means limited to peoples who spoke Indo-European languages. We may instance the conquests of the various Turkish peoples, from the fourth to the fifteenth century—from the Huns to the Osmanli Turks. In our era indeed the Turks have been the greatest of all 'Herrenvölker'.

And it is not only the steppe which has produced Herrenvölker. They may arise anywhere from communities of nomad shepherds who occupy large open spaces, without natural barriers. We may refer to the immense conquests made by the Arabs in the seventh century. Instances in more recent times and on a much smaller scale may be found in the Fulani and the Bahima of western and central Africa. Where no protection is given by nature or by any external power, shepherd peoples must develop their military strength, to defend their flocks. Then defence may turn to aggression; the shepherd becomes a wolf towards his own species. And, when such a community has overcome rival communities of the same character as itself, it is commonly attracted to the conquest of peaceful agricultural communities, at whose expense it may enrich itself by robbery and the slave-trade. The great advantages which the nomads possess against settled communities are those of speed and mobility. Military organisation too is more easily carried out by them. Terrorism and atrocities regularly accompany their movements.

When a country has been conquered, the nomads usually settle down as a ruling class among the conquered population. Their nomadism is given up; but their military organisation is preserved, in order to secure their conquests. And for long ages their young men are encouraged to follow their princes in raiding expeditions, which may lead to further conquests.

It was largely by such processes that the map of Europe was shaped. The former process may be seen in eastern Europe in the devastations carried out by irruptions from the steppe, the latter in central Europe by the expansions of the Celtic and Teutonic peoples and, later, by that of the Osmanli Turks. The conquerors seldom gave much attention to agriculture, but left it in the hands of subject peoples. In later times, when the Teutonic peoples had acquired great power and wealth through the conquest of the Roman empire, the superiority of the conquerors, who continued to be primarily military, to the natives, who were landworkers and artisans, was recognised everywhere.

It is these processes which have supplied the models for modern German ideology. The cardinal doctrine is that the conqueror must be superior to the conquered, and that the German people is proved by its victories in ancient and recent times to be innately superior to all other peoples. Only the mistakes and dissensions of their rulers —due to ·the malign influence of the Church and the insidious operations of the Jews—have prevented them from achieving the domination of the world, which is their due. This is of course the crude form in which the doctrine is preached by political demagogues.[1] But I fear that it differs little from that which is commonly taught in schools. It would be disowned by the more cultured and learned elements in the country; but even among them the gratifying feeling of racial superiority is a powerful factor in their psychology— a factor which leads them to condone the ghastly atrocities ordered by their government. They would not themselves be guilty of authorising such atrocities; but they are prepared to acquiesce in whatever steps their government thinks necessary for the maintenance of German supremacy. Perhaps they may console themselves with Treitschke's words:[2] 'The Germans let the primitive Prussian tribes decide whether they should be put to the sword or thoroughly Germanised. Cruel as these processes of transformation may be, they are a blessing for humanity. It makes for health that the nobler race should absorb the inferior stock.'

[1] Including persons in high official position. We may instance a broadcast speech by Dr Frank, governor of German-occupied Poland, reported in *The Times*, 24 December 1940: 'It is the greatest gift of heaven to be able to call oneself a German, and we are proud to master the world as Germans.'

[2] *Politics*, I, 121 (Engl. transl.).

POSTSCRIPT to p. 154.

The term *Hercynia* (*silva*, etc.) is treated by Latin and Greek authors as a proper name; but this may have been due to a misunderstanding, like the personal name *Veleda* (cf. p. 157). In Celtic the term may have been applied to any oak-forest. The argument based on the name *Hercuniates* therefore must nòt be pressed. It may have been taken from the local forest, now called Bakony—which, together with the valley of the Raab, had presumably belonged in the past to the Aravisci, a Pannonian (i.e. Illyrian) people. But I see no reason for doubting that the Celtic invaders had come to this region through Bohemia.

CHAPTER IX

YESTERDAY AND TO-MORROW

TOWARDS[1] the end of last century the German government embarked on a great policy of expansion, which took two main forms. One was the 'colonial' policy, which aimed at expansion overseas. Actually this movement had begun as far back as 1884–5, when large territories were acquired in Africa. From about the end of the century it began to arouse much misgiving in this country and elsewhere; and dangerous situations arose from time to time, especially the incident at Agadir in Morocco, in 1911. The other form of the policy, however, was in reality more dangerous. It aimed at expansion towards the south-east—through the Balkans, and thence throughout the Turkish empire. The Turkish government was weak, the administration was corrupt, and it was generally believed that the empire was approaching dissolution. The free Balkan states were preparing to take possession of those parts of it (in Europe) in which the populations were of the same nationalities as themselves, though unfortunately they were not in agreement with one another as to the nationality of certain districts. Between the Reich and the Balkans lay the Austro-Hungarian Monarchy, which was itself distracted with discord among its many nationalities; indeed it was itself commonly believed to be near a collapse. The Monarchy was in close alliance with the Reich, which in general guided its policy, and regarded itself as its heir. In the Balkans the chief object of the policy of the Reich was to push Austria forward to Salonica, and to absorb or control the free Balkan states. In Asiatic Turkey the Reich pursued a policy of infiltration, especially by the Baghdad railway project, by which it was hoped to extend German power to the Persian Gulf.

In 1908 a revolution took place in Turkey, which at first seemed likely to revive its power. Then Prince Ferdinand of Bulgaria proclaimed himself king; and the Austrians annexed the provinces of Bosnia and Hercegovina, which they had occupied as a temporary measure since 1878. This annexation brought the Balkan states to compose their differences for a time; and in 1912 they united to

[1] The purpose of the following brief survey is to present in broad outline the chief features in recent history and in the present situation which come within the scope of this book, and in particular to call attention to certain elements which have hardly received sufficient notice in this country.

make war on the Turks, whom they drove out of the whole peninsula, except eastern Thrace. Then the Bulgarians claimed Macedonia and western Thrace as their share; but they were defeated by the Serbians and Greeks. The result therefore was a great increase of territory and power to these two states—which had now become a serious obstacle to the Austro-German advance to Salonica.

War on a greater scale was now generally regarded as inevitable, for Russia had pledged its support to the Serbians. But the immediate cause of the first World War was the murder (in June 1914) of the Archduke Franz Ferdinand at Sarajevo, in which the Austrians charged the Serbian government with complicity. But in any case, owing to the trend of events in the Balkans and the precarious position in Austria—where the emperor was eighty-four years old—the Germans could not have afforded to wait much longer, without endangering the success of their schemes.

In the meantime Italy, though in alliance with Germany, went to war with Turkey in 1911, because the Turkish government had impeded Italian colonisation in Tripolitana. In 1911–12 the Italians conquered all Tripolitana and Cyrenaica, and then seized Rhodes and the neighbouring islands. The seizure of these islands was declared to be a temporary measure—until all Turkish troops had been withdrawn from Africa—but no attempt was ever made to restore them.

There is no need here to enter into the history of the first World War (1914–18). The Germans' complete readiness for war, for which they had long and constantly been preparing, and their policy of taking the offensive and overrunning neutral territories without hesitation—all this, combined with the central (geographical) position of their country, gave them at the outset an advantage which it took their enemies over four years to redress. Temporarily they came into possession, or at least complete control, of most of the regions on which they had set their hearts. Their armies occupied Belgium and a considerable part of France, Russian Poland, the Austrian borderlands and the greater part of the Balkans. They never actually reached Salonica, and only a few of their troops penetrated into Turkey. But their officers were in all parts of the Turkish Empire; and the Turkish armies were usually under their command. All this of course came to an end in the latter part of 1918, when first their allies, and then the Germans themselves, had to sue for peace. But it is to be noted that there was practically no fighting in Germany itself.

The history of the negotiations which followed the armistice

(11 November 1918) is the story of a great conception which led to disastrous failure. President Wilson's scheme (first published on 8 January 1918), on which the negotiations were founded, was designed to settle international relations on a permanent foundation of peace and good will. But, as we look back to it now, after a quarter of a century, we can see that it had one inherent and fatal weakness; and in other respects the circumstances of the time were against it. Nevertheless, with important modifications, it ought to serve as the basis of any future settlement. At least it is difficult to see any reasonable alternative.

The inherent weakness of the scheme was that it made no adequate provision for its own preservation or protection. Wilson and his colleagues, except perhaps the French, seem not to have fully realised that the Reich had a distinctive character—a traditional policy of its own—which it had inherited from the kingdom of Prussia. This character was—and still is—radically immoral. It does not recognise the principles of international law, which are now accepted by nearly all the rest of the civilised world. It does not admit the rights of any other state which conflict with its own interests. It attaches little value to the preservation of peace: on the contrary, it believes firmly in the 'arbitrament of the sword', and for this purpose values its army above all else, and keeps it always ready to take the offensive. It holds that promises, engagements, treaties are binding only so long as they serve its own interests.[1] Much indignation was roused in this country in 1914 by Bethmann-Hollweg's reference to a 'scrap of paper'; but our government should have known that this doctrine was a traditional element in Prussian policy.

The initial mistake was made in receiving the application for an armistice from the Reich. It should have been made clear, before any such application was made, that an armistice would be granted only to the individual states. The Reich should not have been recognised.[2] The other states might have been granted better terms than Prussia, which has been the chief enemy of all other peoples and of peace, through its aggressions, militarism and ill faith. Prussia's influence might have been greatly reduced by limiting it to the territories owned by Brandenburg in 1600; and centrifugal tend-

[1] Cf. Treitschke, *Politics*, II, 597 (Engl. transl.): 'When a State recognises that existing treaties no longer express the actual political conditions, and when it cannot persuade the other Powers to give way by peaceful negotiation, the moment has come when the nations proceed to the ordeal by battle. A State thus situated is conscious when it declares war that it is performing an inevitable duty.' Cf. also I, 66 ff., where the author dwells upon the benefits of war.

[2] As a political institution. I am not speaking of the Zollverein.

encies might have been encouraged in the other states, none of which seems to have had so bad a record. Above all, the connection of East Prussia, whether with the Reich or with Brandenburg Prussia —which arose from the marriage of 1594 (cf. p. 132)—should never have been allowed to continue after the two regions had again been geographically separated by the restoration of Poland. If the Allies had adopted a stronger policy in these respects, it would probably have involved some prolongation of the war, at least in Prussia; but the resistance could hardly have been effective.

At the moment when the armistice was signed Germany was in a state of revolution. During the month of November (1918) all the reigning princes abdicated or were deposed, some of them even before the emperor. Power came into the hands of the Socialist Party, which had never been in office before. The rest of the population seemed to be stunned. But these conditions did not last. It soon became evident that the German people were not ripe for responsible democratic government, and that the revolution had been the work of a minority. The other parties had preferred to acquiesce in the revolution, rather than themselves to take the responsibility of admitting defeat and its consequences. Five years later the old general, Hindenburg, was elected president—virtually as a monarch—and nine years after that they came under a tyranny far worse than that of the emperor or any of his vassal princes.

The Allies apparently never claimed the right to intervene in the internal affairs of Germany. But the Germans may have been led to acquiesce in the revolution by an impression that as a democracy they would get better terms from the Allies. Possibly this impression may have been derived from a rather unfortunate speech by our Prime Minister on 5 January 1918. In any case the expulsion of the princes, except in Prussia, must now be regarded as a misfortune for the cause of peace. If they had remained, they would, as a centrifugal influence, have proved an obstacle to the schemes of nationalist demagogues.

The British and American governments were apparently not well informed about German feeling—especially the growth of nationalist feeling in the period before the war. They seem to have attributed too much importance to the influence of the emperor, and to have placed too much faith in the strength of German democracy. No doubt national feeling suffered a setback in 1918; but they did not realise that this was likely to be merely temporary. The French appreciated this factor much more clearly, though they regarded it merely as affecting their own country. They appealed for a continued occupation of the Rhineland and, when this was rejected, they sought for a pledge of military support from Britain and America, if they should be attacked again. The pledge was given for joint support; and it lapsed when the American Senate refused to ratify the Treaty. This disagreement eventually led to a divergence between British and French policy, which lasted for some years.

Our statesmen seem not to have realised that the war, with all its evils, was a direct result of the military ambitions which the Germans had long been cherishing. Consequently they did not recognise the absurdity of declaring that the Germans and the Entente Powers should have equal treatment in regard to disarmament. If they thought that the revolution would bring about any lasting change in German policy, subsequent events have shown how greatly they were mistaken.

No proposals seem to have been made for the League to have an army of its own or to acquire or occupy territory.

Apart from the negotiations relating to Germany, the circumstances of the time at which it was founded were unfavourable to the League.

Russia after the revolution had withdrawn from the war, and took no part in the peace negotiations. It did not join the League until many years later.

Italy was a source of great difficulty throughout. Italian policy was governed by the desire for expansion and aggrandisement, which was incompatible with the principles of the League. The British and French were not in a position to oppose this policy, because they had agreed (in March 1915) to the discreditable Pact of London. Italy had been in alliance with Germany and Austria down to the outbreak of war in 1914; but, when war broke out, the Italians demanded large cessions of Austrian territory as the price for their military support. The Austrian government refused to grant this demand; and eventually the Italians offered their support to the Entente Powers, in return for which the latter guaranteed their demands—for they feared that France would be gravely endangered if it was attacked from the south-east, as well as from the north-east. The Americans, when they entered the war, refused to endorse this Pact, because only a portion of the territories claimed by Italy was inhabited by an Italian population; the population of the greater part was Croatian, Slovenian and German. In October 1918, when Austria was collapsing, the Croatians and Slovenians established themselves as an independent Yugoslav ('South-Slavonic') state, and called Serbian troops in to help them. On 31 October the

Austrian emperor recognised this state, and transferred to it the Austrian fleet. But that night the flagship *Viribus Unitis*, with the Croatian admiral on board, was blown up in the harbour at Pola by Italian naval officers.

In the subsequent peace negotiations Wilson adhered to the principle that the frontiers should be drawn in accordance with the boundaries of the nationalities; but the Italians demanded the fulfilment of the Pact. A deadlock resulted; and the Italians took little part in the further negotiations. Eventually the question was settled by a compromise (in November 1920), after the Americans had withdrawn. The Italians gave up their claims to Dalmatia, except Zadar, but acquired possession of districts in the north inhabited by nearly half a million Slovenians and Croatians. In the meantime (on 12 September 1919) Fiume had been seized by D'Annunzio with a band of Italian volunteers. Successive Italian governments evaded the restoration of the port, though they did not openly defend its seizure; and it still remains in Italian hands.

The formation of the League of Nations had been an integral part of the peace treaties. But the League did not actually come into existence until 10 January 1920.

The United States, though responsible for the creation of the League, was not a member of it, owing to the refusal of the Senate (on 25 November 1919) to ratify the Treaty—a most disastrous decision which, more than any other event, has been responsible for all the bloodshed and horrors of the last five years.

Russia did not join the League until 1934, and Germany was not admitted until 1926. At the beginning the chief states were Britain France, Italy and Japan; and of these the two latter were pursuing policies directly opposed to the principles of the League. It was therefore a most precarious existence which the League entered upon.

Not only had France failed to obtain the guarantee of protection which she desired; Poland and Czecho-Slovakia, and a number of smaller nations bordering on Germany, were likewise left without protection. The League possessed no forces of its own collectively; and the regulations in the Covenant relating to mutual help proved to be difficult to carry out, even in disputes between members of the League. Italy remained in possession of Fiume; and the unauthorised seizure of Vilna by a Polish general led to the incorporation of that city and district by Poland. War broke out between Poland and Russia in 1920, as a result of which the former annexed certain regions which had belonged to it before the Partition (cf.

p. 25), but which are inhabited by a Russian population. The Poles were successful, and retained possession of these regions down to 1939.

The western Powers, Britain and France, were mainly occupied with 'Reparations' and other financial and economic questions; and they did not work together harmoniously. The French were always inclined to take a stronger line, while the British favoured leniency. The French also strongly supported the movement for a separate 'Republic of the Rhineland', which the British discountenanced. Then, in 1923, the French occupied the Ruhr—another movement of which the British disapproved. In the latter part of 1924, however, the French withdrew, and more accord was reached.

In the meantime German nationalism was recovering. The German army had been reduced to 100,000 men by the Treaty; but potential armies were being trained on a large scale by political parties. It was believed also that a large proportion of the arms, which were to be surrendered according to the Treaty, was withheld and concealed. The movement back to nationalism and militarism became more pronounced each year. Yet successive British governments apparently paid little attention to this movement, while the British public generally were engrossed with domestic questions, and seem to have lost interest in Continental affairs. Our governments, however, continually pressed for disarmament—which indeed had been carried out here very soon after the Treaty. Since Germany had been disarmed by the Treaty, this pressure was tantamount to a demand that our former allies should expose themselves to a war of revenge. The plea which was put forward—'equal treatment for victor and vanquished'—revealed a fundamental misunderstanding of the situation and of German psychology. It is true that the negotiations did induce the Germans to sign treaties of non-aggression with France and other nations—at Locarno in 1925—but subsequent events have shown how much that was worth.

It is hardly necessary to continue the story further—how the results of the war were gradually thrown away through ignorance and groundless optimism. Hitler was appointed Chancellor in 1933, and acquired full power on Hindenburg's death in the following year. But the way had been prepared for him by von Papen, who seems to have had influence with Hindenburg, and had been Chancellor twice during the preceding years. From 1934 at latest it should have been clear to everyone that things were hastening to a catastrophe. We may instance the successive repudiations of treaties and the enormous preparation of munitions, which was itself a direct

violation of the Versailles Treaty. Among other noteworthy incidents which illustrate the character of the new regime we may
instance the massacre of 30 June 1934, including the murder of
Schleicher, the murder of Dollfuss, also in 1934, and the trial for
the burning of the Reichstag in 1933. Worst of all was the persecution
of the Jews, which began in 1933 and was soon followed by the
establishment of concentration camps for the various classes of people
opposed to the new regime. Then came the institution of the Gestapo
and, in short, all the characteristics and machinery of an irrespon-
sible tyranny.

In aggression against foreign nations, however, Italy was the first
to move. In 1935 the Italians embarked on the conquest of Abyssinia, partly to secure possession of that country and partly to avenge
the defeat of a previous attempt at conquest nearly forty years before.
The League of Nations, led by our government, exerted such powers
as it possessed to check the invasion, but received little support from
France. Indeed, there seems to have been a general fear that, if the
Italians were thwarted, they would unite with Germany. It was
apparently not realised that sooner or later the two aggressors were
bound to combine. Then came the demand made upon France for
the cession of various territories; for Mussolini thought that the
domination of the Mediterranean was now within his grasp. The
next step was the seizure of Albania, which took place only a few
months before the outbreak of the present war.

By this time it was becoming clear to all that Germany was con-
templating aggression on a still greater scale. First came the annexation of Austria in the spring of 1938; no action was taken by the
Powers. Czecho-Slovakia was the next to be threatened; and here
Mr Chamberlain's unfortunate activities in the cause of peace merely
had the effect of stripping the Czechs of their defences. The occupation and dismemberment of their country soon followed; and
Poland's turn came next. But now the British and French governments had awakened; and the present war resulted.

Future historians will doubtless wonder why no concerted opposition, no united front, was offered to the German menace. Some
of the causes are clear enough: (1) the reign of isolationism in
America; (2) the Russian revolution and the subsequent strained
relations between that country and the western Powers; (3) the
selfish policy of Italy, which was directed, hardly less than that of
Germany itself, towards aggrandisement and aggression. French
policy and Polish policy will require more explanation. It would
seem that Polish statesmen were deceived by German pretences of

friendship, the object of which was to induce them to a forward policy in the Ukraine, so as to get them embroiled with Russia.[1] Our own government was unprepared and probably ill-informed. At all events the attitude of the general public was characterised by ignorance, negligence and groundless optimism. Even down to 1939 there were many people who believed that the Nazi Party would soon lose their power, and that a change would then take place in German policy.

When the war comes to an end our country and its allies will be faced with some serious problems. It may be well here to compare the conditions, so far as they can now be foreseen, with those which prevailed in 1919.

In some respects the outlook would seem to be more hopeful. Russia stands with the United Nations and is stronger than ever before. The new states in Central Europe, which had barely come into existence in 1919, have all been overwhelmed and ravaged; but in spite of that they will doubtless be in a better position, after twenty years' experience, to contribute to the common cause. Italy's ambitious schemes, which caused so much embarrassment in 1919, need no longer be taken into account. Above all, the true character of German ambitions and of German domination has been made abundantly clear to all the world.

In other respects the comparison is less advantageous. It will take France a considerable time to recover her strength. Much of the attention and the resources of the United Nations will probably have to be diverted to the Far East, where the war may last longer than in Europe. India is likely to be an embarrassment to this country.

If lasting peace is to be assured, the primary object which must constantly be kept in view by the United Nations is that of preventing the resuscitation of German military power. All schemes of economic reconstruction, however desirable, however pressing, must be treated as subordinate to that object.

Next to this main object is the prevention of discord—or, better, the promotion of friendly feeling—among the United Nations themselves. Care must also be taken to prevent the revival of military ambitions in Italy, or the growth of such ambitions in any other nation.

[1] This idea was current among the leaders of German political thought more than half a century ago, long before the restoration of Poland; cf. Treitschke, *Politics*, I, 132: 'It is doubtful...whether Poland will ever arise anew. Certainly never in its former shape, and the insensate obstinacy of the Poles would not accept compensations in the region of the Black Sea.'

The essential conditions of success are (1) the continuance of American co-operation, and (2) the preservation of complete unity of policy—and of action, when necessary—among the United Nations. The question whether the United Nations should possess an army of their own collectively is one which deserves careful consideration, although influential voices have declared against such a suggestion. Indeed, much might be said in favour of the collective possession of certain strategic territories occupied by such an army.

The problem of how to secure peace for the future should be viewed in the first place from the geographical side. Germany, with a population of between seventy and eighty millions—over eighty, if Austria be included—occupies a central position, surrounded by a number of states, of which the largest is slightly more than half its size; but most of them are very much smaller. All of these, except Switzerland, have been invaded and occupied during the present war. In most cases the attack has been made without warning, munitions, food-stores, livestock and other property seized, and many of the inhabitants carried off to work in war factories or, when resistance was offered, shot. In some countries many districts have been systematically devastated. All this is in accordance with the traditions of German (Prussian) warfare, which is essentially aggressive; consequently the fighting always takes place on foreign soil. Potential enemies are overthrown one by one; and even if the war proves unsuccessful, the fact remains that the invaded countries have suffered more and had their populations further reduced than that of the invaders.

The problem is how to prevent a recurrence of these aggressions. It needs no knowledge of strategy to see that what is required is a co-ordinated system of defence under a unified command, which could act without delay and check such attacks by counter-attacks from different quarters. And one would have thought that the most effective way of carrying out such a system would be through the occupation of certain frontier regions, such as Rhenish Prussia, Holstein and Silesia, by an international force strong enough to hold the invaders until larger (national) armies could be mobilised. All these are among the regions which have been appropriated by Prussia within the last two centuries.

If no such system is adopted, the neighbouring states will have, as at present, to bear the onset until more distant nations, the Russians, British and Americans, can come to their rescue; and much destruction and suffering may again be the result. It may be, however, that some measure is contemplated which is expected to render such attacks impossible in the future. The German (Prussian) army has done more injury and caused more suffering to mankind than any other body or institution that we have ever heard of; and no greater benefit could be rendered to the world than its total and final destruction. Are the United Nations prepared to take such steps as will secure this object—steps which must clearly involve some form of prolonged occupation? Or will they be contented, as in 1919, with half-measures—which are bound to lead again to disaster? Is it credible, after what has been experienced in Russia, Poland and elsewhere, that we shall hear any more of the foolish talk about 'equal treatment for victors and vanquished'?

The leaders of the United Nations have declared that war-criminals shall be brought to justice in those countries in which their crimes were committed. But what about the greatest of all war-criminals—the Reich itself—which ordered or authorised these atrocities? Is it to be allowed to continue a career which has been devoted to the preparation of injury to other nations and has twice bathed the world in blood?[1] In 1919 the mistake was made of negotiating with the Reich, instead of with its constituent states. It may be more difficult now to insist upon the independence of the states; but no other course offers any hope of security for the future.[2] A Reich which would be content to live in peace and friendly relations with the rest of the world is inconceivable.

Another mistake made in 1919 was that of encouraging or at least acquiescing in the expulsion of the princes. Subsequent events have shown that the German people are incapable of democratic government. The choice lies only between the dynastic rulers, whose interests lay in their own dominions, and dictators fired by dreams of world conquest. It is of course not unlikely that, when the war is drawing to a close and German prospects are seen to be hopeless, some democratic element will emerge—possibly it may even come into power, as at the end of 1918. But this will be merely ephemeral. How can those who have been trained to massacres and man-hunts become fitted for responsible self-government?

Economic questions will no doubt receive due attention. The most

[1] Two of the four chief characteristics of German policy—viz. the consistent practice of aggression and faithlessness in the observation of treaties—were already fully developed under the imperial regime. The other two—viz. the organisation of the machinery of persecution and the wholesale perpetration of atrocities—are in the main products of the present regime; but cases of 'Schrecklichkeit' were not rare in the first World War.

[2] It would be well also to insist on the restoration of the states and territories annexed by Prussia last century.

pressing need will be that of restoring or compensating in kind for the livestock and foodstuffs carried off from the countries which have been invaded by the German armies. But we need not enter into these problems here.

Is it credible that anyone among the United Nations will again misunderstand the cry for 'Lebensraum'? Events have shown that the expansion desired is to be obtained by superimposing a numerous German ruling class upon the conquered peoples. The chief duty of the latter is to provide agricultural and unskilled labour—for which purpose they are deported to Germany in large numbers.

The League—or whatever it may be called—of the United Nations ought to include among its activities a Bureau of Education. There can be little doubt that the evils of recent years have been largely due to the poisoning of the minds of the young by school teachers, who have been inculcating in them such doctrines as that might is right, that war is a desirable thing, and that the Germans in view of their superiority are entitled to dominate other peoples. It should be the duty of the Bureau to secure the dismissal of all teachers who are imbued with doctrines contrary to the principles of the League and the ethical standards of civilised humanity. If Germany cannot supply teachers free from such doctrines, the Bureau will have to provide otherwise for the education of German children.[1] Apart from this, the Bureau might be of great value in facilitating and promoting the exchange of knowledge between the students and the educational institutions of different countries.

Apart from questions relating to Germany as a whole, another difficult problem is presented by East Prussia, which is a German colony planted outside the limits of the German area and not geographically connected therewith (cf. p. 37). The political connection arose from a marriage between two ruling families (cf. p. 102). Events have clearly shown that the maintenance of this connection is incompatible with the security of Poland and with the peace of Europe.

There are other questions again which urgently require to be settled, though they are not concerned—at least not directly—with Germany. Some of these may be mentioned here.

[1] So far as I have observed, Mr Wallace seems to be the only one of the Allied leaders who has emphasised the vital importance of the educational problem; and I doubt if even he has fully appreciated its difficulty. German leaders have broadcast several times that we intend to take their children (to be educated in Russia, according to Hitler, 1 January 1944). I have not heard of any such intention on our part; but the Germans naturally attribute to us what they would themselves do if they were in our place.

The most serious problem is presented by eastern Poland. This region formed part of the Polish kingdom for over two centuries before the Partition; and it had been connected with Poland for two centuries farther back. In earlier times, however, its connections had been with Russia; and the majority of the population is still Russian. No more valuable contribution could be made to the peace of Europe than a satisfactory and amicable settlement of this question.

Next comes the question of those nations which have followed Germany into the war—not, apparently, through any special affection for that nation, but because they hoped to secure advantages for themselves thereby. Two of them, Hungary and Bulgaria, fought on the same side in the war of 1914–18. What steps should be taken to prevent any recurrence of this policy?

Hungarians and Rumanians have fought side by side in this war under German orders. But there can be little doubt that if they were left to themselves they would fight with one another for the possession of Transylvania, where the distribution of population has produced one of the sore spots of Europe. It is not easy to see how this can be cured, except by a transference of population or by the occupation of certain districts by international forces.

Other adjustments should be less difficult to effect. Rhodes and the neighbouring islands, where the population is Greek, should be allowed to settle their own destiny by ballot. And the wrong done to the Slovenians and Croatians by the treaty of 1920 (cf. p. 171 f.) should be rectified by the same process.

The right of self-determination, however, cannot fairly be pressed in the case of seaports where the population is of different nationality from that of the regions for which they are the natural, and perhaps only, outlets. We have seen this right usurped by violence at Fiume, Memel and Danzig; and we have no inclination to concede it. But the most important case is Trieste, which owes its existence to the fact that it is the seaport—the only seaport—for the East Alpine region, Slovenia and the lands beyond. It is an Italian linguistic island, which extends inland no great distance—perhaps three miles —from the sea. The Slovenian population comes down to the shore, I think, both north and south of the town.

These are only a few of the problems which will require consideration when the war is over. There are plenty of others, strategic, political and economic. Thus, if the United Nations collectively had forces of their own, they could effectively prevent any future attempts by Italy to close the Adriatic or to cut off the western from the eastern basin of the Mediterranean. Again, it would be a powerful hindrance to German aggression and intrigue if permanent political combinations of some kind could be formed between the Scandinavian kingdoms or the northern Slavonic states. Still more beneficial would be a union of all the southern Slavonic peoples, which would prevent the Bulgarians from being dragged into suicidal conflict with their neighbours. Then there are problems relating to the peoples of the Baltic, for which at present no sufficient data are available. But what I would emphasise is that, whatever steps the smaller states may take for their protection, they require the support of the great peace-loving Powers; and it is essential therefore that harmonious co-operation and, when necessary, concerted action among the latter should be secured. I need hardly add that, if this co-operation can be extended to economic and intellectual interests, all the states affected will gain thereby. But until it is established on an efficient and permanent footing the position in Europe will remain precarious.

POSTSCRIPT.

Since the above was sent to Press, great changes have taken place in the military situation; and, consequently, opinion as to the details of the post-war settlement is gradually assuming a more definite form. In a book of this kind, however, it is hardly possible to keep pace with the movement of events. So I have thought it best to make no change in what is printed above. On the whole the general trend of opinion seems to be satisfactory, though I think that more consideration should have been given to the independence of the (German) states (cf. p. 177).

CHAPTER X

OUR WEAKNESS AND ITS REMEDY

WE may now examine the situation as it affects our own country. On the whole we stand well with the peoples of Europe at present. It is recognised that we have no selfish aims,[1] at least in Europe. Our object is peace and freedom for all peoples. Moreover, we were the first to offer effective resistance to the common enemy. We have sheltered the governments and the patriotic elements who have escaped from the Continent. We have made unparalleled efforts in the common cause, and we have suffered greatly, even if not so greatly as the countries which have been conquered or invaded. Lastly, we have enabled America to bring its great resources to support the common effort.

On the other hand, British policy has met with adverse criticism, not without justice, in several important respects.

It was weak during the years 1934–9, especially as regards Austria and Abyssinia. Action would no doubt have been difficult in the latter case while Laval was in power, but it should have been foreseen from the beginning that both Italy and Germany were intending mischief, and that the two would probably join forces before long. When we did intervene—in the case of the Sudeten—the intervention was ill-advised, and its only effect was to injure and weaken a friendly nation.

During the war our action has been necessarily slow, owing to unpreparedness. From 1934 all possible preparations for mobilisation should have been taken in hand. Even during the first year of the war insufficient energy seems to have been shown. The tragedies which took place in the spring of 1940 might perhaps have been averted, if we had been better prepared.

Our Press and the general public were ill-informed and liable to

---

[1] Some governments which have remained neutral during the present war—whether through fear of German attack or to please certain anti-British elements among their own peoples—have defended their neutrality by representing the conflict as one which concerns only the Germans and ourselves. In point of fact, if we had been willing to follow a purely selfish policy and evade our responsibilities to the rest of the world, we could have averted the war from ourselves in 1939, and again probably in 1941, and doubtless gained much selfish advantage thereby. Such a course would have involved danger in the future, but hardly greater than that which we were actually encountering. Our policy may fairly be charged with ignorance and negligence, but not with selfishness. On the contrary it is due to us that the neutral states have been able to preserve their independence.

be buoyed up by groundless optimism; and it is widely suspected that the same was true of our government in the years before the war. Down to 1939, in spite of the repeated repudiations of treaties, it seems to have been generally believed that the differences with both Germany and Italy could be solved by conciliation and economic agreements. At the outbreak of war, and probably for some time previously, the Russian attitude seems to have been misunderstood. French political feeling seems likewise to have been misunderstood even during the first year of the war. And it may be doubted whether our knowledge of other countries was any better. There may of course have been experts in the government service who had a more accurate appreciation of the conditions and the feeling in foreign countries—indeed, it is known that some of them disapproved of the conciliation policy. If some rule or convention prevented their expert knowledge from gaining a hearing, this would seem to indicate a defect in our system of government.

It may be added here that our rule in India and other countries where the population is non-British is regarded abroad with rather widespread disapproval—especially perhaps in America. It has not been tyrannical or unjust, and it has benefited those countries by substituting a long period of peace for what was in many cases a state of chronic warfare. But the resident official class has in the past borne, and indeed commonly still bears, the character of a 'Herrenvolk'—expensive, aloof and unsympathetic; and educated people belonging to those countries feel that they themselves ought to have a larger share—if not the whole—of the administration in their own hands.

Setting aside for a moment the last case, the charges commonly brought against our policy in Europe are those of ignorance, negligence, lack of foresight, unpreparedness. No one can deny now that these charges were well founded for the period before the war; but it is not sufficiently realised that the three last were results of the first. It was Chamberlain's well-meant but unfortunate efforts for peace in 1938 which caused our ignorance of the European situation to be widely recognised; but they did no more than facilitate the development of a catastrophe which had been preparing for many years, but which had been ignored by successive British governments.

The point which I wish to emphasise is not that our government was ignorant of the German preparations for war. They had had warning of this at least as far back as 1935, though they had not paid sufficient attention to it. What I would stress is that apparently they were ignorant of German popular feeling. They seem not to have realised that the Nazi government was fully supported by a considerable proportion of the German people, including the great majority of the younger generation. The same mistake was made before the last war. It was not realised that in general the emperor was acting as his people expected him to act. And the present German government is more dependent upon popular support than the emperor's was. It is not certain that Hitler could have changed his policy, even if he had wished to do so, without risking his popularity with those elements in the population upon whose support he depended.

It was not only our government—one government after another —which was ignorant of the attitude of the German people. The same ignorance pervaded all classes and sections of our people. And, what is more strange, after all that has passed in the last four years, the same ignorance is still widely prevalent. It would seem that our present government, or at least some members of it, have now come to realise the true situation. But we still hear of resolutions passed by trade unions and other public bodies, exonerating the German people from the crimes committed in their name. How can a democracy which is so ill informed perform its functions successfully?

Moreover, it is not only the criminal nation about which we are ignorant. Still less is known of the nations which have been its victims. Except to a limited number of people who have gained some—more or less superficial—knowledge of these countries by visiting them for business purposes or for holidays, most of them are little more than names. There is a widespread feeling that Poland has always been an unfortunate country, and that the Balkans have always been a troublesome part of the world. But there our knowledge ends. Little is known even of Russia. Some believe—or did until yesterday—that no good can come from Russia, others that it may provide us with a panacea for all our troubles. But what definite knowledge have either party of Russia and its history, or of the distinctive and permanent characteristics of Russian life?

Yet these peoples are our allies. In the future we have got to stand by them for our mutual protection and benefit. We have responsibilities towards them. We have to learn to be 'good Europeans', as well as good Britons. How can we discharge our responsibilities towards these peoples when we know so little about them?

Again, how much do we know about India and many other countries which are under our rule? Have we no responsibilities towards them? They have their own needs and aspirations, towards which we could help them, if we knew more about them. But we must confess, I fear, that our knowledge is sadly defective. Is it any wonder that some of them want to be rid of us?

Wherever we turn, the same conclusion is forced upon us. Nothing has been more prejudicial to our security, nothing has done more to prevent us from discharging our responsibilities in Europe and in the empire, than our ignorance of other peoples. It is due of course to an antiquated system of education—an inheritance from times when our relations with the outer world were more limited and less important—a system which neither provides us with the knowledge which is needed nor stimulates us to acquire it for ourselves. Until such knowledge is acquired, and widely diffused among us, we must suffer the disadvantages which naturally fall to the lot of an ignorant person, when he has to deal with better-informed neighbours. But how is this defect to be remedied?

At present our educational system is under review. Important changes have already been made; and others are being discussed. But they are almost entirely concerned with schools, and as a rule more with the social than the intellectual side of these. The knowledge in which we are so deficient is a subject fitted in the first place and more especially—though not exclusively—for higher education.

It is to the Universities rather than the schools that the defect is due. The studies of the Universities have been governed by professional, rather than national, interests. This applies of course very much more to 'Arts' than to 'Science' studies. I am concerned here only with the former,[1] and indeed not with the whole of these. 'Arts' is of course an antiquated and ambiguous term. Some Universities include under this head various subjects, e.g. Law, Theology, Mathematics and Economics, which in other Universities are assigned to different Faculties. But I am concerned only with studies which in foreign Universities are sometimes described as 'humanistic', sometimes as 'literary and historical'—a group of studies which in this country is everywhere, I think, included in 'Arts'. Among them the chief subjects are Classics, English, Modern Languages and History. All of these are taken by large numbers of students, whereas the number of those who take other 'humanistic' subjects is insignificant. It is for these subjects that entrance scholarships are given; and each of them usually occupies the whole attention of the students who take it for a period of four or five years—counting both the time spent at the University and the last years before leaving school.

It is obvious that these four subjects have little or no direct bearing upon the needs of our time. And this fact is recognised in the laws

[1] What is said in the following pages has no reference to 'Science' studies.

relating to military service. Many 'Science' students are granted exemption, on the ground that their work is of national importance; but this is hardly ever granted to 'Arts' students.

Yet Arts, or at least 'humanistic', studies ought to be as valuable to the nation as Science studies—perhaps even in time of war, and certainly more so in the period which follows a war. Their potentialities could not be effectively mobilised in a moment, without preparation. But if they were carefully husbanded and developed, they could be of incalculable value. As it is, they are thrown away. Such studies are treated as something decorative and without practical value, except for the scholastic profession—something apart from the world of reality.

It is often contended of course that the study of the Classics, though not directly of practical use, provides the best foundation for study in other subjects. This may or may not be the case; I am not prepared to give an unqualified assent to it.[1] But in any case the argument is fallacious. The number of persons who pass on from it —at the age of 21–22—to the systematic study of other languages and peoples is extremely small; and the knowledge which these acquire is usually of a strictly professional character, such as is indispensable for official work in certain government services. I fear it is only rarely they acquire the intimate knowledge which is required by the conditions of the present time. English courses cannot contribute anything of value for the purpose we are discussing. Modern languages courses have a certain value for the study of language and literature, though as a rule very little[2] for that of the peoples themselves. But the number of students who take any language except French, German and Spanish is extremely small; and not very many take Spanish. History courses have a wider scope. But they are almost always limited to western and west-central Europe, and very little linguistic knowledge is required. Subjects and periods which involve a knowledge of any languages except Latin and French are in general avoided, though German, Italian and possibly Spanish may be required in some optional subjects which are taken only by a small number of students.

An appreciable proportion—perhaps about one-third—of the entrance scholarships in our Universities are awarded on the results of examinations in these subjects; and about the same proportion of the best brains among the youth of our country devote their time

[1] There is much to be said for it as a school subject, but not for making it occupy also the whole of a student's time at the University.
[2] In some Universities more than in others.

at the Universities to continuing their study of them.[1] They are among the most popular subjects in our Universities. It is true that other 'humanistic' subjects may also be taken; but no entrance scholarships are available for these, and students are generally discouraged from embarking upon them, because such subjects are not likely to be of service to them in their subsequent careers.[2]

The most promising of our students, when they have taken their degrees, frequently pass on to research. In the subjects which they have studied they have little prospect of being able to do more than explore some literary or historical minutiae which have not received sufficient attention from previous investigators. In the meantime by far the greater part of the modern world—perhaps more than nine-tenths of it—remains neglected and unknown; and so also all the ancient world, except Greece and Rome. But they are not in a position to undertake work in these wider fields of study. They have had no training to fit them for it; they do not know the languages; nor as a rule can they get advice here. If in spite of these drawbacks they are resolved to widen the scope of their studies, they must go to Germany, or at least devote long study to work which has been done by German scholars.

So it has come about that in our knowledge of nearly all the peoples of the world our Universities have been left behind by those of Germany and other foreign nations. And the indifference shown by them is no doubt largely responsible for the ignorance and lack of interest which prevails among the general public.

The four 'popular' subjects noted above may have seemed an adequate provision for education in 'Arts' subjects last century, when our University courses in these subjects assumed more or less their present form. It was then thought—and the same view is still widely prevalent, I fear—that knowledge of foreign peoples and of the peoples within the Empire was a matter only for officials in various government services who had received some special training for the purpose. The feelings of foreign and colonial peoples did not concern the Universities. The study of remote countries and useless languages could be left to foreign scholars, who had nothing better

[1] Some Universities allow students to divide their time between two subjects; but both of these are usually chosen from the popular ones.

[2] The scholarships and the hope of obtaining posts, especially in scholastic life, are two of the chief factors which determine the popularity of a subject. Very many students also prefer to continue subjects with which they have become familiar at school. They are afraid especially of new languages, believing them to be beyond their ability. I have found that, when tested, this belief almost always proves to be groundless. It is due to an antiquated educational tradition, which appeals only to memory, and not to the intelligence.

to do. The education of our own young people should be directed towards qualifying them for professional careers,[1] without regard to national or imperial interests. As for the general public, what was the use of trying to provide them with information for which they had no desire?

The experience of two ghastly wars, with all the mistakes which have been made through ignorance, both in war and in peace, should have taught us a different lesson. We can no longer live in isolation. Our safety and welfare and that of our allies demand mutual protection and help; and this can be secured only by a firm understanding, which must be based on mutual knowledge. The same is true of our relations with the non-British peoples within the empire. Everywhere the object should be to replace ignorance, misunderstanding and suspicion by a knowledge and understanding, not only of the political, social and economic conditions under which other peoples live, but also of their feelings and aspirations—such a knowledge as will enable us to appreciate and respect their feelings, even when they are in conflict with ours.

Our future and that of the world in general will be precarious for many years. All will depend upon our capacity for intelligent and friendly co-operation with other nations. On the other hand, there are signs enough that, just as after the last war, industrial disputes and schemes of reconstruction will divert our attention from foreign and imperial interests. No form of government is more liable to external danger than an ignorant and ill-informed democracy; and our only safeguard against the negligence which, as before, is bound to lead to disaster, lies in the acquisition and widespread dissemination of the knowledge of which I am speaking.

For this purpose it is necessary to secure the best brains in the rising generation and to provide them with such a training as will enable them to obtain the best possible knowledge and understanding of foreign peoples. Such knowledge and understanding cannot be acquired without learning the languages of the peoples concerned; and consequently this linguistic knowledge must be acquired—not for its own sake, but as a necessary means to the understanding of the peoples, their history, institutions, conditions of life and ideas.

I do not mean such a training as might in, say, a year's time

[1] Hence the restrictive regulations of all kinds and the excessive attention paid to examinations. Owing to the latter the majority of University teachers have their time fully occupied; and many of them are overworked. Time which might be devoted to research or to encouraging the better students has to be spent in 'tutorial' work, which is mainly concentrated upon enabling those who are backward or slack to pass their examinations.

qualify a candidate for official work in one of the government services. I mean the best course of study which can be obtained in a subject—equal if possible to the best courses in Classics which are available at any of our Universities. Such courses should not be reserved for those who are intending to enter government services, but should be open to all who are willing and qualified to take them. It may reasonably be hoped that many who have taken such courses will later contribute by their writings or by lectures to the dissemination of the knowledge they have gained. Encouragement should be given by scholarships and prizes. Among the better students research should be encouraged by every possible means.

Care should be taken not to copy the Universities in herding students by hundreds, like sheep, into a small number of pens. In view of the fact that we now have interests and responsibilities in nearly all parts of the world, the scheme of studies should be worldwide. The events of the last few years, however, have shown that the following regions require special attention: (1) Central Europe, with the Balkan Peninsula; (2) Russia; (3) the Near East (or 'Middle East'); (4) India; (5) the Far East, especially China; (6) Africa, or at least large portions of it; (7) Latin America. The Dominions and the United States likewise claim a greater share of attention than they have received in our educational system; but they differ from the regions just enumerated in the fact that they require no special linguistic study. In other respects too they are less unfamiliar. I shall leave them out of account therefore in what follows.

It will be seen that the four chief subjects in 'humanistic' studies contribute hardly anything to the study of any of the regions we have specified. Some of them, it is true, have a certain—though quite inadequate—provision[1] made for them, outside these chief subjects, while others are practically ignored in our educational system.

Let us first take India, though properly it does not fall within the scope of this book. There are hardly any peoples whom it is more important for us to know and to understand than those of India; yet I fear that in our schools and Universities Indian studies have been almost wholly ignored. Last century, it is true, chairs of Sanskrit were established in several Universities. But the number of students who have taken a full course in this subject has been very small—

---

[1] In the following paragraphs I have spoken only of provision for teaching. The provision for scholarships, etc., which is even more important, is very difficult to ascertain. But I fear that in most of the subjects noticed practically no funds are available for this purpose.

perhaps about one student per year in each University, and about half of these have been Indians. A somewhat larger number have taken a small amount of Sanskrit in connection with Latin and Greek. But both the full and the elementary courses are purely linguistic.[1] For Indian law and history and for a number of modern languages courses are provided in several Universities; but these, except perhaps in London, are of a professional character—intended for probationers in the Indian Civil Service, and usually limited to one year. So far as I am aware, there are no professorships in these subjects.

It is clear then that no attempt is made by the Universities, except perhaps London, to provide for Indian studies as our national interests demand; and even in London, I think, the courses are for the most part purely linguistic. How much importance is attached to these studies in some Universities may be gauged by the fact that all teaching in them, including Sanskrit, has been suspended during the war. This absence of interest in the Universities is reflected by a general ignorance and indifference in the country. A different feeling might have prevailed, if the Universities had taken Indian studies seriously.[2] Much might have been done, not only to make India better known, but also to remove prejudices and to bring about a more respectful and friendly attitude in the relations between the two countries.

Next take Africa. I am not aware that any University in this country possesses a professorship in any African subject except ancient Egypt. Lectures on some African languages are given in a few Universities; but I think that, except in London, they are of a purely professional character, and intended for probationers in various Civil Services. Some Universities also have lectures on African anthropology. But on the whole it must be confessed that African studies in our Universities are in their infancy.[3] Can they be said to exist at all in our schools? Yet many parts of Africa are moving fast. Important works have been produced by Africans on the history of their peoples; and it is clear that a feeling of national consciousness is arising. The Africans will soon be requiring Universities of their own; but in the meantime they look to us for help. Relations with Africa are important for us; but if good relations are

---

[1] It is perhaps worth remarking that most of the books chiefly used seem to be American or German, except those which are produced in India itself.

[2] E.g. by providing scholarships and research studentships on the same scale as for Classical studies, or even to the extent of a quarter of that amount. There are few subjects, if any, which more urgently call for research than Indian studies. What is done to encourage such research?

[3] Are any funds available for scholarships, etc., in these studies?

to be maintained, we must learn to know the Africans and to understand them. They are backward in civilisation. But are we Germans, that we should regard them as a permanently inferior race, and rule them for the sake of exploiting them? All traces of the 'Herrenvolk' idea should be got rid of. Neither should we indulge our own conceit by assuming that they must regard our presence among them as an unqualified blessing to them. What we should learn to acquire is a more respectful attitude, which can be attained only by knowledge and understanding. It is urgent therefore that a serious and widespread study of African peoples—not only their languages, but also their history, institutions and ideas—should be initiated without delay.

What about China? Professorships have been founded, and courses of instruction established in several of our Universities; but I fear that the number of students taking the subject has been almost negligible up to now.[1] Such knowledge as the general public possesses seems to be derived mainly from newspapers, and from stories and dramatic pieces which are too often of a silly character. Yet China has a longer unbroken history than any other nation in the world. Its culture, thought and art deserve the closest and most widespread study. Our relations with it in the near future will be at least as important as those with any other nation. Our ignorance therefore is deplorable. No doubt the language presents great difficulties. But these are overcome by missionaries and merchants, and consequently cannot excuse the neglect shown by the Universities—which some day no doubt will come to be recognised as a national misfortune.

Again, what about Russia? The position, I fear, is not much better, although here there is no excuse to be found in any insuperable linguistic difficulties. Lectureships—very few Professorships—and courses of instruction in Russian have been established in a number of Universities. But the number of students, though larger than in Chinese, is still lamentably small. Among the general public a good deal of superficial knowledge, relating to present conditions, is available from books and journals.[2] But the more intimate study of Russia, which is demanded both by the interests of its history, literature and art, and by the importance of our relations with it, and which should be the special duty of our Universities—this is still very far indeed from receiving its due share of attention. It may not be possible for some time to come to provide satisfactorily

[1] And will of course remain so until funds for scholarships, etc., are available. Is it necessary to point out that in so vast a subject provision should be made for post-graduate, as well as undergraduate, study?

[2] A good deal of useful information has recently become available through pamphlets, which draw largely from official publications.

for Chinese studies; but there ought to be no delay in giving a great expansion to Russian studies, in schools as well as in Universities.

The study of the peoples and languages of central and south-eastern Europe—apart from Germany and Italy[1]—seems to be almost wholly ignored in all our Universities, except London. Elsewhere, so far as I know, all that can be found is that a few Universities have lecturers in (modern) Greek and that lecturers in Russian sometimes include courses on some other Slavonic language among their duties. Even the history of east-central and eastern Europe seldom receives attention. It is only in the University of London—in the courses called 'Regional Studies'—that these peoples and languages are satisfactorily provided for. I do not know how many students are attracted by them, or what means are available for enabling or encouraging students to pursue such studies. What I do know—and anyone can see for himself—is that the neglect shown by the other Universities is reflected in a widespread, indeed almost universal, ignorance among the general public.

Yet the study of these peoples, their history, institutions and literatures, in itself presents attractions enough to repay all the attention we can give them. Moreover, it is clear now that their interests are closely bound up with our own. In the period of reconstruction we could help them, and they would probably be glad to receive our help, even after our misguided intervention in the Czecho-Slovakian crisis of 1938. But what help can we give that will be of any value, in our present state of ignorance? And how much use have we made of the opportunities given to us by the fact that for several years many thousands of their ablest and best informed people have been resident among us?[2]

The same remarks apply to the peoples who are our nearest neighbours. I have not specified these peoples above; but they certainly ought not to be ignored.[3] French is widely known in this country, France and the French people perhaps less widely. But the number of people who know Dutch or the Scandinavian languages is quite small, while the knowledge we have of the peoples themselves, including even the Belgians, is usually more or less superficial. If

---

[1] Even in these cases the course is usually limited more or less to language and literature. The number of students who take Italian—where such a course is available—is usually, I think, very small.

[2] All that I have heard is the naive comment that they will have had the opportunity of learning our language and ways.

[3] They ought to be studied widely, though of course not exclusively, as subsidiary subjects. For this purpose they are of the greatest possible value in connection both with historical studies and with the study of other regions. A knowledge of the Dutch language and of Dutch colonisation is important for various regions, especially the Far East.

we had had a better knowledge and more intimate relations with them, it might perhaps have been possible to foresee and provide against the tragedies which have taken place during the last few years. At all events we must try to avert the recurrence of such disasters in the future by establishing more intimate relations with them—not merely military and commercial relations, but also social and intellectual. I think that these peoples themselves would welcome such a movement; for there can be no illusions now as to the meaning of German friendship. They are the peoples most closely akin to us both in origin and in present cultural conditions; and they richly deserve all the attention we may give them, not only for practical reasons, but also because of the intrinsic interest of their history and their intellectual achievements.

The knowledge which is most urgently required at present is that of foreign peoples as they now are—their present conditions, industrial development, social and political ideas. But, except for purely commercial purposes, this knowledge is not enough. If we are to gain their respect, we must know something of their past history, which to the majority of peoples is more of a reality than ours is to us. In India, except among the Moslems, Sanskrit occupies a position similar to that of Latin in western Europe. But it is of greater importance than Latin now is; for Indian society in many respects corresponds to that of Europe in the Middle Ages, rather than the twentieth century. In Sanskrit all religious, philosophical, social and legal ideas are rooted; and without study of it Indian ideology is incomprehensible. Our attitude to Sanskrit studies,[1] which is sprung from ignorance and intellectual indolence, allows access only to those elements in the population which have been affected by European influence.

The same ignorance and indifference pervade all our studies, wherever linguistic knowledge is required, in Asia, Africa, and in Europe itself. For examples we need not go beyond our own islands[2] which, with their three peoples and languages, provide us—if we had only known them—with an ideal nucleus for a cosmopolitan empire. Celtic ideologies are rooted in early literatures of great and varied interest and in historical traditions reaching back to remote times. Yet Celtic studies have been treated with contemptuous

---

[1] Cf. p. 188 f. It might be of interest to compare the number of Professorships of Sanskrit and the number of students taking it in this country with the corresponding numbers for Germany and America. In some of our Universities the number of teachers had been reduced, I believe, before the war.

[2] I have called attention to the claims of our native studies in *The Study of Anglo-Saxon*, especially pp. 23 ff., 42 ff.

neglect by our Universities as 'without practical value'; and consequently they are very little known to the general public in England. Observe the effects of this attitude in our present relations with Ireland; and note the parallel with India.

Even English antiquity has not fared much better. It is true that the Anglo-Saxon language is taught to thousands of our students—though in a form which is commonly not much better than a waste of time. But what do these students know of our early history, institutions or art? For instance, we claim, not without good reason, that democracy is an English institution. But its origin and early history—questions of importance in our experimental times—are commonly ignored or misunderstood. Again, it is generally recognised that early Rome is worthy of study. But who would trouble himself about the early history of London?

Take again the early history of civilisation, in its original home, the Near East, to our knowledge of which such valuable additions have been made in our time. British archaeologists have played a very important part in these discoveries. But I fear that the impressions which the new knowledge has produced upon our Universities and schools, and through them upon the general public, have been slight and ephemeral.

It is clear that our education is in need of reform. We cannot rest content with the limitations now imposed upon our knowledge. Kemal saved the Turks by pulling off their blinkers and setting them to learn the ABC. Have we a statesman who is capable of rendering a similar service to us?

If our empire is to continue, we must produce a new ideology, to take the place of the old imperialism—an ideology as remote as possible from the German type. All idea of a 'Herrenvolk' must be eliminated, and replaced by that of an association of free peoples for mutual benefit and protection. Such an idea already underlies our relations with the Dominions, not all of which are wholly, or even predominantly, British in population. The same kind of relations must be established with those parts of the empire, in which the British population is negligible or non-existent.[1] These non-

[1] Much may be learned from the Russian constitution relating to the various classes of Republics and Autonomous Regions contained in the Soviet Union—which deserves very careful study. In an empire so heterogeneous as the British it must not be assumed that any particular form of government, e.g. our own form of democracy, is necessarily the one best fitted for all peoples, including those which have had no political experience and are perhaps still almost wholly illiterate. Every case needs special consideration. My plea is not for this or that form of government, but for a better knowledge of the peoples and their circumstances—which may serve as a sounder base for changes in the future.

British peoples must be convinced that to remain within the empire will be to their own interest, and will not mean a one-sided exploitation of them in our interest. Similarly those foreign peoples, outside the empire, who are in alliance with us must be convinced that it will be to their own interest, as well as ours, to maintain close and friendly relations with us.

It is a widespread fallacy in our country, and one which has led to disaster in the past, that financial or commercial connections are, or ought to be, sufficient for the maintenance of such relations. Much can no doubt be effected by such means; but they cannot by themselves bring about that intimate knowledge and understanding of the peoples, which is required to make these relations lasting. In point of fact many foreign and colonial peoples are eager to learn our language and to get to know all they can about us. It is for us to learn their languages and to get to know all we can about them.

How then is this knowledge to be acquired?

There can be no doubt that great expenditure will be involved. But the cost, whatever it may be, will be less than that of another war, and less than the loss which we should be likely to incur, if through ignorance and neglect we should lose our associates and allies within and beyond the empire. The expense then must be faced; but what kind of organisation is to be employed?

Something might perhaps be done by the Universities in the future, if not at once. A large proportion of the best intellects in the youth of the country are to be found there; and many promising students would probably be willing to take up the new subjects, if funds were available for that purpose. The Universities also possess endowments which are available for research, as well as libraries, museums and other facilities for study.

It is unlikely, however, that the Universities would be willing, or even able, to cope with a comprehensive scheme such as is now required. The primary object of the Universities, at least in 'Arts' studies, is to provide for professional interests; and the idea of providing for national interests in these studies would be novel and not likely to commend itself. And apart from other considerations, it is unlikely that any University could afford to introduce more than a few new subjects without very substantial subsidies from the Government, while the Government itself could hardly be expected to finance the scheme as a whole at more than one centre.

From a practical point of view the choice would seem to lie between one University and a new institution founded specially for the purpose. And, as between these two alternatives, I think that on the whole greater advantage would be derived from the latter. It is true that the connection with a University might be expected to prove beneficial in some important respects, as I have noted. But against these is to be set the fact that the supervision of these studies would be only one of many interests which would claim attention from the University. They would presumably be subject to the authority of a Central Board, of which few, if any, of the members would have any knowledge of them.

Further, the provision for these studies should include not only the training of students and the promotion of research; the dissemination of knowledge among the general public should also claim a large share of attention. And this latter duty could hardly be performed by a University, except to a limited extent by way of extramural teaching.

I think therefore that a comprehensive scheme such as I have in mind could be carried into effect most satisfactorily by an organisation specially constituted and financed for the purpose, under the control of a management in sympathy with its objects and able to give its undivided attention to them. Let us call it an Institute of Imperial (or Commonwealth) and International Studies. Its objects would be to promote the knowledge of these subjects by training students and encouraging research in them, and to make such knowledge accessible to the general public. It may not be out of place to sketch out in broad outline how I think these objects could best be accomplished; and consequently an attempt in this direction will be made in the Appendix which follows.

The Institute would have to be centred in one place, though some devolution of its activities should be kept in view wherever possible. At its centre it should seek to provide something in the nature of a University Honours course in studies for which no provision, or no adequate provision, is made by the Universities themselves. No attempt should be made to compete with the Universities in the four subjects specified on p. 184 f., for which ample provision is made by them. But where Universities provide courses[1] on subjects which come within the scope of the Institute, efforts should be made to secure some kind of co-operation with them.[2] And even when a

[1] E.g. the courses called 'Regional Studies' in the University of London, which are, I believe, organised by the School of Slavonic and East European Studies. These courses seem to approximate more nearly to what is required than any other University courses that I know of, though apparently they make no provision for initiation into original work.

[2] The Institute would of course retain the general direction of the students and also the control of the scholarships and other funds, so as to prevent the possibility of their being diverted to other studies.

University has no such courses, but has teachers qualified to conduct them,[1] some kind of liaison might with advantage be attempted.

It may be hoped that in course of time the Universities themselves will come to realise the value of these studies, and be willing to take an active part in supplementing and extending the work carried on by the Institute.[2] With the resources at their disposal, especially in endowments for research, they could of course contribute greatly to the promotion of these studies.

The first and most essential requisite is the provision of funds available for scholarships and studentships. The practicability of any such scheme as I have in mind is dependent upon such provision; for without it none but those who have private means can embark upon these studies. Examinations of some kind would be necessary for the awarding of such emoluments, and also for the purpose of securing that proper use was made of them.

The number of teachers required would depend to some extent upon the question whether it would be possible to secure the co-operation of the Universities. If such co-operation was available, the teaching given by the Universities might be almost sufficient in some subjects, though more usually it would have to be supplemented, perhaps by a subsequent course at the Institute. For many peoples and countries, however, the Institute would have to supply all the teaching. In any case, therefore, the number of teachers required would be very considerable.

It would be of the greatest benefit to the country and the Commonwealth if some such scheme as I have outlined could be initiated during the period of demobilisation. I suspect that many of those whose education has been interrupted by military service would welcome the provision of new lines of study, in the subjects which I have indicated. And there can be no doubt that the Commonwealth would gain greatly by having—in the course of a few years—a reserve of persons possessing such knowledge, from whom the Government overseas services could be recruited.

It would be impossible of course to get the 'Institute' into full working order at such short notice. The most that could be done would be to secure the funds necessary for the scholarships, to

[1] E.g. the School of Oriental and African Studies in the University of London, which includes a considerable number of Asiatic and African languages within the scope of its activities. Most of the courses, however, seem to be concerned, at least mainly, with language and literature.

[2] Many teachers individually might be ready to encourage new studies; but I do not think that the prejudices of the administrative authorities and boards would be easily overcome.

ascertain what facilities were available at various Universities, and to obtain expert assistance in the awarding of the scholarships and in advising the scholars. But I do not know whether even so much as this would be practicable. Whatever might happen later, it is hardly to be expected that such a scheme would be warmly welcomed by the Universities at first.

I am under the impression that in the conditions which are likely to prevail before long our country could, if it chose, become the intellectual centre and clearing-house, not only of the empire, but also of the world. It is improbable that after the war there will be the same readiness as in the past to resort to Germany for instruction. In 'Science' studies the future doubtless lies with America which, owing to her superior wealth and resources, is bound to secure a lasting supremacy. But in 'humanistic' studies we are in a better position, owing to the length, the variety and the riches of our past. In Europe, and even in our own islands, we can study at first hand the works of our ancestors, which attest the growth of civilisation for thousands of years. And not merely material civilisation. Here also are the conditions, the environment, the localities, the home, in which the social and intellectual culture of to-day grew to its maturity. And at present we are more advantageously placed than any other nation in Europe. Our country has not been devastated by invasion; and our colonial empire and our intimate relations with our allies give us an unrivalled opportunity.

But are we in a position to take advantage of the opportunity? I fear the answer must be 'No—certainly not at present, and probably not for some considerable time to come.' We are unprepared for such an eventuality. In 'scientific' subjects the value of knowledge is now generally recognised. But in the subjects with which I am concerned it is not recognised either by our statesmen or by our educational authorities. 'What good would it be to us if our country did become the intellectual centre of the world?' 'Why stuff our heads, or our students' heads, with knowledge of that kind?' If the value of this knowledge had been recognised, I think that many of the troubles and disasters which have befallen us recently might have been averted. But we were unprepared. And we shall be equally un- prepared to take advantage of the opportunities of peace.

It is to be hoped that a change of feeling will take place before it is too late. My belief is that the acquisition of this knowledge is a matter of necessity to us. Without it we cannot gain the respect of the intellectual world. But more than that, we cannot hope to maintain our position, or to carry out our imperial and international responsibilities. Perhaps we shall not be able even to support ourselves.

Our hope for the future depends on our being able to work in harmony with our friends. Are we going to delude ourselves into imagining that henceforth no difficulties will arise with, for example, Russia or China? Such difficulties can be overcome by mutual goodwill—if we make a serious effort towards a fuller understanding of foreign nations. We have to recognise that international relations are no longer the concern of governments only, and that the governments themselves are dependent upon their peoples. We must learn to realise and appreciate the difficulties of other peoples, and be ready to help them if they require our help. We must learn to respect their characteristics and traditions, their national feelings and ideologies, even when these differ from our own.

Within the empire we must discard the old imperialism. There must be no more talking—or thinking—about 'natives' (in a disparaging sense) or 'British Possessions'. In place of this we must adopt a new ideology—a new imperialism, if you like—based on the idea of an association of free peoples. The Atlantic Charter must be made applicable to the peoples of the empire, as well as to other peoples. Sore places may show themselves, as in India; and they may tend to multiply and become aggravated. Some of these peoples may wish to be entirely free from our control. We may be convinced, not without good reason, that the severance of relations between them and us will be detrimental to them—and their relations with one another—as well as to us. But if the association between us is to continue, they also must be convinced. The sores must be healed—not by financial remedies alone, but by the growth of mutual understanding and respect. Only by so doing shall we have our cosmopolitan empire established upon secure foundations—which may be more lasting than finance or force of arms.

For these reasons it is essential that we should set ourselves to acquire a better knowledge of foreign and colonial peoples without delay. Some new organisation seems to be necessary for the purpose; and in the following pages I have outlined a scheme. We need not expect that it, or any such scheme, will work miracles for us. But it should help us forward in the right direction.

APPENDIX

AN INSTITUTE OF IMPERIAL AND INTERNATIONAL STUDIES

I T may be convenient to outline briefly the kind of scheme which I have in mind for the 'Institute' suggested on p. 195.

We will begin with the training of students.

A full course at the Institute should occupy not less than two years. But it should be preceded, if possible, by preliminary study at a University. And part of the course itself might in some cases be spent at a University, if facilities were available. A 'full course' should include the detailed study of a country or region—its geography, history, antiquities, art, literature, education, social and political conditions, industries and trade. But students should be allowed a good deal of choice among these subjects. It should also include some subsidiary subjects, e.g. a less detailed study of other regions, as well as subjects of a more general character. A knowledge of the language or languages of the chief region should be required.

Provision should also be made for those who may wish to take short courses in some special subject of limited range.

The necessary funds would of course have to be supplied in the main by the Government. And in view of the national importance of these studies and the serious losses we have suffered through ignorance, there should be no stinting of expense,[1] especially for the endowment of scholarships and research studentships and fellowships. By this means an attempt should be made to attract to the Institute as large a proportion as possible of the best intellects among the youth of the country, both men and women.[2] An appeal might be made to local authorities to supplement the Government endowments by providing scholarships for students from their localities.

Study at the Institute should be regarded as a form of national service and, if a sufficient standard is attained, should exempt students from other forms of national service,[3] in the same way as exemption is granted to students in science and medicine.

One of the chief objects of the Institute would be to provide well-qualified

---

[1] There can be no doubt that the pre-eminence gained in the course of last century by German learning was due largely to the unstinted support given by the various governments. It is said that at the beginning of this century 70 per cent of the expenses of the Universities—which were at least twenty-one in number—were defrayed by state subsidies. Our governments have never adequately recognised the value of knowledge; and this has been the cause of most of our misfortunes.

[2] It is of the greatest importance that more women should take up these subjects, and also that more openings should be given to them in the overseas services. Backwardness in these respects is contrary to the public interest.

[3] In this respect also a lesson may be learned from German experience. Intellectual activity in German Universities was without doubt greatly stimulated by the fact that a very material reduction of military service was gained by success in the 'Abiturienten' examination.

recruits for certain government services, especially[1] the foreign, colonial and Indian services. I do not mean that it should set out to supply a professional training; its object should be to provide a liberal education, of a standard similar to that of a University Honours course, in subjects with which members of these services should be familiar. But this education should not be limited to candidates for the government services. It should be available to all who are interested in foreign and colonial peoples, whether they intend to be merchants, missionaries, settlers or journalists—not excluding even those who expect to spend their lives in this country. Special encouragement should be given to those who are likely to undertake research; and the need of raising the standard of knowledge in publications of all kinds should also be constantly borne in mind.

The funds available should be distributed (in scholarships, stipends, etc.) among the various regions in proportion to our interests, commitments and responsibilities. So far as I can judge, it would seem reasonable that not more than half should be spent on the study of Europe, while of the remainder one half should be devoted to Africa and the Near East and the other to India and the Far East. In Europe about one half should go to the west, together with Latin America, and the other half to eastern and east-central Europe, including all the Slavonic lands. The largest items would presumably be for India[2] and Africa, owing to the multiplicity of the peoples and languages involved. China would probably come next, and then Russia and the lands where Spanish and Arabic are spoken.

As regards actual courses of study, though it would be out of place here to enter into details more than I have done above, it may be suggested that for those who are taking a full course the 'Regional Studies' established in the University of London for eastern Europe might in general—with modifications—serve as a model for all regions. The important consideration is that sufficient latitude should be allowed to suit the requirements both of those who are interested mainly in present economic and political conditions and those whose interests lie in the history of the nation, its records and antiquities. The full course would probably as a rule be accompanied by subsidiary subjects, consisting partly of a less detailed study of some other region or regions and partly of more general subjects or studies covering larger areas: but a student should not be debarred from taking more than one full course. Time limits, such as are fixed in most Universities, might be dispensed with. Certificates of a somewhat detailed character should be awarded for success in all examinations, and should be taken into account as qualifications for government services.

Regulations relating to residence should be less rigid than in a University. It might often be beneficial for students to interrupt their course by a period of residence or travel—perhaps for as much as a year—in the

[1] Not exclusively. Courses such as I am recommending should be found useful, e.g. for members of certain branches of the fighting services. Again, a course on the early history and antiquities of our own country should be of great value for certain branches of the 'Home' services, e.g. those which are connected with the preservation and study of ancient monuments and records.

[2] The proportion for India might perhaps be reduced to a certain extent when that country attains self-government. I presume that then the 'Home' services there would be provided for internally, as in the Dominions. The same remark may perhaps apply to certain Colonies.

region which they are studying. For well-qualified students grants should be available to defray their expenses.

In other respects also it would be well to break with the traditional usage of Universities. In the study of many regions, and in their subsequent residence there, students will have to depend largely on their own efforts; and it is essential that the habit of working by themselves independently should be begun as early as possible—even from the age of sixteen or seventeen, while they are still at school. All forms of cramming or 'spoon-feeding' should be discouraged. Lectures, which in some Universities amount to fifteen or even twenty hours a week, and prevent any consecutive work, should be kept down to less than half that number. Full treatment of a subject in lectures is a survival from the time when satisfactory books were not yet in existence; and now it should be reserved for subjects in which this is still the case. In most subjects now a lecturer may carry out his duties more effectively by directing the reading of his students, to which of course he may contribute criticisms and supplementary matter. It is as a rule only in learning a language,[1] and especially in learning to speak it, that more frequent teaching is required. The extent to which a student can develop his own powers of initiative and criticism is a good test of his value for responsible work.

In order to obtain an entrance scholarship a student should have to show knowledge of a high standard in subjects which belong to the usual curriculum of schools, especially history, geography and languages, which should include a reading knowledge of German. But they should also have to show that they have tried to acquire for themselves knowledge in a wider field—outside the school curriculum, but connected with the work of the Institute. It would hardly be possible to insist on a high standard in this latter. But even smatterings of knowledge, which one acquires for oneself, have their value, whatever professional teachers may say to the contrary.

Scholarships should also be available for older students, including those who are self-educated. In this case somewhat different qualifications might have to be accepted, though they should include evidence of ability to learn languages, as well as some knowledge of geography and recent history. Sometimes also older students might be enabled to attend the Institute for short periods by grants made by local authorities for a specific purpose.

It would be well if a beginning could be made, as soon as possible after the end of the war, by offering grants for study at the Institute to men and women in the forces whose education has been cut short. As I suggested on p. 196, this would have the effect of providing a reserve of well-qualified recruits for the overseas services and also of disseminating knowledge which is so much needed more quickly than could be done at ordinary times.

The co-operation of Dominion Universities should of course be invited at the outset. In some subjects it might be possible for part of the course to be taken at a Dominion University, just as at a University in this country.

Efforts should also be made to promote relations with colonial and foreign Universities and colleges, e.g. by encouraging correspondence between students of the Institute and students belonging to the region which

---

[1] But in many languages a reading knowledge can be acquired without a teacher, if suitable books are available. The student will then be able to get rid of that dread of languages—due in the main to antiquated and pedantic methods of teaching—which has contributed so much to the futility of our 'Arts' studies.

they are studying. This would be helpful not only for improving knowledge of the languages on both sides, but also in facilitating the exchange of information and ideas.

Encouragement should be given not only to students of the Institute who wish to visit foreign and colonial lands, but also to students from foreign and colonial lands who visit this country. In addition to the courses of study available for students who belong to this country, many students from overseas might perhaps appreciate a special course for them—a 'Regional Study' of the British Isles, their history, antiquities, institutions, literature and art, with reference to places of interest in these islands.

I have sketched out above a scheme by which students could be enabled to acquire a knowledge of foreign and colonial peoples far in advance of what they can acquire at present. It would be the first duty of the Institute to provide such an education. Next comes the duty of promoting research, by which our knowledge may be constantly extended. There remains yet a third duty, that of making known to the general public the knowledge which has been acquired. This duty can be carried out to some extent by lectures, but much more by the publication of books and periodicals. It is a question worth much consideration whether the Institute itself should undertake such publications, and thus make itself responsible for their general accuracy. But in any case the production of such books and articles will be one of the ways in which those who are educated at the Institute will be able to render valuable service to the country.

Some of the books should be short and of an elementary character, others more advanced and detailed. All should be well illustrated and supplied with maps. They should also give reference to books where fuller information can be obtained. They must not take the form of propaganda; but they ought to be of great use to those who are intending to study at the Institute by giving them information which will enable them to choose a region for study and to acquire some preliminary knowledge of it. But it may reasonably be hoped that both books and articles will also reach a wider circle of readers, among whom they may kindle the desire of learning more about colonial and foreign peoples, and thus do something towards lifting that pall of ignorance which is both a danger and a shame to us.

The above scheme might doubtless be improved in many respects; but it would be out of place here to enter into further detail. My business is to call attention to the need for such an organisation as I have suggested and to indicate—in broad outlines—the form which I think it should take.

POSTSCRIPT

Since the above was sent to Press, it has been announced in *The Times* (8 February 1945) that an Inter-Departmental Commission has been appointed to examine the facilities available in this country in universities and other educational institutions for the study of the languages, histories and cultures of the countries of the Near and Far East, of Eastern Europe, and of Africa.

The announcement goes on to say that 'the Commission will consider what advantage is being taken of the existing facilities and whether additional facilities are required'.

'It must be our aim', a Foreign Office statement says, 'to strengthen and broaden the ties which already bind this country to other lands. After the war it will be more than ever necessary for the people of Britain to study the languages, traditions, and current problems of the more distant countries of the world. It is hoped that more British scholars will be encouraged to make the past and present achievements of other nations a subject of serious study and research, and that British people who go abroad in Government service, on business, or in other capacities, will be able, before leaving this country, to learn something of the habits and languages of the people among whom they intend to work.'

The names of the Commissioners are appended.

This is very good news; it is satisfactory to learn that the Government is now awaking to realise the need for such study. One criticism may perhaps be ventured. Why are Western Europe and Latin America excluded? Is it assumed that the study of these countries is already adequately provided for? Since the study of the past, as well as the present, is included, it may be pointed out that the early history of our own islands is as much neglected as that of foreign countries. What facilities for such studies have our students, including those from the Dominions and Colonies, as compared with those which foreign students have for their own early history? I would therefore respectfully call the Commission's attention to what I have said on pp. 191 ff., above.

In some directions a certain amount of progress has been made during the past year. In African studies one Professorship has been established, and some (Government) research studentships are now available for students from this country. I believe also that the subject is now taught in some schools. For other studies I have no definite information.

But I understand that an appeal for large additional funds for such studies is now being made by one or more institutions connected with the University of London. This also is very satisfactory, as showing that one University at least is awake to the needs of the time. It would seem too that the reason given on p. 195, above, for preferring an independent institution to a University loses some of its force in this case; for I understand that the institutions in question are to a large extent autonomous. Their funds are apparently under their own control, and cannot be diverted to other purposes by the University.

Nevertheless I do not feel inclined to withdraw the proposal which I have outlined above. The fact that these institutions are bound up with one University cannot fail to contract seriously the field from which prospective students will be drawn. Even if it is intended to attract graduates from other Universities, a large proportion of their ablest students will probably be excluded. It should be borne in mind that the Universities collectively— some of course more than others—have at their disposal an immense store of potential intellectual force, much of which is now allowed to lie unproductive. The object should be to draw from this store as much as possible.

Other considerations have also to be taken into account. If I am correctly informed, the appeal is only for the endowment of teaching posts, not for scholarships or research studentships. My view is that the latter—both the scholarships and the provision for research—are even more important than the former. Another very serious objection is that, if I understand rightly, the appeal is for the study of languages only, not for that of the peoples themselves, as defined on p. 187 (cf. p. 199) above, and in the terms of the Inter-Departmental Commission. If this is really the case, the object for which the Appeal is made would seem to fall far short of what is required. But there may be some special provision, of which I have not heard. Lastly, I do not know whether any action is contemplated to make the knowledge of foreign peoples more accessible to the general public. An institution connected with a University would seem to be less fitted for this purpose than an independent national institution.

The Appeal deserves all success; but in view of these considerations I do not think that, however successful it may be, it will remove the necessity for an organisation on different lines and more far-reaching in its operations. The two organisations need not come into conflict with one another. Where they cover common ground, there ought to be no insuperable difficulty in bringing about co-operation between them.

INDEX

Only the more important references are included

EXPLANATION OF THE MAP

Linguistic boundaries are marked in red lines.

In order to avoid the over-crowding of names in small spaces the following abbreviations are used:

A.: *Altaic (or Turco-Tataric) family of languages*
A. 1: Ottoman (or Osmanli) Turkish
A. 2: Kazan Turkish
A. 3: Baškir Turkish
A. 4: Čuvaš
A. 5: Crimean Turkish

B.: *Baltic group*
B. 1: Lettish (or Latvian)
B. 2: Lithuanian

C.: *Celtic group*
C. 1: Irish Gaelic
C. 2: Scottish Gaelic
C. 3: Manx
C. 4: Welsh
C. 5: Cornish (extinct)
C. 6: Breton

F.: *Finnic (or Ugro-Finnic) family*
F. 1: Finnish (with Karelian)
F. 2: Estonian
F. 3: Lappish
F. 4: Čeremis
F. 5: Mordvin
F. 6: Votjak
F. 7: Zyrjän
F. 8: Hungarian (or Magyar)

R.: *Romance (or Latin) group*
R. 1: Portuguese (with Galician)
R. 2: Spanish
R. 3: Catalan
R. 4: Provençal
R. 5: French
R. 6: Italian
R. 7: Sardinian dialects
R. 8: Alpine dialects
R. 9: Rumanian

S.: *Slavonic group*
S. 1: Russian
S. 2: Bulgarian
S. 3: Yugoslav (or Serbo-Croatian)
S. 4: Slovenian
S. 5: Slovak
S. 6: Czech
S. 7: Polish
S. 8: Sorbian (or Lusatian)

T.: *Teutonic group*
T. 1: English
T. 2: Frisian
T. 3: Dutch
T. 4: Low German dialects
T. 5: German
T. 6: Danish
T. 7: Swedish
T. 8: Norwegian
T. 9: Icelandic and Færoese

In regions where an intrusive language is spoken by the majority, but not the whole, of the population, the survival of the old native language is denoted by initials and figures enclosed in brackets.

For the Balkan peninsula reliable information as to the present distribution of languages is not available. The boundaries indicated on the map are political frontiers.

In Russia the boundaries marked in the map are those of the Autonomous Republics, etc., which take their names from the languages spoken in them.

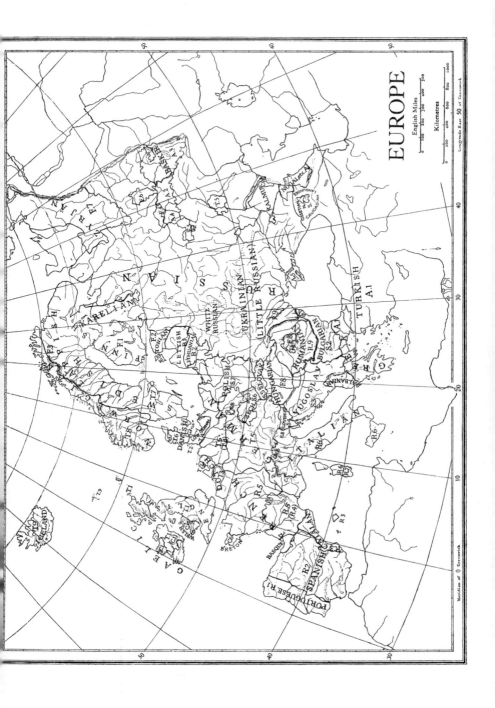

EUROPE

English Miles

0   100 200 300 400 500

Kilometres

0   200 400 600 800 1000

Longitude East   50   of Greenwich

Meridian of   0   Greenwich